B. F. Skinner

TIME

B. F. Skinner Says:
We Can't Afford Freedom

B. F. Skinner

Benign Anarchist

Daniel N. Wiener

Allyn and Bacon

Boston • London • Toronto • Sydney • Tokyo • Singapore

Other Books by Daniel Wiener
Dimensions of Psychotherapy (with Stieper)
Short-term Psychotherapy & Structured Behavior Change (with Phillips)
Discipline, Achievement & Mental Health (with Phillips)
Training Children in Self-Discipline
Practical Guide to Psychotherapy
Classroom Management
Albert Ellis: Passionate Skeptic

Copyright © 1996 by Allyn & Bacon
A Simon & Schuster Company
Needham Heights, Massachusetts 02194

Library of Congress Cataloging-in-Publication Data
Wiener, Daniel N. (Daniel Norman)
   B. F. Skinner : benign anarchist / Daniel N. Wiener.
     p.   cm.
   Includes bibliographical references and index.
   ISBN 0-205-17348-9
   1. Skinner, B. F. (Burrhus Frederic) (date).   2. Psychologists—
United States—Biography.   I. Title.
BF109.S55W53   1996
150. 19′434′092—dc20   95-23600
[B]   CIP

Credits: Various excerpts in this book are from *Particulars of My Life* by B. F. Skinner, Copyright © 1976 by B. F. Skinner, Reprinted by permission of Alfred A. Knopf Inc.; *The Shaping of a Behaviorist* by B. F. Skinner, Copyright © 1979 by B. F. Skinner, Reprinted by permission of Alfred A. Knopf Inc.; *A Matter of Consequences* by B. F. Skinner, Copyright © 1983 by B. F. Skinner, Reprinted by permission of Alfred A. Knopf Inc.; *Walden Two* by B. F. Skinner, Reprinted with the permission of Simon & Schuster, Inc. from the Macmillan College text *Walden Two* by B. F. Skinner, Copyright © 1948, renewed 1976 by B. F. Skinner; *The Selection of Behavior* by Charles A. Catania and Steven Harnad, Copyright © 1988 by Cambridge University Press, Reprinted by permission of Cambridge University Press. Photo on page ii © 1971 Time Inc. Reprinted by permission.

Printed in the United States of America
10 9 8 7 6 5 4 3 2 1   99 98 97 96 95

To my wife Phyllis and my son Jon,
who supported my effort with
interest and devotion.

Contents

Foreword

There is little doubt that B. F. Skinner, or "Fred" as his friends knew him, became widely influential and certainly the best-known American psychologist of his generation.

We were born in the same year (1904) and took our Ph.D.s at about the same time, although at different universities. Because Skinner had little teaching experience during his graduate years at Harvard, his academic promotions were slower than mine, but the early signs of recognition that he had received, such as appointment as a Junior Fellow of the Harvard Society of Fellows (1933–1936) and the Warren Medal in Experimental Psychology in 1942, showed his early prominence. These were followed by the Distinguished Scientific Contribution Award of the American Psychological Association in 1958 and the Gold Medal Career Award of the American Psychological Foundation in 1971. These awards attest to his continued recognition. He also received numerous honorary degrees, was recognized through election to the National Academy of Sciences, and received the President's Medal of Science for scientific achievement.

All of this does not mean that all of Skinner's hopes were satisfied along the way. For example, his major early book, *The Behavior of Organisms* (1938), did not sell well. Although 800 copies had been printed, only 80 copies were sold in the first four years, and there was a residue until his friend, Fred Keller, began doing experiments along the lines Skinner had initiated and thereby produced a market for the book. Later, a number of operant behaviorists became a large and loyal body of disciples, with their own organization and journals.

Skinner all along showed the qualities of heroes of folklore, as recounted in Campbell's book, *The Hero with a Thousand Faces* (1968). These include a time to find himself, which in Fred's case was a "moratorium." After graduating from college, he tried (unsuccessfully) to become a writer in Greenwich

Village. A chance meeting soon launched him on his career. His encounter with Watson's *Behaviorism* led him into graduate study in psychology and to the development of his own operant behaviorism.

Although he continued to hold firmly to his beliefs, Skinner was always cordial on a personal basis and was not without a sense of humor. Once at a dinner party in his honor, when he was presented a gift in the form of a "Skinner box" made of plastic, I offered a toast to him for having chosen of his own free will to accept determinism. His reply was, "I can drink to that!"

The detailed biography presented in this book gives an accurate account of B. F. Skinner's career and his influence, and will be welcomed by his many admirers.

Ernest R. Hilgard
Stanford University

Preface

My thoughts about B. F. Skinner have simmered for many months now since completion of the manuscript for this book. They have blended and clarified, and it is time to state conclusions—and an introduction to the life of this most eminent behavioral scientist.

Skinner's ideas are presented clearly and are tightly argued in his writing. He was proud of his concise prose, which he edited with great care. His issues are as large, important, and effective as he could construct them. His personality, which is the central subject of this biography, remains complex, somewhat uncertain, and often modified in its presentation as new information appeared.

As are most people with grand ideas, strong convictions, and tenacious efforts to enlarge their influence, Skinner has been constantly attacked by adversaries criticizing most of his views (usually without trying to substitute their own) and attempting to establish in every possible way that he is fatally flawed. To define as clearly as possible what B. F. Skinner stands for and why it is so important, one must often slight details and concentrate on why he is a giant in behavioral science ranking in this century with Freud. Although Freud and Skinner are opposites on the importance of introspection, Skinner considered them fundamental allies in propagandizing for the primacy of environmental influences on human behavior.

Skinner himself chose to believe that his most distinctive contributions were "out of the laboratory," the subtitle he initially chose for this book. It was because of his applications of the idea that human behavior could best be explained by his view that animals were behaviorally molded by acting at first tentatively, then with increasing definition in the rewarded directions.

So well accepted has this idea become that it is applied throughout our society, from our government, which gives financial rewards to countries that support its policies on matters such as nuclear disarmament, antiterrorism, and making peace; to athletic coaches who systematically compliment their players' successes; to Congress, which gives bonuses for overall compliance with federal speed limits (rather than penalizing violations); to mental hospitals and schools, which grant privileges to reinforce desired behavior. So pervasive are these ways of thinking that users often do not realize that they are unwitting Skinnerians. One newspaper publisher learned of behavior modification methods in a Harvard business course but had no idea where they had originated. Interestingly, Skinner published his seminal book on behavior modification 57 years ago, before the publisher was born.

Skinner's ideas are widely known, discussed, applied, misinterpreted, and misapplied. The personality that gave birth to them and determined their nature can be readily dismissed (and is, even by him); he believed that the ideas should stand by themselves. However, a psychologist should be able to trace the origins of creations to the humans who produced them. Skinner's traits of originality, tenacity, intelligence, independence, vitality, contentiousness, one-mindedness, and bravado can be related to his genetics and environment, albeit imprecisely, especially since he was not much interested in such etiology.

Above all, Skinner wanted to proceed rationally to lead a satisfying life for himself and to prescribe for others how to do likewise. By that, he meant that one should strip a problem to its bare bones and try most logically to solve it. He was increasingly impatient with humankind's blind march toward self-destruction—like lemmings pushing mindlessly to drown in the sea—through international wars, nuclear weaponry, willy-nilly governing policies, a libertarian anarchy, and thoughtless impulsivity in the name of exercising freedom, which was not calculated to sustain satisfaction.

A major feature of his personality was described in his Epilogue for the final volume of his autobiography, *A Matter of Consequences* (1984), where he abjures the need to analyze his feelings. He believed they had little to do with the ideas that he esteemed, and he did not want feelings to distract from the validity of those ideas. His ideas and practical creations are what he wanted to be remembered for as his contribution to the world. But it was his personality that stamped his huge influence on our society—his fierce desire and skill for extending his impact on the world. Without the nature of his personality, B. F. Skinner might have died, as do most of us, influencing only our tiny circle of immediate family and friends.

Finally, there is the present subtitle of this book, *Benign Anarchist,* taken from concluding notes in Skinner's autobiography. There he characterizes his effort to achieve the design of an ideal community that will bring maximum satisfaction to its inhabitants. The plan in *Walden Two,* in accord with what he believed about human behavior, is to accomplish its purpose without the imposition of outside power via a dictator, a police force, or any other coercion. He insisted on his own autonomy, and equally that for others.

That is the way Skinner answered his critics who insisted he was dictatorial, even malevolent, in imposing behavioral design in our society at the expense of human "freedom." Freedom must have its referents so that it is not merely whimsy, at the mercy of random social influences that are as likely to come from commercial advertising as from ethical values. Thus, the subtitle *Benign Anarchist* takes form. Here is Skinner's design of a rational society, and here are the ways to accomplish it. But he will not dictate it, he insists, nor will he even participate in its imposition. That is up to the humans populating society, as they choose to use such methods.

Now for a personal note. Skinner's daughters, Julie and Deborah, were intensely loyal to him and loving, and saw him as an extremely sensitive and giving father. Eve, his wife, also intensely loyal, provided no grist for criticism of him. She consistently maintained her distance from his work as well as from his attitudes when they did not impinge upon her. Eve firmly protected her own interests as an individual. She also tried to take care of her husband although, until they were old, he had acted like the prime protector of her as well as their daughters. All three women shielded their personal interactions from public observation.

Skinner's courtesies and support for me extended well beyond what the situation required. He even advised me: "I hope you won't let a publisher tell you too much of what to say." Ever since taking his classes at the University of Minnesota, I strongly identified with him and his struggle to prevail in his field. I present here what I know of him as objectively as I can, yet I also hope that my admiration and respect clearly show through.

I knew Skinner's earliest colleagues and students at the University of Minnesota, and although they uniformly respected his creative work, a few did not like him personally because he seemed aloof and self-centered. But all these individuals wanted to contribute what they could to an accurate portrayal of the great psychologist they were privileged to know. They include Minnesota's Herbert Feigl, William Heron, Marian Breland Bailey, William and Kay Estes, John Carroll, Stuart Cook, and Gail Peterson. Harvard's Richard Herrnstein, Edward Pattullo, Brendan Maher, Robert Epstein, John Kenneth Galbraith, and Harry Levin also provided exceptional personal statements. Paul Meehl was an invaluable source of information about the Minnesota years. Other friends also helped generously: Ernest Hilgard (who wrote an early review of *The Behavior of Organisms*), Margaret Vaughan, Evelyn Segal, and Fred Keller.

My wife Phyllis and my son Jon were ideal, sensitive, informed editors. Margie Kirwin helped immeasurably in preparing the manuscript. Lawrence Young aided greatly with references. Robert Epstein organized Skinnerian artifacts in a small museum bordering Harvard, edited Skinner's diaries in *Notebooks*, and created invaluable indices to his autobiography. Eve, Julie, and Deborah Skinner also provided vital assistance in answering my questions. I wish also to thank the following for suggestions on the manuscript: Georg Eifert at West Virginia University, Timothy Hackenberg at the University of Florida, Ernest R. Hilgard at Stanford University, and Joseph J. Plaud at the University of North Dakota. My gratitude is also extended to John Cowles, Jr.

Finally, I wish to thank Susan Badger and Mylan Jaixen at Allyn and Bacon for their support, and Susan Hutchinson and Lynda Griffiths for their detailed oversight.

We are all controlled by the world in which we live,
and part of that world has been and will be
constructed by men. The question is this:
are we to be controlled by accidents, by tyrants,
or by ourselves in effective cultural design?

—Skinner (1972)

▶ 1

Roots and Childhood

"I think the things we discover are lucky finds," B. F. Skinner in old age said of his achievements. "I don't think you go out knowing what you're going to find, then look until you get it."[1]

While Skinner consistently wrote about the fortuitous events, accidents, and serendipitous leaps that had led him to his behavioral principles, he also began early to shape the highly controlled, goal-directed life that characterized his maturity. At the same time that he was committed to encouraging spontaneous occurrences, periodically he made pithy and practical assessments of his current status and future plans in his notebooks.

This kind of inconsistency, between encouraging spontaneity to yield creative outcomes and planning to make things happen, is a key to understanding Skinner. Otherwise, one might force a consistency on his life that would not reconcile the varying ways those who knew him best interpreted his personality. He could be seen as feeling or unfeeling, controlled or spontaneous, autocratic or democratic, arrogant or humble. He was all of these.

Skinner was a romantic, sensitive, compassionate, lonely human being wanting to accommodate to authority yet also to deny its influence on him. He shared the universal desire to be loved, but he could not express it fully except perhaps with his daughters who, when young, were the most helpless and dependent humans ever in his life. As they continued to mature, they engendered their father's protectiveness. Skinner couldn't even bring himself freely to punish his rats. He made his way like an innocent in the vast world, attending to its minutiae and gaining its attention, while overtly denying a wish to be accepted and loved. That desire might be expressed but rarely, when he felt rebuffed by those he liked or respected.

He must have been shaped in these ways during his childhood, yet it is not obvious just why and how. No one was in a better position than he, when he wrote his autobiography, to discover how his desires and relationships developed. He did not choose, however—indeed, apparently did not even think—to find out from those who knew him in childhood and youth why he grew up in this manner. He apparently never even asked that kind of question.

Early, Skinner adamantly sought autonomy. He tried not to depend on anyone for anything. Rather than compete with his younger brother, he seemed to recognize but ignore Ebbe's (Edward James) superior charm and strong hold on his parents' affections, which solidified up to the death of his brother at age 16. Skinner showed serious ambivalence about the death.

One can imagine little Fred (a nickname derived from Burrhus Frederic) exploring the huge mysterious world beyond his horizon, oblivious to what might lie over the edge. Driven by insatiable curiosity, he experimented with what lay before him. All of his life, he delighted in his discoveries that were like "lucky finds," as if he were chancing upon a marble or coin. One such find occurred in his university laboratory just because he was running out of food pellets to reward his rats and had to space out the food supply to last over the holiday weekend. That produced one of his major discoveries—that intermittent reward worked better than continuous reinforcement.[2]

Was Skinner fond of Susquehanna, the small Pennsylvania town where he was born and lived until he left for college at age 18? He was always reluctant to discuss his feelings and he tried to rely in his autobiography only on events and people described at the time they occurred in his life. The small town provided his only world to explore as a boy. He described it factually and with little expression of emotion for any of its features or his adventures in it—except for one high school teacher.

He did describe in fine detail (Skinner, 1976a) the town's physical characteristics. His backyard, for example, "offered black cherries, red cherries (shared with the robins), purple plums, green plums, Concord grapes, currants, raspberries, rhubarb, horseradish, and mustard." He wrote further of the nearby trees, plants, flowers, and small animals (p. 51). But he was far less forthcoming about the human beings who flourished in the neighborhood. He mentioned them rather flatly and without the glow of discovery and pleasure he found in the landscape and his own constructions. He mentioned their work, products, and tools, sometimes in precise detail, such as the carpenter who "simply glued pieces of wood together, but the glue was hot and hence presumably stronger than the kind I used" (p. 54). He wrote few personal reflections about the inhabitants and their interactions with each other and with him.

It is no longer possible to find out how that lad looked to others; he neither asked around nor remembered being told when he was young or in old age when he wrote his autobiography. He showed little interest in the attitudes of those around him; they may have been as oblivious of him as he was of them. But he would have been noticed in his small town surrounded by relatives. He would count as one of only 2,500 or so inhabitants. He could not be lost or hurt, dangerous or endangered, without being observed and handled in some way by his family and neighbors.

The attitudes of others toward him would not interest him unless they frustrated or facilitated what he wanted to do. By the time he began his autobiography, few who had known him were still alive and accessible. In company with other famous people, such as novelist/poet Vladimir Nabokov, Skinner was too preoccupied with describing documents and his own memories to consult with others.

In Susquehanna, he developed habits he would use to handle new situations he encountered after he left home. His exceptional vitality unfolded rather mysteriously, since his known genetics were not outstanding in that respect, nor apparently in intellect. Both sides of his family were rooted in northeastern Pennsylvania near the Susquehanna River. They lived humbly, had no outstanding members, and were relatively uneducated and uncultured. Few of them had ever wandered very far during the prior two generations after their arrival in this country. One grandfather (Skinner) had come from England, the other grandparents all from New England.

The community took its name from the river. It was established shortly after the Civil War when the Erie Railroad built a depot and shops there. It offered employment to settlers, eventually drawing his grandparents and parents. Life in Susquehanna, as in most other U.S. small towns, was radically different from urban living, sharing more with villages around the world than with large cities. Americans who identify with big cities seldom appreciate this distinction.

Small-town dwellers get used to firsthand transactions with those who serve them. They tend to be suspicious of slickness, special talents, or high aspirations. Their social lives center around nearby family and neighbors, and their personalities become more evident than in bigger communities. There seldom is public transportation; the residents usually walk to places in town. Cars, bikes, and other vehicles are used to get into the country, to nearby cities, and to cabins "out a ways," which may amuse city folks who think these small-town dwellers are already out quite a ways. They can hardly maintain privacy, much less anonymity. Their reputations are soon made and unmade by their histories. They become independent in maintaining their homes, cars, and yards, and in making and fixing their things. They are reluctant to use the services of others if they can possibly do the work themselves. Lovely natural beauty is usually nearby, and also nature's bounty, in vegetation, fruits, and animals.

In cities, personal incompetence is abetted by the easy availability of helping services. Where there is no public charity in small towns, private charity is more needed and available. Where professional counseling is scarce or unavailable, people tend to find help from friends and relatives, physicians, ministers, and lawyers—or to struggle harder on their own. Reared this way,

Skinner, as an adult, would be distinctively independent in an ordinary urban environment.

Both couples of Skinner's grandparents lived in nearby communities. Grandmother Skinner came from poor dirt farmers, was not very bright, had little education, and was untalented even in the cooking that consumed much of her time. She aspired "to be a lady" and to make her son (Fred Skinner's father) into "a great man." She even pinched his nose to make it "more distinguished" (Skinner, 1976a, p. 8).

Grandfather Skinner, born in England, spoke with an accent. He was often looking for work and took a wide variety of jobs from painting to selling but never found any he stuck with, and, according to his wife, he had "absolutely no ambition" (1976a, p. 10). Both pairs of grandparents seemed to get along harmoniously. Grandfather Skinner grew deaf prematurely, a deficiency Fred also developed in middle age.

The Burrhuses, Fred's mother's family, were a cut above the Skinners. Her father served in the Civil War. He was a carpenter foreman for the railroad and good at carving. Fred remembered him for his zest for life. He gave his grandson coffee and extra spending money and encouraged him to go out with girls and to go dancing. He owned cars but never a house. In photographs, Fred bore more resemblance to his Grandfather Burrhus than to his own father. They had the same high broad forehead, slender well-articulated build, and somewhat dashing appearance, which Fred cultivated as an adult.

Grandmother Burrhus left a sealed envelope to be opened after her death but after Fred's father read it to himself, he threw it into the fire uncommunicated to the others. Fred believed it reported some "sinning" by his grandfather. Grandmother Burrhus was the only grandparent or parent to read much fiction. But it was the good food she served Fred that impressed him most. As an adult, he valued good food and encouraged his wife to learn to cook—but never did much of it himself. Eve became an excellent cook.

Skinner's mother, Grace Burrhus, was born in 1878 and graduated from high school at age 16, second in her class of seven. (Interestingly, his father, as well as Fred himself, also finished second in their classes.) Immediately, Grace took a job as secretary to a railroad executive. Attractive and able to sing and play the piano moderately well, she spent a fair amount of time in Susquehanna after high school with her husband-to-be in social activities and theatrical productions.

William Skinner, Fred's father, was born in 1875 in Starrucca, Pennsylvania, before his parents moved to nearby Susquehanna. He was an only child, pushed to achieve by his mother. He was called "bumpy" and considered arrogant all of his life, even though he tried to be congenial and political. As an adult, Fred also was considered arrogant—he had an aloof manner—but his father was uncomfortable and felt socially inferior in a way his son Fred sometimes felt but seemed to overcome. William often regarded himself as a failure and felt depressed; he was both consoled and depreciated by his wife. Sensitive to his parents' humble background, William drew in more polished relatives when courting his wife-to-be.

After high school, William Skinner began to work in the railroad shops and apprenticed as a draftsman. He did not stay at it long, however, but began to "read law" with a local attorney. This permitted him to finish his legal education after one year of schooling instead of two and to take (and pass) the bar exam at age 21, gaining him a somewhat inferior certificate to practice.

Fred's father and mother married in 1902 in their own home, which they had brought and furnished beforehand. It was a simple inexpensive house in which a bathroom had been installed to replace the outhouse. It needed further extensive improvements to be equipped with even modest comforts; even so, it remained old fashioned and somewhat shabby. The Skinners lived in that house for 20 years, through Fred's last year in high school. His father furnished a shop at home and made things out of junk lying around, a habit Fred also practiced all of his life. Fred was born in this home in 1904, healthy, although his mother complained to him without explanation that she almost lost her life in the process. His only sibling, brother Edward James (Ebbe), was born $2\frac{1}{2}$ years later.

William Skinner practiced law in his own office and led a highly regular life. The home ran according to his work schedule, but his wife otherwise directed their lives. Both pairs of grandparents lived nearby, a half mile apart, but were not especially close to each other except on holidays. Fred was surrounded by family members, saw them frequently, and probably gained security and comfort from their presence. He and his brother usually played together as children with common toys and games, and their own inventions. When they were little, their mother sang comforting lullabies and other songs to them and both parents read them stories, often from the blood-thirsty Grimm Brothers' fairy tales. Fred retained fond memories of the furnishings of their home and of the excitement of his parents dressing up to go out.

His father aspired to political influence and gave speeches on national issues, which were then reported in the town paper. He was a very conservative Republican which, combined with his aloof, intimidating manner, contributed to his losing all of his election campaigns in this working-class area. Like his son later, he felt lonely with his unpopular opinions, but was nonetheless sure of them. With a wide variety of cases in the small town, his legal practice flourished more than his income. When he defended a railroad strikebreaker charged with murdering a picket, however, he gained unwelcome notoriety. By defending the man successfully, Skinner's father doomed any further local political aspirations. Grandfather Skinner's reputation as antilabor had been established in a previous incident when, because he was a foreman, he refused to strike.

Although he appeared to take his disappointments well, Skinner's father often felt like a failure. Reporters and others described him as a success, but he frequently became discouraged because he thought he had reached his professional limits in his thirties. He constantly turned to his wife for support, which she provided, though her efforts were undermined by her frequent criticisms of him.

Skinner's mother's life was devoted to community service, where she gained loyal friendships. She kept a good figure and posture all of her life; as an adult, Fred emulated her pride in appearance. His picture on the back cover of the first volume of his autobiography shows him dapperly dressed in horn-rimmed glasses, turtleneck sweater, and plaid jacket. He wanted picture-taking for this biography postponed until he regained his presurgical appearance, which was not much different after his hair again flourished.

Despite her professional support when her husband was depressed, Skinner's mother referred disparagingly to his efforts to write, and also to a genuinely heroic incident when he rescued two girls from drowning. She also compared her husband's shorter height with that of the taller Fred's. Confiding his problems to his wife, Fred's father never achieved the self-confidence he sought. A friend who had known them both well remarked that "Grace made quite a man of Will Skinner" (Skinner, 1976a, p. 45). Fred inferred that she was frigid but that she had no doubts of her husband's fidelity. When Fred was at Harvard, his mother visited and told him of his father's jealousy about her attentions to her son.

Skinner wrote more favorably about his mother than his father. Beginning in adolescence, Fred preferred the company of women to men. Except for his wife, daughters, and mother, however, he often treated women as sexual objects, somewhat like an adolescent, without committed affairs. Toward the end of his life, one woman urged him to change this, and also his use of sexist language. He did work on the latter.

He had no apparent reason to fear or be jealous of his father, who was no threat in any regard, and not mean, tough, or punitive. Fred seldom acted intimidated by him or any other authority. He believed his father wanted to be close to his sons but didn't know how. He did encourage their athletic activities and later tried to get Fred to study law but was little involved with them otherwise. He also tried to instruct them in sex but by the time he tried they knew more than he could at least talk about.

Clearly, Fred had more to gain by pleasing his mother than his father, given her dominance in the home, although he never seemed to rebel against either parent. He did briefly comply with a couple of onerous tasks from his father: collecting delinquent phone bills and serving legal papers. Without enthusiasm, he later collaborated with his father on a book of corporate liability cases.

Fred's formal religious training was not remarkable, but his early moral upbringing within his family traumatized him. He suffered torments about the devil and hell when he lied to avoid punishment for such offenses as using a "bad word" or stealing a quarter. His father often told him of the punishments for criminality, perhaps a reflection of his own depression since he had no realistic cause to do so. As an adult, Fred remained "afraid of the police and [bought] too many tickets to their annual dances."[3]

Extremely attentive to correct behavior and conventional superstitions, his mother imbued Fred with such irrational habits as not stepping on floor gravestones. Despite his apparent disregard of others' opinions, Fred was sensitive all of his life to what others thought of him. He occasionally brooded briefly, though that was usually all he did about it. Faith and guilt were major ingredients in his early religious education and he was tortured by his most minor misdeeds. "I think I described my petty thefts and my sexual practices in an effort to avoid appearing as a saint"[4] he noted of his autobiography (Skinner, 1979), written much later than the events and apparently to correct for a tendency toward self-righteousness. After he left for college, he seemed to have left his guilt behind and it only occasionally manifested itself strongly again.

When Miss Graves, his admired high school teacher, also became his Sunday school teacher of religion, he turned away from religion and to humanities instead. She attracted him to the history and literature of religion rather than the dogma. His parents never showed much interest in religion, although they attended church regularly. Eventually, Fred announced to Miss Graves that he no longer believed in God, and he became more interested in ethics and humanism for the rest of his life.

He was practically never punished physically although he was occasionally reprimanded, ridiculed, or threatened—mildly, but enough to make an impression on him. He remembered the lessons about morality but had a benign attitude toward the enforcement of rules. If he could easily get around them, he did—for the rest of his life—without making a big fuss. He did develop a deep antagonism to punishment, which he articulated especially later when rearing his own children. Incorporating it into his theory, he declared that punishment was inefficient because it produced delayed adverse effects, and he maintained that stance firmly thereafter.

Skinner did not like the exercise of authority by others or—later, when he had power—by himself. While his parents' efforts were certainly mild, he nevertheless resented them. He went out of his way later in life to avoid exercising his own power as a teacher, chairman, or project director. There was little physical aggression in his life—practical jokes, yes, but no gangs, fights, or even strenuous competitive team sports for him. In his small town, there were few strangers to push against. "We were not physically aggressive toward each other, or toward more distant acquaintances. . . . I do not remember ever striking anyone or being struck" (Skinner, 1976a, p. 83). Tightly controlled emotions also helped him to rule out any fights.

About sex, he stated that "my innocence . . . was extraordinary" (Skinner, 1976a, p. 63). There was both a primness in his family and a paucity of intimate conversations with other children. He noted that the Italian and Irish boys in town talked freely with each other about sex. Despite being surrounded by farm animals and rural earthiness, he remained largely ignorant about sex until college. He looked up sexual words, he overheard jokes and stories, and he was excited—and anxious—when he glimpsed live girls' legs and sexy pictures in the *Police Gazette*.

Around age 11, Fred learned to masturbate and at first worried that he might have broken his penis when it declined. He felt "demeaned" and "defeated" by ejaculating and noted that in other ethnic groups, boys seemed less inhibited about it. Intercourse was delayed for him until college and then only once. Here, as in other areas of his life, he was a loner, teaching himself by reading, limited personal events, and overheard conversations, and responding furtively to the excitement of it.

Sexually, he remained somewhat arrested at this level through his maturity, wanting to see and hear about sex and practicing an unfocused shallow promiscuity. He acquired pornography later but he mentioned it to me only once, casually, and also that he kept a kind of sexual diary. Although he ordered Halderman-Julius's "Little Blue Books" he said that he never bought the sexually titillating titles in the same catalog.

Born the same year as Fred, and his closest friend up to the time they left for college, was "Doc" Miller, whose father was a homeopathic physician. Doc also planned to become one. Fred promised Doc that if Doc died, he would dedicate a book to him. Doc did die at age 25 and Fred dedicated the first volume of his autobiography to him 47 years later. Doc, in his early adolescence, had nothing to do with girls and "somehow it added to my strong feeling of admiration and awe that I supposed him above all that" (Skinner, 1976a, pp. 117–118). Fred himself *wanted* to be above it too but couldn't make it.

Doc's family belonged to the same church as the Skinners but took it more seriously. Fred and Doc talked over improvised phone wires and telegraphs, sold elderberries, and horsed around. Skinner wrote that he was comfortable with Doc as with no others. "With a friend like Raphael Miller my behavior was easy, natural, and wholly uncontrived. . . . But with more distant acquaintances my behavior was rather calculated" (1976a, p. 171). It is not clear why this intimacy was reserved to Doc.

Miller isn't mentioned for the over four years between high school and when Skinner arrived at Harvard for graduate work where Doc was already in medical school. True, they had gone to different undergraduate colleges, but after such prior closeness, it was strange that they were so totally out of touch with each other for so long. This "out of sight, out of mind" reaction was typical of Skinner's friendships throughout his life. Except for Fred Keller, later in his life, Skinner had little personal correspondence despite his other prolific writing. With rare exceptions, he acted indifferent about maintaining close ties.

Skinner noted but never described a brief homosexual episode in his young adolescence with Doc, which he remarked was never repeated as they both drew closer to girls. He expressed sensitivity, however, to how his close later friendship with Fred Keller at Harvard and afterwards might be misinterpreted by others as sexual.

Because he was $2\frac{1}{2}$ years older than his brother and was clearly superior in knowledge and inventiveness, Skinner believed their relationship was more friendly than competitive. Yet his brother Ebbe, at age 7, wrote under the inscription in a book given to Fred by his grandmother, "Your a BOOB" (Skinner, 1976a, p. 65). On the whole, however, they played together often and equally. Ebbe tried harder to please their parents. Fred also remarked about Ebbe's greater popularity and athletic ability.

Beginning quite young, Fred usually got his way through reasoning and planning. He was trained in good manners by his mother, who worried constantly about what others would say. The rewards of pleasing others ripened with age. People he did not offend he usually charmed and impressed with his self-sufficiency. Even when young, he was quite calm and rational about getting what he wanted with minimal interference from his emotions.

Acquaintances of great achievers have often remarked about their extraordinary energy, inventiveness, curiosity, and autonomy. *Seeds in the Wind* (Braybrooke, 1989) records the exceptional drive that led children ages 7 to 16 to create, in part at least, in order to impress others. But their early productions were often far afield from what they became notable for: a poet was first a painter, George Bernard Shaw tried to draw, Anthony Burgess wrote music. What characterized them all, however, was their desire to express themselves in whatever form they could. Sometimes they were good at what they tried early, sometimes bad, but they were impelled to do *something* to gain notice. They kept experimenting until they found a medium in which they could excel.

That was the youthful history of Skinner. He tried a variety of ways to gain attention: selling shoes and magazines; inventing various aids such as a pants-hanging device and a shoe arch support; publishing poems, news items, and fiction; playing his saxophone to sound like human singing. He was full of ideas and was not afraid to experiment with almost anything he thought of. He used his special mechanical interests and skills all of his life. As a child, he also made an elaborate hydraulic system with water flowing in and out of several crocks, and a small steam engine run by alcohol. He tried to create a system to extract oxygen from water, capable of rescuing a submarine crew, and to invent an adjustable reed for musical instruments. He sustained none of these projects for very long, but he was clever at consummating new ideas from odds and ends of material that lay about—as he did later in his university laboratories. He had access to his father's shop at home that was better than the manual training equipment at school.

Of his writing, he noted (Skinner, 1976a): "The things I wrote were no more original than the pictures I copied with stencil or pantography" (p. 93). Most important was that he kept trying to write and publish as a child. At age 10, he got his poem printed in the *Lone Scout* magazine for boys:

When you're getting ready for a hike
And the weather's looking fine
And you've got your eat kit packed chock full
With your fishing rod and line,
Who's the fellow that steps up and says,
'It surely looks like rain'?
He's the pessimist and joy killer.
I don't believe he's sane! (p. 93)

Skinner kept on with his writing, mostly derivative and trivial stuff, at times injecting a peculiar style, as when he replaced every *you* with *ye*. He never found anything very interesting to write about, however. He did get a job on the local newspaper and learned something of the craft of a reporter and printer. He wrote cleverly at times, often satirically, making fun of local events. But his writing never soared; his imagery remained pedestrian and his ideas were trite. He did not ask for nor profit from criticism. He never seemed to realize until the final year of trying to will himself to be a literary writer, between college and graduate school, that he had not found anything of importance or passion to write about, nor the talent to fly on wings of feelings or imagery. Mostly, Skinner wrote about solitary activities, critically or cynically about the world. His were the common reactions of smart young boys contemptuous of conventions, considering themselves completely rational, yet unable to accept their frustrated but uncontrollable longings.

In his eighth-grade English class, after having heard his father casually mention that some people thought Shakespeare's work had in fact been written by Bacon, Fred announced to the class his commitment to that notion. He then set about documenting his opinion with various arguments he found in books at the library. Conspicuously and tenaciously, he maintained this position throughout high school and into college before finally dropping it.

Fred enjoyed high school, often arriving early to look at materials the class would be working with that day. The principal took special interest in him, and, in brief conversation just before graduation, called Fred into his office to declare, "You were born to be a leader of men. Never forget the value of a human life" (Skinner, 1976a, p. 147). Fred never knew what the principal meant, since he had shown no signs of leadership, played on no team, nor advanced as a boy scout. Nonetheless, he impressed observers, even that early, that he would make his mark in the world. There was something about his demeanor, self-containment, assurance, and assertiveness that suggested his potential for "leadership" in some as yet unpredictable way. Even his parents showed a kind of respect for him.

Skinner had few playmates and spent time mainly with his brother. "It was a very good relationship," he remarked. "He teased me, and that bothered me, but I don't remember ever getting angry enough to strike him or do anything else that would be aversive. He was closer to my father and mother than I, and I found it difficult to take his place after he died." Yet Fred tried to be a good family boy even if he felt skittish about that role. On trips he sent newsy letters home signed "Lovingly."[5]

His early memories were leavened with his attempted objectivity when he wrote of his life. Fred was not swept along by feelings from his childhood and youth. He seldom compared his bucolic boyhood with his sophisticated life after college. He almost always managed to enjoy himself and rarely expressed special affection or nostalgia for his past. Apparently, Fred revisited Susquehanna only three times as an adult, mainly to observe the setting of his early life for his autobiography. He profited from all of his environments, growing from and enjoying whatever life brought him.

His family and community largely lacked intellectual and cultural stimulation except for music, classical and popular, which he enjoyed all of his life. Eagerly, he sought out and profited from stimulation from his high school teacher, Miss Graves. Her father had been a teacher of astronomy who expressed unpopular views such as favoring evolution and atheism. Moving up to teach advanced classes as Fred progressed, Miss Graves taught Fred art, religion, penmanship, astronomy, and English literature. Later, Dean Saunders at Hamilton College similarly enriched the cultural background Fred sought.

Despite Miss Graves's teaching, Fred began college feeling like a bumpkin. His rural background suited his childhood, but urban and academic living that comprised his later youth was far more sophisticated. He never regretted either. He adapted so well to his new environment that it became difficult to place him as originally rural. Only in his late sixties, when he began to write his autobiography, did he revisit his rural roots where he had developed his insatiable curiosity, inventiveness, and independence.

It is difficult to imagine Skinner being contented in his simple small-town environment for long. He made the transition to a more cultural life quickly after he reached college. But the decision to attend college had to be his own. No one, not even his parents, advised him on it or knew how to go about entering college. Grandmother Burrhus probably spoke for his relatives and friends when she remarked that Fred should either work for the railroad or become a lawyer like his father.

Inchoately, he pushed himself along, reaching out beyond where he was.

He did not relate well to people. If he had, there might have been someone who would have encouraged him to move ahead educationally. Miss Graves might have helped but she was seriously ill. He thought he was probably rather obnoxious as a student, sure of himself, self-centered, showing little respect for conventions and formalities. These traits would put people off. Later, as a professor, he noted that a graduate student he found objectionable was probably like himself when he was young.

Getting good grades was never a problem for Fred, and his parents took them for granted. He displayed neither boredom nor trouble making, even though he had no courses in arts or mechanics, which appealed to him especially. Cultural programs at school and in town were minimal and primitive, but what did appear became major events in the community—light opera, Chautauqua, science demonstrations, and so on. Social activities tended to be communitywide: fairs and picnics, Civil War veterans' speeches, small circuses, Fourth of July programs—the same as now in many small towns (except for the change in wars involved).

Fred's musical education was paltry. For over a year, he took piano lessons but his father discouraged them for fear they would divert him from more important (though unspecified) alternatives. Nonetheless, he was devoted to music all of his life. His mother sang and his father had played the cornet. As an adolescent, Fred returned to the piano, which he associated with falling in love, then took up the saxophone and played in a small jazz band for movies and dances to earn money. He played whatever classical music he could find for the saxophone. Music remained an integral part of his life thereafter—his main recreation. As an adult, he played piano, harpsichord, and clavichord at home with small string groups of colleagues and students.

As with music, in art he developed his taste for the sophisticated and classical on his own. At first, he practiced drawing with his father's drafting tools. Eventually, he learned to appreciate good painting. By his last years in high school, he was making show cards, painting with watercolors, and drawing in charcoal. He continued to work with watercolors later in his life and encouraged his younger daughter to pursue her interest in art.

He built himself a little reading room at home out of an old packing case, a kind of precursor to other boxes such as the baby-tender and his later personal sleeping box from Japan. He began to write his first novel at age 13 in the romantic spirit of a man who could win a lovely woman. He daydreamed about becoming a famous novelist, poet, and songwriter, and attempted them all, trying to become notable for *something*.

Aware of ethnic and class differences in Susquehanna in religious practices, family traditions, and celebrations, Fred knew that ethnically common people like his family were only part of the population in which the Irish and Italians were conspicuous, and that Catholics and Protestants often lived differently. His reactions were objective, almost scientific, all of his life, and free of common prejudices.

His religious education had more effect. Observing injustice in the world as a child, he decided that punishment and reward in an afterlife would balance what happened on earth. He considered this theory of compensation to be a great revelation, though he later dropped it. Briefly, he took some religious principles seriously. He tried through spiritual power to levitate when he was about 12 years old, and decided to prove the value of Presbyterianism by showing that it was the religion of great composers. He failed at both. He became and remained an atheist for the rest of his life.

His brother died shortly after Fred entered college (Skinner, 1976a, p. 210). Fred had returned home to Scranton (to which his parents had moved after he left for college) for Easter. Ebbe complained of a severe headache and in agony asked Fred to get a doctor. Upon arriving, the doctor immediately pronounced Ebbe dead. Although diagnosed as acute indigestion, later it seemed more likely that it was a cerebral aneurysm. Traumatic as the death was, before Fred's eyes, he expressed mixed feelings about it afterwards. He anticipated demands from his parents that had previously rested on Ebbe. In his early abbreviated autobiography, Skinner (1967) wrote that "when [Ebbe] died suddenly . . . I was not much moved. I probably felt guilty because I was not" (p. 388).

The editor of Skinner's later extended autobiography, Robert Gottlieb, thought the sentiment was too unfeeling, and Skinner (1976a) then wrote, nine years later, that "I submitted to that tragic loss with little or no struggle. . . . But I was far from unmoved. . . . Escape had been the dominant theme in my departure for college. And now . . . I was to be drawn back into the position of a family boy. It was a position I had never wanted, and it was to become increasingly troublesome in the years ahead" (pp. 209–210). Actually, it is difficult to see how his brother's presence made much difference in the way Fred later related to his parents, although they probably became more generous to him financially as their only child.

Although he had seemed objective in observing his family up to this point, Skinner's reaction to his brother's death seemed extremely insensitive given their close relationship. He seemed far more feeling about the deaths of Miss Graves and, later, Sister Annette Walters, and others such as his student Norman Guttman. In fact, death drew his strongest expression of feeling—but not his brother's death.

Above all others, Miss Graves drew out Fred's emotions. He remembered her as attractive and bright eyed, then aging into spinsterhood. Pursuing her father's interests, she kept a notebook of observations on flora and fauna, and had an intellectual life with her parents far beyond what any other families in Susquehanna had, Fred observed. To Skinner, she stood for culture, representing a model of scholarliness and culture, which became his own hallmark.

He searched out her notebooks after her death. In his junior year in high school, she had a relapse of tuberculosis, and by his graduation, she was forced to resign. Skinner visited Miss Graves once after her retirement, as she lay dying.

The most moving scene in his autobiography described that visit (Skinner, 1976a, pp. 154–155). He called his emotion "close to love." He thought for the first time that Miss Graves was beautiful. He sensed her as a human being. He thought she "infected" him with more than a love of literature and art. In closing his tribute to her, he quotes the poem by Emily Dickinson he found in her notebook:

> *They might not need me—yet they might.*
> *I'll let my heart be just in sight;*
> *A smile so small as mine might be*
> *Precisely their necessity. (p. 155)*

Although his emotional attachment was evident in his autobiography, Skinner denied it in our later conversations. It is not the only time he denied feelings that seemed obvious to an observer, both positive and negative ones. The negative ones toward ex-students and admirers who came to disagree with some of his views were especially adamant until toward the end of his life—William Estes, Marian and Keller Breland (though he mellowed toward them), and Richard Herrnstein. They had been close but he remained disappointed with their disagreements with him. Despite his ambivalence, he still valued their friendship, however. But his positive feelings, except toward his wife and daughters, were more often neglected or denied, as with even Miss Graves.

His later disavowal of his positive feelings for Miss Graves was also extended at times to his brother Ebbe, Fred Keller, William Heron, Richard Elliott, and others. His interpretations of his feelings were inconsistent. The positive ones especially were at times obscured; he found them easier to express toward women than men but not unequivocally toward either. What was the matter with his emotions, anyway? He seemed choked up about them, at times almost embarrassed—except where his daughters were concerned.

A kind of bravado may have given rise to his appearance of self-centeredness, arrogance, and coldness, as if to say "Who cares?" from a first-born whose position was usurped by his more attractive and tractable younger brother. Such analysis is purely speculative, but it bears on a key question about his personality—his overt rejection of emotionality and his sometimes parodied cool-headedness (or cold-heartedness).

Skinner observed consistency and stability in his life from his early years on. While the "Dark Year" between college graduation and graduate school when he tried to establish himself as a literary writer marked the most radical intentional shift in his life, he thought that his prior and later development were concordant. "I don't think nature pays any attention [to] what is the nature of the oak. . . . It grows and dies."[6] He viewed his own evolution similarly, mainly as consistent and inevitable.

Soon after he began graduate school, Skinner's position about science hardened and remained relatively unchanged thereafter—except for some mellowing as he aged. "You can say I'm just stubborn" but well before, in his youth, "the lines of my interests in life . . . were very well established. . . . I was always interested in music . . . I remained relatively inactive in politics for a long time. . . . My religion was established then and has not changed [nor] my methods of work."[7]

ENDNOTES

1. B. F. Skinner, personal interview.
2. Ibid.
3. Ibid.
4. Ibid.
5. Ibid. See also Skinner, 1976a, pp. 134, 210.
6. B. F. Skinner, personal interview.
7. Ibid.

2

Finding Psychology
College and the "Dark Year"

No one in Skinner's family had ever attended a liberal arts college nor had talked with him about attending one. Even his attorney father had taken his law degree partly by just "reading" for it in a lawyer's office, with only one year at what was known as the New York Law School. Nonetheless, Fred assumed that he would go to college, even that he was expected to, though by no one specifically. However, no relative or friend had any idea of where he should go, how to choose, or even what one needed to get in. One bright teacher suggested Hamilton College (New York), to which Skinner then made his only application.

At first, his father tried to get Fred to take a legal course by correspondence. He would have liked his son to work in the Skinner law firm—consonant with baby Fred's birth announcement in the local newspaper: "Wm. A. Skinner & Son." But law simply did not interest Fred, despite and perhaps partly because of his father's brief efforts to draw him into it. Certainly, his father's disappointment about his own practice would not have endeared his profession to his son, nor would the distasteful office errands he gave Fred to run for him.

Writing became Fred's major interest early on. He wrote advice for living well, tall stories, reminiscences, and news stories, pursuing any form he thought might fit a market. Mostly, the writings were published in the local paper, but occasionally in a national magazine. Skinner also had other, more regular jobs for pay, such as trying to collect telephone bills for his father. He hated this job, juggled funds to his father's dismay, and was relieved of the work. He also disliked serving legal papers for his father. With his friend "Doc" Miller, Fred briefly and unsuccessfully started a bicycle repair business. His most serious job was as a salesman at a shoe store. There, he developed a device to spread sawdust. There, he also practiced, on one client, as a "practipedist" (with printed cards), making a shoe brace. He stole pennies from the shoe store as well. Playing saxophone for dances and movies and working at the shoe store were his main sources of income the summer before college.

As a youth in high school, Fred did petty embezzling on several jobs. He was open and casual in describing it in his autobiography (Skinner, 1976a). Many children probably do it on a trivial scale—but few admit it. Why did Skinner mention it? Once he said that he thought it made him seem more human, more "one of the boys."[1] Perhaps he wanted scrupulously to cover all aspects of his behavior and didn't mind having such minor transgressions known. In any case, Skinner apparently suffered no significant consequences then or later, except perhaps when he narrowly avoided censure in old age for his overt sexual aggression.

His relationships with girls in high school were almost entirely conversational. He took them out, he petted a little, mainly their legs, he fantasized romantically and sexually, but took no serious sexual initiatives. He remained a fumbling innocent until after he finished college, although while there he had his first intercourse, with a prostitute.

Skinner took difficult courses in high school and graduated second in his small class, just as his father and mother had. The last year, his classes were physics, geometry, English, Cicero, and American history. Unlike many bright students, he was no rebel in school; he never had trouble there. He liked school and he had an open attitude toward its new experiences. Fred's school high jinks were limited to his undergraduate years at college.

As Skinner was finishing high school, his small town was going into a decline. After World War I, the railroad, which dominated the town, began contracting its yards. The library closed. No new industry developed, despite frequently revived hopes for which his father was a conspicuous booster as he delivered his numerous public speeches. His father's career also seemed blighted. He lost another election—in fact, he failed in all races he ran for various offices. His practice was on a plateau. He was blackballed from becoming a Mason for some unknown reason, but probably because he had offended a member. His wife became irritable. Then, suddenly, a case he handled was favorably observed and he was offered and accepted a much better job and income than he had. He became counsel for the railroad—in the substantial city of Scranton. That required the family to move from its geographical roots in small-town Susquehanna and upgrade its style of life.

Thus, Skinner's imminent departure for college was immediately preceded by the family move to elevated living conditions and status in a new city. His parents promptly became upper-middle class, with a much better home, new furnishings, a maid—and the insecurity of unaccustomed social standing. His mother especially was impressed and tried to take on habits and attitudes she considered appropriate to their new status. She upgraded their home and her own appearance.

Hamilton College required applicants to have taken a modern language. Not knowing that, and since his high school taught none, Fred had to study French on his own before he could be admitted. He promptly did so, and passed all of the qualifying exams. By any measure, he was sufficiently smart. He entered the college in the fall of 1922 and adapted to it quickly and well according to his dutiful letters home. He began with zest for college activities and enjoyed his new freedom from home and family.

His independence had been tolerated in Susquehanna, except for his mother's cautions about conforming to social conventions and his father's concern about a career and possible moral delinquencies. Fred's father had observed a few minor misdeeds of his son, especially with money, but his warnings about consequences were exaggerated—and ignored.

In college, Fred had a sense of relief from even such minimal constraints as he had experienced at home. To have felt such a release, he must have been more concerned about his parents' judgments than he had indicated. After college, when he returned home to live while trying to become a writer, he concluded, "I must break from the family and set up some way of living in which I can respect myself" (Skinner, 1976a, n.p.). But it was Fred, not his parents, who sought to make a refuge of his home, when he could think of no other place to go and support himself while he tried to write.

Usually, Skinner seemed to be cheerful, optimistic, and appreciative of whatever goodies were available to him intellectually. Only during his college years did he also enjoy horseplay and practical jokes. Once he got into trouble by inventing and publicizing a supposed visit to campus by Charlie Chaplin. Another occasion involved commencement high jinks that threatened his graduation. His friends and he were supposed to deliver sardonic orations, but, to his dismay, only he ended up doing it.

Even these limited ways he acted out at college suggest that he must have felt more inhibited when he lived at home in Susquehanna than he realized. Despite acting as a free spirit and susceptible to few parental demands, he felt even the minimal limitations at home acutely enough to feel and act unleashed at college.

Fred joined an inferior fraternity before he knew its standing. He stayed on anyway, despite the brutal hazing he received. He did poorly in all extracurricular activities he attempted, even the band, and so he continued to depend on self-generated recreation. His activities almost always were intellectually stimulating or inventive. He seldom participated in any common social doings; in fact, he tended to be contemptuous of them. The course of his life might have changed if he had succeeded in some group program and identification at college. It was his best opportunity up to that time to become part of a social body other than his family—and the Saunders family who befriended him at Hamilton. Mainly, he continued to create his individualized life, staying aloof from others except when they shared his specific interests.

Although Hamilton College and its nearby city, Clinton (NY), were also fairly small and unsophisticated, the academic setting provided advanced cultural background for Skinner. For his first college year, he felt like something of a hick in his speech and manners. He used words such as *tremenjous* and *crick,* he didn't know about tipping, and he hadn't learned not to volunteer answers in class. Partly because he was not sensitive to his peers' attitudes and remained aloof from them, he, like his father, gained a reputation for conceit.

Skinner wrote a lot of poems that later sounded "maudlin" to him. He printed a number of them in his autobiography, not entirely ashamed of them, including even one he judged to be among his worst. His poems were neither very good nor bad, but he wanted desperately to be a writer who was read. Mostly, they seemed clever—he got them printed in a nearby newspaper and in college publications. That characterized most of his writing while he was still trying to be literary. His style imitated others, this one simulating one of his heroes, Christopher Morley (Skinner, 1976a):

> *She let me take a book on love:*
> *She told me she enjoyed it—but*
> *She must have read it hurriedly:*
> *I found some pages yet uncut. (p. 269)*

He longed for female companionship and turned to writing poetry to express his loneliness and yearning, and at times to appeal to girls he liked. He also was a romantic, falling in love with the mere sight of a girl.

During his first Easter vacation from college, his 16-year-old brother suddenly died almost before Fred's eyes. His feelings about his brother were as tightly leashed as they were in other close relationships. And feeling unwillingly drawn into the position of a "family boy" "was to be increasingly troublesome in the years ahead" (Skinner, 1976a, p. 210). Pretty much left alone, he still worried about being beholden to anyone, and thought he had to fight against it. He dedicated the first volume of his full autobiography to a friend who played a much less intimate and pervasive role in his young life than had his brother.

While at Hamilton College, Skinner became acquainted with Dean Saunders and his family, which he believed to be the most important event in his life there. Again, as with Miss Graves's family, the Saunders home was scholarly and cultured. All the children were prepared at home for college, and Skinner was asked to tutor the youngest son in mathematics. He found this family, like the Graves family during high school, helped to satisfy and provide a model for his cultural aspirations in a way that his own family did not.

Dean "Stink," as his students affectionately called him because he taught chemistry, became the closest thing to a model father for Skinner to pattern himself after, although he would never admit it. Saunders was devoted to science, astronomy, and hybridizing peonies. The latter interest may have influenced Skinner to try landscape gardening after graduation, in desperation for productive work after fiddling around with writing. To give the menial work status in his parents' eyes, he said it was to build himself up physically, and he even talked with his employer about educating himself in landscape architecture. But he developed an allergy to grass and thus ended the prospective gardening career.

The period between college graduation and graduate school was designated the "Dark Year" by Skinner. He tried desperately to write but never could do so to his satisfaction—a realistic appraisal of his output which was sparse, intermittent, and led nowhere. Cutting his losses after this strenuous but ineffectual effort, he then abandoned the notion of a writing career except for a wisp of hope that never completely died. His father had agreed to support him for one year while he wrote a novel, and extended it another year while Fred lived hedonistically in Greenwich Village and traveled in Europe.

Before settling in with his life's vocation, he thrashed about despairingly for a way to support himself. He tried making ship models to sell, he tried landscape gardening, he contemplated something else that excited him momentarily—then promptly forgot what it was before he could even record it. Even during his college years, Fred vacillated in his outlook. He was cynical, lonely, and unfulfilled romantically, which he tried to satisfy with sentimental poetry. He read and wrote a lot, cultivated his friendship with the Saunders family, and floundered at efforts to make his mark in a generally unsatisfying place.

Skinner's practical jokes, triggered by a growing self-confidence, skirted danger to his continued enrollment. A private detective was hired to track down the perpetrators of the Chaplin hoax of which he was a major instigator. The college president warned him and his friends who were bent on disrupting commencement to settle down or be denied their degrees. As he was finishing college, he still thought of himself as a writer, boosted by his nostalgia about Miss Graves, the cultural background and interests of the Saunders family, his cleverness at writing which he published in college magazines and papers, and favorable comments he received from Robert Frost.

College had done little to interest Skinner in psychology. He wrote, "The only formal instruction I received [in psychology] lasted ten minutes" (Skinner, 1967, p. 397). It involved a philosophy professor who had studied under the famous experimental psychologist Wilhelm Wundt. He wrote a term paper on Hamlet's madness for which he read about schizophrenia, but he "should not care to have the paper published today" (Skinner, 1967, p. 397). Skinner also wrote a play about a quack who changed people's personalities with endocrines.

He noted that with so little background in scientific psychology, it was only his extraordinary luck that kept him from becoming a Gestalt or a cognitive psychologist. Fred referred to his desultory reading in the classical literature of psychology, which eventually seemed largely irrelevant to his practical nature. The latter eventually led him toward the science of animal behavior via which he committed to psychology. He had, after all, tried as a boy to manipulate the behavior of small animals; he liked to exercise control, which he had not learned how to do with humans; he had an early appreciation of science through Miss Graves and Dean Saunders; and he always tried to plan and direct his own behavior.

Despite reading and thinking about psychological analysis and reading Proust, even in French, it was the writings of the more rigorous scientists such as Ivan Pavlov and John Watson, and philosopher Bertrand Russell, that appealed most to Skinner. That was not merely "extraordinary luck." He was already receptive to science because of his pragmatic intellectual bent even while he still wanted to become a literary writer.

The summer before his senior year, Skinner attended the Middlebury School of English in Vermont (Bread Loaf School). There, he had lunch one day with Robert Frost who asked him to send him some of his work. Skinner sent three short stories. He did not hear from Frost until the following spring. Frost wrote encouragingly, and later published his letter to Skinner. This boost heavily influenced Skinner's life for a year after he graduated from college—and further fueled his lifelong yearning to become a literary writer. He cited it for the rest of his life. Frost wrote:

> *You asked me if there is enough in the stories to warrant your going on. I wish I knew the answer to that half as well as you probably know it in your heart. . . . All that makes a writer is the ability to write strongly and directly from some unaccountable and almost invincible personal prejudice. . . .*
>
> *Those are real niceties of observation you've got here and you've done 'em to a shade. "The Laugh" has the largest value. That's the one you show most as caring in. You see I want you to care. . . . I wish you'd tell me how you come out. . . . I ought to say you have the touch of art. The work is clean run. You are worth twice anyone else I have seen in prose this year. (Skinner, 1976a, pp. 248–249)*

Skinner clung to the message for the rest of his life as the most acceptable validation of his never fulfilled eagerness to succed as a literary writer.

Frost advised him well, although Skinner knew too little about what he lacked and what Frost was saying to be able to assess and apply it. He simply never did know himself, others, and writing itself well enough to "write strongly" and with beliefs that he could sustain in literary writing (except for *Walden Two,* which was technical and dry).

Fred had been unsure of what to do after graduation. Eventually, he told his parents he would like to live at home for a year and write a novel. His father replied with a well-written, at times eloquent, plea for his son to equip himself to make a living and not become an arrogant, hermitic artist, aloof from people, living on crusts of bread.

His father wrote, "I believe you . . . have the ability . . . to study and master about anything you care to undertake. . . . [But] suppose . . . that your dream does not come true. Are you going to be disappointed and feel sour and enter other lines with lack of interest and distaste?" (Skinner, 1976a, pp. 245–248). His father was projecting on his son his disappointment with his own life, although he apparently never expressed what he would have preferred to be rather than a lawyer. In this letter, Fred's father was certainly wise about his son and his life, and he may at other times also have offered more good advice to Fred than Fred remembered or would admit to.

Skinner never replied to Frost. He apparently never tried to put Frost's advice to work, nor did he ever even comment on its contents except for its complimentary nature. He seldom ever acknowledged the advice he got from others and he rarely used it. He did admit that there had been "influences" in his life but he generally left them obscure. For the year he had assigned to it, he tried to write but was never able to sustain hard or productive work. S. R. Coleman (1985a), who studied Skinner's writing during this period, concluded that his "creative writing . . . is surprisingly meager. Nothing . . . is as good as the three stories he sent to Robert Frost. . . . Most are unfinished or spoiled by heavy-handed irony or exaggerated characters" (p. 82). "Social discomfort," and "mockery of the social climber" were characteristic (p. 82). Sinclair Lewis's *Babbitt* was a major model.

By fall of his "Dark Year," Skinner's father offered him a job with a "fabulous salary" managing a self-insurance bureau. Fred couldn't stand the thought of staying in Scranton, however. He corresponded with his old friend, Dean Saunders, of Hamilton College, during this time, full of dissatisfaction with the world. He diverted himself to reading, playing the piano, and listening to music. Finally, with his failure at literary writing stonily confronting him, he did a laborious hack job for his father, abstracting thousands of coal board grievance decisions, his father's arena. A book resulted, which was privately published with his father listed as co-author. Writing itself was no problem for Fred when the material was laid out for him as it was. Creative imagination was the stickler. The volume succeeded as a guide to corporation defenses against employee complaints.

Another factor in his failure as a writer, perhaps the most painful defeat of his life, was the distraction of his home and parents. For the rest of his life,

Skinner gave productive attention to his work environment and schedule. It is surprising that he did not anticipate or acknowledge the difficulties imposed by his return to his home in Scranton. He would be reluctant to admit to not controlling his environment. He did try to ensure his privacy by constructing a separate room at home in which to live and work.

He felt the debacle keenly. First of all, he had a duty to produce because of his commitment to his father for the year of his support. There was no external stimulation, but he thought he could transcend that deficiency. And around him were tempting diversions he believed he could control: listening to music, making ship models, reading haphazardly, working as landscape gardener, and earning money by writing the book with his father.

Finally, however, Skinner decided that "I had proved beyond any doubt that I could not make my way as a writer" (Skinner, 1976a, p. 283). It was an impulsive decision, unusual for him. He then lived for six months in Greenwich Village around artists and available women, and went on to Paris for the rest of what became his two-year "vacation," only the writing half of which he called his "Dark Year."

The months he spent away from work, in New York and Europe, were rich in sensual and social experiences. But Fred quickly tired of them, writing to Dean Saunders, "I am goddam sick of it. I have read, studied, worried, sunk into ecstasy, wallowed in depression, languished in boredom. If nothing else comes of it, I am satisfied that I shall never feel that I am missing life, if I grow to live quietly."[2] He had certainly discovered how he did *not* want to live. He found more serious intellectual alternatives thereafter. Yet he enjoyed at least the sex and free spirit of Greenwich Village, though not passionately enough to continue with it at the expense of a serious career.

Skinner had already concluded that he had nothing important to write, but rationalized his failure by deciding that literature itself could not advance knowledge of the world. Only science could do that, and psychology was the science that would give him an understanding of human behavior that literature and his life had not. But it was his nature, outlook, personality, and life experiences that failed him, not the conditions of literature itself. His life did not generate the material to excite him to write. The content that engaged him deeply turned out to be the science of behavior, and not human emotions.

Field animals had attracted him as a boy, and he had tried to train them. The mechanics of human behavior also interested him. Skinner had experimented with methods to ease his way at home with various devices such as a machine that smoked for him when he was not allowed to do so, and papers he wrote on Hamlet's madness and about a quack who changed people's personalities with hormones.

It was his reading, prompted at first by literary interests, that directed Skinner to psychology. Proust sharpened Skinner's habit of objective self-observation and appreciation of distortions of memory and perception. Ivan Pavlov and Jacques Loeb intrigued him with their original observations about animal and plant behavior influenced by the environment. And he was introduced to the rigor and excitement of scientific behaviorism through John Watson and Bertrand Russell. Informed of the importance of Watson's behaviorism in an article by Russell, Skinner read Watson for himself. That stimulated an interest in animal behavior that he retained for the rest of his life. In Pavlov, he found his model for a dedicated experimental scientist.

H. G. Wells had most sharply confronted Skinner with the choice between a literary and a scientific career, epitomized in a *New York Times* report in 1927. Wells was quoted as saying,

> *I have before me . . . a very momentous book. It is entitled "Conditioned Reflexes," and it is by Professor Pavloff [sic]. . . . I find—that one has at least attained the broad beginnings of a clear conception of . . . the convoluted gray matter of the brain. . . . I have an admiration and affection at least as strong . . . for . . . George Bernard Shaw. . . . I come somewhere between them . . . I have been amusing myself . . . with that . . . game of the "one life belt" . . . to which of the two would you throw it?. . . . I was manifestly obliged to ask myself, "What is the good of Shaw?" "And what is the good of Pavloff?" Pavloff is a star which lights the world, shining above a vista hitherto unexplored. Why should I hesitate with my life belt for one moment?*

Wells chose "Pavloff," and Skinner agreed.

In the fall of 1927, Skinner finally chose psychology as his field for graduate work. He had to choose something since the grace period he had accepted from his father (and an extra year besides) to become a writer had expired. He needed something novel. He had been derisive of much that was conventional; he didn't seem to take seriously a manual job such as landscape gardening.

Behaviorist psychology was fundamentally at odds with existing forms of psychology that were based mainly on the mind and introspection. Skinner was intrigued when he read in the iconoclastic Bertrand Russell whom he admired: "Dr. Watson's Behaviorism is the spearhead of this attack" on traditional philosophy. Later, at a party in Minnesota, seated next to Russell, Skinner remarked that Russell's *Philosophy* had converted him to behaviorism. "Good heavens," replied Russell, "I thought it had demolished behaviorism" (Skinner, 1979, p. 224). Regardless of Russell's intent, Skinner remembered only that his attention had been directed to this new cutting edge theory in psychology that was given respectability by an admired philosopher but was not (yet) popular.

Furthermore, Skinner (1976a) had decided that the kind of writing that fit in with his idea of pure literature was objective writing. Thus, his interests in psychology, writing, and science were meshing nicely with his cynicism about conventional views in these fields. It also provided him with an excuse for failing to write literature: It was the deficiencies of the field itself.

Skinner was ripe for a frontier of science, which he found in the unconventional science of behaviorism. Though he was still largely uneducated in psychology and science when he appeared at Harvard in the fall of 1928 for a graduate school education, he had already determined his orientation. He would thereafter pursue, develop, and, within limits, argue for behaviorism as tenaciously as he had insisted in high school that Bacon had written the works attributed to Shakespeare.

ENDNOTE

1. B. F. Skinner, personal interview.
2. From Skinner's unpublished correspondence with Dean Saunders.

▶ 3

Harvard Graduate School

Becoming a Psychologist

To the great relief of his father who had been supporting him while he tried to begin a serious literary career, Skinner decided to enroll in the Department of Philosophy and Psychology at Harvard University. His father had only the foggiest notion of what psychology was as a profession or what his son could do with it. But at least Fred was getting on with his life at a noted university, and climbing out of the rut of failure at writing, a flirtation with manual labor, and a fling at frivolous living in Greenwich Village and Europe. As Fred put it, "I was escaping from an intolerable alternative" (Skinner, 1979, p. 37). He referred to having been living in a state of suspension with his parents.

> I didn't plan my life. . . . At the end of my college career . . .[it was] touch and go. . . . I had a successful repertoire of college behavior . . . second in my small class of 50 . . . I made a great mistake . . . I tried to go home and write in my family's ambiance. It was a disastrous year. I didn't do a damn thing. It was awful. I did everything except write. I found reasons for not writing. . . . I built myself a little room on the top floor. I partitioned myself off some open space there. . . . I was going to write a novel but I didn't know anything about how. . . . It was a fantastic waste of time. I capitulated and went out and got a job working as a landscape gardener . . . I didn't know where the hell I was going to go. I even talked to a landscape gardener about how many years it takes to become [one] . . . anything at all that would have given me an out.[1]

Skinner continued, "I earned some money writing a hack book on work-man's compensation"[2] with and for his father, which he believed earned him much of his college expenses. He also "thought of going back to Hamilton College to study English."[3] Then, through a Hamilton professor, he turned to reading Pavlov and Russell, and on to Watson's "Behaviorism."

I then declared myself as a behaviorist. Nothing that I planned. . . . Watson convinced me of that . . . I found Fred Keller . . . I was very close to Trueblood [another student] . . .[they] were very good behaviorists . . . that kept me going . . . that got me into constructing what turned out to be the operant box with rats pressing levers. . . . Here [Watson's book] was some-one fighting a battle. . . . I wrote a review of a book "The Religion Called Behaviorism" . . . and sent it off.[4]

Here again is Skinner proclaiming the accidental nature of his life, and how coincidences in various combinations at different times shaped his career. What stands out is that his first and most emotional choice was to write literature, and he still suffered at the end of his life from the terrible pang of that failure.

Watson's passionate fighting words on behalf of his new science of behav-iorism gripped Skinner at a highly vulnerable period following his most abysmal failure. It gave him an "out" at that crucial time. He could go to graduate school to study this intellectually stimulating theory endorsed by the most famous and socially rebellious contemporary philosopher, Bertrand Russell. Although his personal behavior was conventional, Skinner considered himself something of an intellectual freebooter all of his life, a kind of Sinclair Lewis or Sigmund Freud run amok in the severely constrained world of experimental psychology.

Among a dozen or so centers of American psychology, Harvard's depart-ment "may not have been the most American [it was heavily derived from Europe] but it was probably the most prestigious" (Keller, 1970, p. 29). Keller observed that getting admitted to Harvard's graduate school was simple: a letter of recommendation, a personal introduction to the chairman of the department, a brief interview, and a bachelor's degree regardless of specialty or distinction. Skinner thought that the high reputations Harvard and Colum-bia had in psychology at the time were outdated.

Nonetheless, Harvard was initially somewhat intimidating to Skinner with his mediocre cultural background and education. Also, it operated in the tradition that newcomers should fend for themselves, and its "erudition, remoteness, and austerity" (Keller, 1970, p. 29) put off new students. Although he never admitted it, it must have had a daunting effect on Skinner. He lost weight and his heart skipped beats, the latter eventually clearing up after a physician assured him his heart was in good shape. The heart symptom reappeared much later in his life while he was touring to promote *Beyond Freedom and Dignity* but never turned out to be serious.

Constantly making the best of life as he found it and denying difficulty in adapting to new circumstances, Skinner would not admit to the stress that Keller diagnosed. Skinner proceeded vigorously with his research, turning himself into a capable student in his field who enjoyed his work and gained confidence as he devised progressively more productive experimental procedures. He savored his exciting discoveries, which popped up frequently. Once, for example, the pellet [food] dispenser to reinforce his rats jammed, and he discovered an extinction curve for learning as he spaced the pellets. He also noted the effectiveness of intermittent reinforcement when, after spacing the pellets, he found that was more reinforcing than feeding the animals each time they performed as he wanted them to. He reported these results at an American Psychological Association meeting in 1932. He wrote of reinforcing learning rather than conditioning it.

To spur him on when his energy flagged, Skinner would start to read in Edwin G. Boring's (a distinguished psychology professor) book titled *Physical Dimensions of Consciousness*. It "infuriated" him with its "refusal to recognize the possibility of a science of behavior" (Skinner, 1979, p. 94). Introspecting, Boring and his ilk described events in the brain as a conscious process, contrary to Skinner's views.

In opening the second volume of his autobiography, *The Shaping of a Behaviorist* (1979), Skinner observed, "Harvard University takes little or no interest in the private lives of its graduate students" (p. 1)—not even helping them find living quarters, which Skinner had trouble locating. Feeling so far behind in the new field he had chosen, he at first imposed a severe study regimen on himself. But he corrected himself when he wrote his autobiography, remarking that "I was recalling a pose rather than the life I had actually led" (p. 5). Life then, he thought, was really easier than he felt it to be at the time. In a short time, he acclimated very well to psychology and Cambridge. Indeed, it quickly seemed like his home territory, so much so that many people who knew him over a period of years thought that he had always been at Harvard.

Recalling his student days, Skinner wrote,

> It is hard to live in New England without becoming a New Englander. If I read any paper, it was the Boston Evening Transcript, *whose readers, said T. S. Eliot, "sway in the wind, like a field of ripe corn." Every day I passed that statue of Ralph Waldo Emerson. . . . I visited Emerson's study. . . . I visited the Alcott House and drove past Hawthorne's. . . . Then I discovered Waldon Pond and I began to go there. (Skinner, 1979, p. 114)*

Fred also continued to depend on his parents. His father contributed financially all of his life to Fred's major purchases. He asked his mother to make a cover and cushions for his bed and to do his laundry regularly—not unusual for college students of that time. For a short time, he earned money by summarizing Italian and German scientific articles for *Psychological Abstracts.* Never, however, did he like doing routine tasks for others. As a graduate student, he worked very little for pay.

Later, Skinner decided that he had led a more amiable life interacting with students and faculty than he first recalled. He especially noted any behavioristic influences he found around him but was reserved in his attitudes about them. S. R. Coleman (1987), who much later examined and discussed with Skinner his early experimental work, found little evidence of a clearly behavioristic commitment until after Skinner obtained his doctorate degree.

In his autobiography, Skinner wrote, "I was not entirely untouched by these introspective predilections [of my professors]. The whole field of psychology was new to me and much of it fascinating" (1979, p. 10). "All this would have been anathema to John B. Watson, and to me, too, in my soberer moments" (p. 10), Skinner wrote of his general theoretical stance. "I was a *behaviorist,* and for me behaviorism was psychology, converted by Bertrand Russell who had written, 'It will be seen that the (Russell's) above remarks are strongly influenced by Dr. Watson, whose latest book, *Behaviorism,* I consider massively impressive" (p. 10). Russell struck Skinner as more sophisticated about the meaning and significance of behaviorism than Watson.

Beginning to build a library, Skinner's first three books were Bertrand Russell's *Philosophy,* John B. Watson's *Behaviorism,* and Pavlov's *Conditioned Reflexes* (Skinner, 1979, p. 4). He did not fully accept Watson as his mentor. For one matter, "Watson . . . had spent too much time on a behavioristic explanation of mental life. The subject matter at issue was *behavior"* (p. 94). Besides, Watson gradually became sharply controversial for both his extreme antigenetic views, which Skinner never shared, and for a promiscuous sexual life that lost him his academic position and any prospects for one. Skinner never commented on the latter except to remark that Watson had been treated unfairly.

In a paper delivered to the American Psychological Association convention in 1988, John Burnham reviewed Watson's colorful, erratic life in detail. Watson had publicly abjured belief in God and lived a sexual life that led Burnham to conclude that "he may have been one of the great lovers of all time." He powerfully influenced people, liked to shock them (as in soliciting funds for his behavioristic "baby farm"), and said that Freud used his analytic method to put down others because he himself felt inferior. Watson ended up as a successful advertising executive where his charm and eloquence were richly rewarded. He was a strong advocate for scientific objectivity but did not practice it. According to Burnham, there were countless contradictions between his theories and his behavior, yet he became the most powerful symbol of behaviorism until Skinner.

Perhaps Watson should have become known as a "radical behaviorist" rather than Skinner, in the sense of applying behaviorism. After all, Watson had written, "Give me a dozen healthy infants, well-formed, and my own specified world to bring them up in, and I'll guarantee to take any one at random and train him to become any type of specialist I might select" (Skinner, 1979, p. 331). The reservations he included about so strong a position never caught up with his claims. Later, Skinner said that "although as a psychologist I was concerned with behavior, that did not of necessity make me a behaviorist" (p. 331). To the end, Skinner was reluctant to label himself, and he objected to the designation that his beloved daughter Julie chose for their field: "behaviorology."[5]

When Watson died, his reputation for loose living and inconsistent theory led several prominent psychologists to refuse to write his obituary, including R. M. Elliott, chairman of the Psychology Department at Minnesota, and the eminent neuropsychologist, Karl Lashley. Edwin G. Boring eventually got Woodworth to write it. Woodworth cited mostly others' views rather than his own. A year after Watson's death in 1958, Skinner wrote in a *Science* magazine article that Watson was "to be remembered for a long time. . . . for a too narrow interpretation of self-observation, for an extreme elitism, and for a coldly detached theory of child care, no one of which was a necessary part of his original program. His brilliant glimpse of the need for, and the nature and implications of, a science of behavior was all but forgotten" (1959b, p. 190). Equally harsh criticism was to be turned on Skinner, but neither Watson's nor Skinner's role in proclaiming a science of behavior is likely to be forgotten.

Watson was treated at least as critically as he was respectfully by Skinner who would not admit of a mentor or father figure. Watson's name will long be associated with behaviorism, as will Skinner's, but Skinner sought to be distinctive rather than merely associated with a previously named theory. Watson was clearly Skinner's professional "father," but Skinner was ambivalent about the relationship—nor did he ever cultivate a friendship with Watson.

Skinner did write, "I think Watson has got a raw deal from the behaviorists who have shied away from him because of the reputation that followed from his later activities."[6] Yet, just as Watson must be credited with announcing the science of behavior, Skinner surely also deserves a unique place as fleshing out the science experimentally as Waston never attempted to do. Skinner, incidentally, might well have been damned as Watson was for his sexual peccadilloes had he lived around the same time and had the occurrences become more public.

In addition to his own reading, Skinner was drawn to behaviorism by fellow students. He joined especially with two graduate students, one of whom was Charles Trueblood, who was running maze experiments but was "timid" and "not inclined to defend his position in public" (Skinner, 1979, p. 13). Much more important to Skinner was Fred Keller, who gently but firmly defended his own behavioristic position. "It was largely because of Fred [Keller]," Skinner wrote, "that I resisted the mentalistic predispositions of the department and remained a behaviorist. . . . Nevertheless I went on writing notes which were scarcely behavioristic in tone" (p. 14).

Skinner's advocacy of behaviorism did not become robust until he completed his doctorate. He sharpened his thoughts and tone as he prepared to write what became his magnum opus, *The Behavior of Organisms*. He may deliberately have curbed his tongue until his book was out in which he could present his thoughts in the most orderly and cogent fashion to establish his reputation as the leader in the field. Although his autobiography traces various elements which, from early in his graduate education, influenced him toward behaviorism, he had not yet clearly committed himself exclusively to it. He continued to reflect other theories presented by his professors.

Skinner frequently argued with his teachers. The head of the psychological clinic, Henry Murray, told Skinner much later that Skinner had written Murray the rudest letter he had ever received. What Skinner had written him was a Freudian interpretation of Murray's use of the word *regnancy* as if Murray had inadvertently left off a first letter, *P*. Skinner analyzed that as an unconscious block revealing Murray's hidden thoughts about pregnancy (Skinner, 1979).

In a letter to his parents, Skinner wrote of one of his classes, "Two or three of the other men and I monopolized the time. . . . I made two or three sharp observations about some errors" about which Skinner observed "I could scarcely have known what I was talking about. I had had no undergraduate courses in psychology and had been a graduate student for only one month" (1979, p. 14). Still struggling with his desire to produce literature, he wrote that "small polemics against literature continued to appear in my notebook, but so did . . . many examples of Proustian recall" (p. 14). This kind of ambivalence toward literature cropped up for the rest of his life.

From the beginning, psychology in the Department of Philosophy and Psychology at Harvard did not inspire Skinner. He did, however, enjoy the challenge of the intellectual ambiance and the opportunities to learn from and speak among intelligent and knowledgeable colleagues and professors. It was a very formal, conservative department devoted to the study of reflexes and psychophysical measurement—"brass instrument psychology" William James had earlier called it. But Skinner was allowed the freedom to experiment and disagree as he struggled to find a voice and stature for himself.

The academic and intellectual leader of psychology at Harvard was the head of the psychological laboratory, Edwin G. Boring, known to colleagues as "Garry"—but not to Skinner until after he acquired his Ph.D. Keller, who took most of the same courses with Skinner, was cooler and more objective about their classes and instructors. Skinner wrote much more sharply of their merits and deficiencies and especially of his disagreements with them, some expressed openly, some not. His opinions hinged particularly around whether they were sympathetic to behaviorism and to external scientific measurement rather than introspection—and whether they contributed to his education and interests.

In a 1988 interview, Skinner reported, "I wasn't a behaviorist, I didn't know a thing about behaviorism, but I was a dedicated behaviorist just as a stance." He reviewed his history of contentiousness: It "attracts me . . . something to argue about. I became a big arguer for behaviorism before I knew anything at all about it. . . . Nobody in our department believed in it at all [but] the precedent had already been established of face to face arguments with the staff as if we were equals . . . amazing."[7]

Skinner tilted with Murray and his clinical (Freudian) interests and he criticized defective laboratory apparatus to experimentalist Carroll Pratt. Striking out into new territory, he was especially attracted to a newcomer named William Crozier, who had been hired to head physiology and was "building an empire" by insisting on larger quarters, training a young staff, and using a textbook discussing the conditioned reflexes of Pavlov and also spinal reflexes. Also attracting Skinner to Crozier was the opportunity to construct apparatus, the freedom to do research, and the encouragement to study insects under controlled conditions. Skinner's first published scentific paper (Skinner & Barnes 1930) was on the locomotion of the black ant under various conditions in Crozier's laboratory.

Keller was far more enthusiastic and objective in describing the strengths and idiosyncrasies of their professors. He wrote about his and Fred's schooling like a literary writer—which he also had wanted to be. Skinner, on the other hand, singled out those who especially influenced or interacted with him, commented critically about them, and showed less interest in describing the overall ambiance or an objective picture of his schooling.

Skinner spoke and wrote little of his feelings about Keller other than a benign friendliness and how they changed over the years as Skinner grew more important professionally. Keller's comments were more revealing. Although Keller maintained his independence, he made frequent comments about how many activities they shared at college. Once he remarked how he longed for the opportunity to go off on vacation alone with Skinner.

Obviously, Keller had a "crush" on Skinner that he both tried to curb and wanted to develop further. Skinner was aware of the connotations of their friendship, that it might be misinterpreted as sexual, and told me that he wondered what others thought when the two of them embraced each other at meetings. They even studied together—Keller's comment about it is the only one that indicated Skinner did not always study alone—and Keller reported wryly that while he was the coach for a group of students who met in his room,

Skinner got an A whereas Keller got a B+ from Boring in a class in which Keller wanted to excel.

Keller noted that he and Skinner corresponded regularly at first when Keller left Harvard for a job at Colgate. Keller wrote Fred about personal matters, such as problems with his wife, but Skinner didn't respond personally. "I never felt I did him any good," Keller commented, but "I learned a lot from him" and "I was a sounding board for him."[8] The personality differences between the two men persisted all their lives, even as their friendship endured mainly through Keller's efforts. One was a sensitive, appreciative student and steady scholar, the other was more narcissistic, tenaciously pursuing his personal research for his own theory, and working indefatigably to enlarge its applications

Skinner took notes on influences that affected his dedication to scientific discovery, his interest in building apparatus, his focus on animal behavior, and his rigorously objective, open-ended curiosity. As they pursued their academic careers, Keller placed Skinner as his admired ascendant colleague, personally and scientifically, just as Keller had been respectful of his professors when he was their student. Keller recognized and articulated the danger to his independence, however, when Skinner offered him (and he rejected) a job at Indiana when Skinner was appointed chairman there. Keller worried that he might all too easily fall further under Skinner's spell.

Keller's close friendship with Skinner from graduate days on was a major factor in Keller's academic career. Not only was Skinner's influence obvious in Keller's teaching but he was also frequently asked questions about Skinner because of their known close relationship. Skinner's most obvious reciprocation consisted of appreciating Keller's always strong support and encouragement. Keller willingly provided his reactions to Skinner's ideas and manuscripts.

Closer to Skinner over many years than anyone else, Keller was often asked questions about his best friend. He was, however, a somewhat reluctant source for biographical material about Skinner because of his sensitivity to the rather one-sided impact, his chronic caution and discretion, and Skinner's denial of emotional reactions and apparent indifference to giving or receiving confidences. Besides, Keller was an illustrious psychologist in his own right and he made Columbia a major center for behavioristic teaching, research, and publications.

Keller apparently provided no revelations about Skinner to anyone. Even in his nineties, he was guarded and ultra-discreet in what he would say about Skinner's personal life. He hedged, for example, on knowledge of Skinner's extramarital escapades and about Skinner's relationship with his wife Eve, which more casual friends were willing to appraise. Keller was friendly and invariably courteous, yet Skinner knew him as tougher than he seemed. As graduate students, they had lived in the same building, sharing food tastes, bicycling, writing, and rebelliousness against parents, religous views, and college conventions such as physical education and chapel. They were "tamely un-American," said Keller (1970, p. 34). Their social and political activities were quite conventional.

Most radically, they were "budding *behaviorists*," Keller wrote (1970, p. 35). Skinner was guardedly a loner, as Keller saw him, not discussing his hopes, plans, or experiments until he had hard results in hand. Keller further saw Skinner as a "systematist" and experimentalist. Belatedly reading *The Behavior of Organisms*, he was surprised that Skinner had so highly developed his research-grounded theory. Skinner's commitment to behaviorism had been more in his thoughts than on his tongue or pen as a fellow student. Keller was stunned to note how far along Skinner had moved in the book in his commitment to behaviorism.

Although Skinner had led a robust sexual life in his second year off after Hamilton College, financially supported by his father, he took a temporary recess from women during his graduate years. Trying to catch up in psychology, he wrote that he was too busy with his intellectual and professional pursuits to socialize frivolously, especially after his two wasteful prior years. Besides, Harvard was almost entirely male at the time and did not facilitate meetings between men and women. The three years he worked on his Ph.D. were probably his most barren, sexually, since his adolescence. He met only one woman he considered marrying. After gaining his degree, he quickly resumed his sexual escapades, daily regaling his fellow counselors in the dormitories, including John Kenneth Galbraith, with stories of his latest adventures.

Upon arriving at Harvard, Skinner resumed his friendship from his adolescence with Raphael "Doc" Miller, who was in his second year at Harvard Medical School. At first, Doc was Skinner's model of a virtuous student: hardworking, focused, and accepting of and meeting college standards with minimal carping. Miller, however, soon proved to be in more need of help than Skinner. He became seriously psychosomatic and depressed. Skinner tried to reassure him, but eventually accompanied him home. A rare personal intervention for Skinner, he demonstrated clinical sensitivity and skill despite his failure to get his friend to stay in school. Doc never did return to Harvard, although he recovered his spirit and his desire to do so. But that summer, he died at age 25 in a boating accident while still at home. Much later, in 1976, Skinner fulfilled his early promise to dedicate a book to him, the first volume of his autobiography, *Particulars of My Life*.

Although pleased with his psychological acumen enough to describe it in his autobiography Skinner added, "Nevertheless, I was determined to be a *scientific* psychologist!" (1979, p. 27). Essentially, he rejected clinical psychology, calling its Harvard head, Henry Murray, a "literary psychologist." He dismissed as unscientific the Freudian and Jungian explanations of behavior that were popular among his peers. Accommodating to the time and place, however, Skinner indulged in analytic descriptions of behavior in casual conversations and was exceptionally receptive to Freud, whose work he once described as "scientific."

The difference in psychology between 1926 and now, Keller wrote in 1970, "started at Harvard University, during the late twenties and early thirties, in the experimental and theoretical labors of Burrhus Frederic Skinner" (p. 36). Ending his description of their years at Harvard, he quoted from Skinner's inscription to him in *The Behavior of Organisms*: "To Fred Keller—for friendship and faith when they were most needed—Burrhus" (p. 36). It was one of Skinner's rare tributes. (For all his life, Keller called his friend by his true first name [his mother's maiden name] to distinguish him, Keller said, from the other Freds in the world.)

Early on, Skinner was attracted to and studied environmental factors that influenced animal behavior. In experimental psychology at Harvard, reflexes were discussed as if they were largely self-contained, and environmental influences were ignored as if they were irrelevant. There was a long history to the isolated consideration of *stimulus* and *response*. Skinner, by studying environmental influences, was giving a different meaning to the concept of "reflex" as used by his advisor, Boring, along with most other academic psychologists. Skinner constructed his own apparatuses, eight or nine different kinds for the experiments he devised. As a student, he had not yet found the theory that would encompass his ideas but he obviously enjoyed inventing equipment and tabulating his animals' responses. Meanwhile, he was accumulating the background in his self-directed and often fortuitous reading—and laboratory results—that would undergird his thesis arguments.

Later, Skinner would argue forcefully against the commonly held belief among scientists, even to the present day, that experimentation should formally follow steps of hypothesis, deduction, experimentation, and confirmation. Describing his earliest laboratory conduct, in 1952, Skinner wrote, "I never attacked a problem by constructing a Hypothesis. I never deduced Theorems or submitted them to Experimental Check. So far as I can see, I had no preconceived Model of behavior. . . . Of course, I was working on a basic Assumption—that there was order in behavior if I could only discover it" (1952, pp. 221–223). Many discoveries had always occurred in science accidentally, as in the relatively recent case of penicillin, but no one had stated as clearly the rationale for encouraging and exploiting the appearance of serendipitous results.

Luck, accident, naive curiosity—they were Skinner's strike points and he became increasingly confident in advancing them as his role in psychology became more secure. Theory, he wrote in 1950, was not necessary. Throughout his life, however, he was also determined to find the lawfulness, the order in nature, as the basis for the prediction and control of animal behavior.

More important to Skinner's graduate school research than any psychology professor was physiologist W. J. Crozier. Crozier became Skinner's dissertation adviser, although Boring formally held that title and presumably oversaw the writing. While never becoming a disciple of Crozier's (or any one else's), Skinner was influenced by his quantitative approach, use of animal subjects, and physiological measurements. He also liked Crozier's use of small numbers of subjects and nonstatistical analysis. Skinner's first published research derived from experiments in Crozier's laboratory on ants traveling up a slanted surface. In the same lab, Skinner later worked with the movement of squirrels and rats, of note chiefly because of his cleverness in building boxes in which to run the animals and constructing equipment to record their movement.

Fred was learning how a wide variety of stimuli affected his results and of the need to control such variables as sound so that he could more purely concentrate on, say, an animal's locomotion and control of its rewards. He needed to construct a soundproof box, for one thing, and to study a more limited kind of behavior than locomotion. He also needed to find a way to record when the rat pressed for food and under what circumstances. He constructed the box and measuring methods in applying to the National Research Council for a fellowship to continue his work. After he obtained his doctorate in 1931, Skinner was ready to use his apparatuses, which remained essentially the same for many years. One major improvement, however, was to substitute a lever for a plate for the animal to press. His Minnesota colleague, William Heron, thought that was one of his most important contributions in the laboratory. It was the key to reinforcing behavior promptly with food.

Skinner never did apply very sophisticated statistical analysis to his data. It didn't interest him; in fact, he poked fun at those, including his early student and later colleague, William Estes, who did apply complex mathematics to their data. He preferred to control and predict the single case without calculating the *tendencies* of a group. He was attracted to concrete individual findings more than to general trends, and he settled on criteria of orderly behavioral change, observable results, and facilitating conditions for his study of learning. In *A Matter of Consequences* (1984), he noted "that Bush and Mosteller had wasted 'vast quantities of impeccable mathematics on vast quantities of peccable data' " (p. 124).

As a student, Skinner had not yet formulated his notions about "operant" behavior differentiated from "respondent" behavior, and conditions for the reinforcement and shaping of behavior that the experimenter wanted to produce. The materials for his breakthrough were present but not yet their clear, systematic presentation. He was, at first, fully engaged in building equipment, measuring responses, and attempting to find and describe orderliness in animal responses.

In *The Shaping of a Behaviorist*, he wrote, "I was confirmed in my choice of psychology as a profession not so much by what I was learning as by the machine shop" (1979, p. 31) in the psychology building. Fred had the run of the place and was delighted with the tools he found that he had never before used. "The shop became my center of activity," he noted (p. 32). There, he made his first silent release box for rats. He thoroughly enjoyed building the mechanisms for his experiments. It was as if he had finally found the best use for inherited mechanical skills he had merely played with until then.

Skinner was still fumbling for a theory of his own on how animals learn. As in his literary career with styles and forms, he experimented with the tools of the lab and developed his skill in using them. He tried different voices, searching for the one that he liked most and would give him greatest influence. With great reluctance, he continually laid aside his interest in writing literature, deciding his prospects were better in psychology. As usual throughout his life, Fred was ever ready to think anticonventionally—in this situation, to change psychology as it was being taught in terms of reflexes relatively independent of environmental influences. He eschewed close relationships and social activities in order to concentrate on creating a new theory. He studied hard what interested him, including physiology and neurology.

Skinner progressed fast with his courses, though he had no sense of mastering the psychology—or the German or statistics—that he had to take. It was like a game that he barely managed to endure, noting, "Nor was I ever to learn much more psychology at Harvard" (Skinner, 1979, p. 14). Thereafter, he signed up (with few exceptions) for research courses that required only that he pay his fees and work independently. He worked without supervision, occasionally producing a sketchy report.

By the end of his graduate training, Skinner was acknowledged to be the most outspoken student against predominant views in the Psychology Department. Although his two friends joined him in arguing persistently for behaviorism, he stood alone in his confrontation with Boring, the most powerful figure in the department, on his thesis. He was also outspoken in his efforts to broaden the interpretation of animal behavior beyond conditioned reflexes and toward a theory of reinforcement he would make his own. His friend Keller lacked the determination to fight for his own thesis as he first wrote it, as Skinner had done for his own.

Trueblood and Keller were more sophisticated graduate students who, like Skinner, questioned the static conventional psychological views of the department. Keller rebelled but with more grace, and Trueblood with more timidity. They agreed in wanting to study animal behavior as it was affected by surrounding influences, but only Skinner had the bravado for confrontations. Recognizing his initially inadequate education in psychology, Skinner laid out a regimen of dedicated, heavy study. His schedule was more rigorous than ever before. Rising at 6:00 A.M., he went to classes, libraries, and laboratories during a strictly programmed day until 9:00 P.M. when he went to bed. He did little except study psychology and physiology for two years, although he later softened his application of this strict plan.

The conventional program in the department was easy for him but generally dull. The exception was the weekly colloquiums. There, he found excitement, challenge, and free rein to argue for a psychology of behavior based on natural laws rather than free will or conditioned habits. As always, Skinner tried to sharpen his language to reflect his thoughts precisely, but he found himself speaking of feelings and using other mentalistic words that he did not like. Finally, he decided "that in using the vernacular I was no more a traitor to my science than the astronomer who comments on a beautiful sunset knowing full well that the sun does not 'set' " (Skinner, 1979, p. 80). "Burrhus," Keller noted, "says a thing in its most extreme form and takes some of it back if he has to" (p. 80).

Skinner was allowed to pick and choose among course offerings, although he had to prepare himself for the standard exams. Informality prevailed; he even wrote a smart-aleck letter to Murray, his professor for abnormal psychology. At a party, Skinner argued against philosophy with an old man unknown to him who struck up a conversation. He later learned that it was the eminent philosopher, Alfred Whitehead, who told Skinner that a young psychologist should pay attention to philosophy. Skinner replied that what was needed was a psychological epistemology.

When it came to writing a thesis, Fred took the advice of a friendly faculty member and decided to submit a lesser study than he wanted to do. To get the requirement over with as soon as possible, he would describe factors affecting a limited reflex. Afterwards, he could then proceed on his own to more comprehensive work on a "science of behavior." It is common enough for faculty to advise restraint to ambitious graduate students from spending more than minimal time on a thesis. After taking such counsel, however, few students follow through later when they are free to pursue research as they please. Most do not then follow their originally most creative ideas. But Skinner promptly did just that.

Skinner had his Ph.D. in three years, in 1931. He claims not to have celebrated it; in fact, he seems never to have celebrated anything much—birth, honors, anniversaries, and such. But it did unleash him to work in complete independence. His desire for autonomy, demonstrated since childhood, now became clear, concrete, and focused, and dominant for the rest of his life. His goal was to shape animal behavior—and to change the world. After receiving his doctorate, he continued on at Harvard, on a fellowship. It was designed to support outstanding students who wanted to continue their own research without having to take a conventional academic job right away.

Although Skinner never made much of it, probably the most dramatic chapter in his life was his confrontation with his advisor Boring about his thesis. Was he courageous, confrontational, antagonistic, stubborn, or arrogant? To have to choose one word would illustrate the difficulty of capturing his personality. At the least, it was a uniquely fearsome risk for a doctoral candidate. Considering the rigid and arbitrary doctorate process at the time and the powerful tenacity and stature of his adversary, Boring, Skinner's insistence on submitting his thesis essentially as he conceived and wrote it seemed foolhardly. This is especially true since Boring submitted a detailed critique that called for changes. Skinner stared down Boring, whom he assumed would become his lifelong enemy. Boring blinked—he withdrew from the committee and let his student have his way.

S. R. Coleman (1985b) wrote a blow-by-blow account of the episode in his article, "When Historians Disagree: B. F. Skinner and E. B. Boring, 1930." In brief, Skinner's haphazard reading in psychology and poor organization of his knowledge clashed with Boring's systemization of the field, which produced his definitive volume called *A History of Experimental Psychology.* Most students were intimidated by Boring's manner and presence. He looked tough, was built like a wrestler, and spoke authoritatively. Seldom was he crossed. He was thorough and careful in his presentations, and in his extended controversy with Skinner he wrote long, well-documented notes and letters. Yet Skinner never winced, apologized, or compromised.

The disagreement turned on several factors vital in Boring's career: his sense of history, his great-man interpretations of progress in psychology, and his insistence on a well-defined common understanding of the reflex and its cruciality in learning. Mostly, he was impatient with Skinner's unsystematized study and single-minded redefinition of the reflex, which enlarged its context to include environmental factors.

Boring opened the joust by sending Skinner five typed pages requesting extensive changes in Part I of his thesis: to correct its inadequate historiography and style, particularly its poor organization, its superficial arguments, and its flowery language. Without any interaction with Boring, one month later Skinner had his critical discussion of the reflex accepted for professional publication—a novel move that gave credibility to his work outside his thesis committee.

Toning down his critique after his failure to get Skinner to modify Part I of the thesis, Boring wrote of Part II:

> *Dear Skinner: I have no criticisms that you would wish to accept, and I have many fewer that you would not wish to accept than I had of Part I. . . . I do not mean to be harsh, but your very versatility and you[r] polemical [cleverness] make it necessary for some older people to tell you bluntly where they think the trouble lies. Otherwise you might go through life doing half-baked work which wins applause from the uncritical and the unsophisticated . . . never realizing that your work was superficial. . . .*
>
> *I am not angry with you, but I was shocked by our conversation this*

morning. . . . You have very unusual experimental ability; you have excep-
tional drive; you write well, your enthusiastic personality will make you a
stimulus to others, you think clearly when your drive does not carry you away.
The only flaw in this gem [is] that he is too clever always to be thorough . . .
and that he believes, because human beings can not be purely rational, that
tricky sophistical argument is justified if the end is justified. Am I just
old-fashioned?[9]

Despite an intense yet politic letter to influence Skinner, and three more notes
and letters from Boring, Skinner refused to change the thesis, replying that
"most of our disagreement can be made intelligible with a single assumption:
namely, that you approached the thesis with a particular Aufgabe . . .[namely]
that I was offering a Behavioristic broadside."[10] After stating that the final
judgment of the thesis "will be up to the committee," Skinner then quoted to
Boring these slightly altered lines from Thomas Hood: "To them I shall submit
it—Owning her weakness./Her evil behavior./And leaving with meekness/Her
sins to her Saviour" (Skinner, 1979, p. 73). The oral exam on the thesis went
well enough and Skinner had qualified for his degree without Boring's further
intervention.

The bare bones of this exchange bespoke a probably unprecedented
stubbornness of a Ph.D. candidate with his advisor. It had to be extremely
reinforcing to Skinner's demand for autonomy in that tough scholarly environment—because he won entirely. Boring totally capitulated by asking the
department chairman to leave him off Skinner's thesis committee, then accepted the thesis as it was and offered Skinner a valued postgraduate fellowship. The oral exam itself was "plain sailing," with Skinner's only discomfort
coming from Gordon Allport, who asked, "What are some of the objections to
behaviorism?" Skinner later wrote, "I could not think of a single one" (Skinner,
1979, p. 75).

Skinner apparently never considered the worst that might happen—that
his thesis would be turned down. When asked, he said he thought he would
have enough support from other faculty members to get through. Many other
graduate students have been struck down by their advisor—or another member of the committee. The autocratic power of faculty members had not yet
been seriously challenged by student rebelliousness. At that time, at some
institutions, one adverse committee vote could sink a thesis and even a career.

It was perhaps the most dangerous act of his professional life because, as
a student, he had little standing. His support within his committee, however,
included Crozier, the head of physiology, and Skinner already had the prestige
of a publication taken from his thesis (incidentally, not an approved procedure). Boring may well have felt constrained by these two factors but he was
also scrupulously fair and respectful of Skinner's creativity and hard work,
which Skinner, in his fighting stance, did not recognize. Yet Boring always

supported him thereafter, though still occasionally critical of the same Skinner weaknesses he perceived then. Skinner did not appreciate this fact for years.

Incidentally, Skinner's comrades in dissent in supporting behaviorism, Trueblood and Keller, submitted more traditional and cautious theses, fairly conventional in subject, conclusions, and format. Skinner had found his voice as an advocate for his increasingly distinctive and bold views. No one thereafter would be able to obstruct him professionally in the pursuit of his research and theories. He might still be frustrated in other ways—such as recognition, pay, and occasionally publication—but he would not be deflected by the voluminous repetitive criticism he received to the end of his life.

In written support of Skinner's application for a National Research Council fellowship following completion of his doctorate, Boring referred to his balky student's "effervescent brilliance," his "feverish industry," and his "ebullient enthusiasm," referring to Skinner as "the best of five Ph.D.s which we have had . . . in the last nine years." Continuing, Boring wrote of Skinner's "possibilities of genius," his "delightful personality, and with all his assurance and enthusiasm never creates antagonisms." There is "one serious defect—a desire to found a school or a science of behavior upon research of the type he is doing."[11]

Skinner said he didn't know what he would have done if his committee had insisted on changes. He remarked that he had no serious doubt of his success. Reminded during our conversations that Boring had strongly supported his first academic appointment five years after he completed his degree, to the University of Minnesota faculty, Skinner expressed ambivalence about his fate at Harvard. When he had to leave it, Skinner at times claimed both to understand why Harvard did not try to hire him for its faculty (no appropriate vacancy) and to feel annoyance that it did not make him an offer (if it had really wanted him). He assumed that Boring was the obstacle.

Getting a good job or making money for a comfortable living never much affected Skinner's plans, however insecure he may have felt from time to time. Rather blithely, he expected to obtain what he needed or wanted. In his dedication to his work, he was becoming a stereotypic heroic scientist such as Boring so admired, even while Skinner rejected this concept and role. He considered himself only a fleck in the march of science, he disliked deference, and he was strongly antiheroic in interpreting how science progressed. It is likely that Boring had recognized the attributes that made Skinner's future bright and wanted to anticipate and participate in it despite his difficulties with this pup.

As a Fellow at Harvard, Skinner soon resumed a more social life, mentioning in his autobiography for the first time that he had "made love." When the woman broke off the relationship, Fred branded his arm with an *N* (her first initial), which lasted for years. He discovered from a typist that he had a reputation for conceit, which worried him and which he promptly blamed on a fear of failure, which was his father's chronic anxiety. Such a fear showed itself rarely, however. Nor did he seek the kind of support his father depended on from his wife.

Fred continued to be an inveterate inventor of frivolous as well as important devices. He built toys for the children of friends, he made a kite that released confetti, he made a puppet that tossed a balloon in the air and kicked it, and he continued to make playthings for his animals in boxes, which utilized the same cleverness and whimsy that had characterized his life from childhood.

Skinner was supported by a National Research Council fellowship for two years in the department of general physiology of the medical school at Harvard. For three subsequent years, he was a Junior Fellow in the prestigious Harvard Society of Fellows. It subsidized the most promising postgraduate students who wanted to continue to study or do research at Harvard before embarking on academic careers. Midway through the second year of his initial fellowship, Skinner "drew up plans for the second thirty years of my life" (Skinner, 1979, p. 115):

November 17, 1932

PLAN OF THE CAMPAIGN FOR THE YEARS 30–60

1. *Experimental description of behavior . . .*
2. *Behaviorism vs. Psychology . . .*
3. *Theories of Knowledge . . .*
4. *. . . By far the greater bulk of time should go on 1. (p. 115)*

About his first goal, he wrote to Boring, "I am trying to define a special science concerned with describing the behavior of organisms, and I want to save and to define the reflex as the logical instrument for that description." He didn't know yet whether it was psychology, noting that "I want to define a science of the description of behavior (does it include psych?—I have no idea!)."[12] In fact, from then on, for the rest of his life, he intermittently denied identifying with both the profession of psychology and its professional organizations.

In the historical survey of reflexes for his thesis, Skinner noted that they were assumed to be innate, involuntary, and unconsciously performed. He stated that these were "unscientific presuppositions" and that a science of behavior should be carried out independently from conventional experimental psychology. Basing his emerging theory on animal experiments, he gave as an example the decline in food-seeking behavior in rats that were sated. While on his fellowships, he made a lever-pressing apparatus in the "problem box," eventually called the "Skinner box" (over his objections), which became a vital device for life-long experiments.

Skinner did not believe in systematic thinking and theorizing about research ahead of his experiments. His method was to experiment in the laboratory in whatever ways interested him, with skepticism about proclaimed truth, in theory or in history. In this sense, his behavior was the antithesis of Boring's views of what it should be. Eventually, Skinner made this concession to Boring's criticism: He acknowledged in an introductory note to his thesis that it "undertakes eventually to frame an alternative definition [of the reflex], which is nevertheless not wholly in despite of the historical usage." Boring was specifically arguing against behaviorism in the late 20s with its "extravagant claims [and] little patience for philosophical niceties" (Skinner, 1979, pp. 70–74). Even before the thesis confrontation, Skinner and Boring were adversaries in departmental colloquiums.

Skinner's last gasp in the literary field—and a first move toward the course in the Psychology of Literature, which he created at the University of Minnesota—was a 1934 article in the *Atlantic Monthly* entitled "Has Gertrude Stein a Secret?" Although his fifteenth published article, it was his first outside of a professional journal. In it, he described Stein's experiment in automatic writing, which he discovered she'd done for a psychology course at Harvard when she was a student at Radcliffe. Later, she denied ever participating in the project and of being influenced in that direction in her later writing.

Skinner decided that Stein had continued with something close to automatic writing later in her career, quoting her own original statement, which she had apparently forgotten, about her writing in the college experiment: "The stuff is grammatical, and the words and phrases fit together all right, but there is not much connected thought" (Skinner, 1934, n.p., 1979, pp. 132–134). Even so, Stein denied that she was a successful subject for automatic writing. In any case, Skinner was to take up the idea of environmental influences that produced language of one sort rather than another, and this was the first instance where he applied the idea to an analysis of someone's writing.

As he approached the end of his Harvard fellowship in the spring of 1936, Skinner had no job in prospect. He tried hard to get an academic appointment somewhere, enlisting the support of senior professors at Harvard. Academic openings were few and he ignored his best early offer from a YMCA college. Eventually, he was offered a position at a major university, albeit at low pay. It came from the chairman of the Psychology Department at the University of Minnesota through the intervention of Boring. Richard Elliott, a loyal Harvard graduate, had been appointed to his position when the department was established at Minnesota in 1919 (and held it until his retirement in 1951).

Elliott wanted to appoint his first Harvard Ph.D. and he was offered a brilliant one to boot, according to Boring, who highly recommended Skinner. Elliott got permission from his dean to hire Skinner for $1,900, a slight boost over the regular beginning salary. The offer was made despite some faculty opposition (informal since there was no voting process) because of Skinner's total inexperience teaching—a fact Skinner did not know until our interviews. In one of Elliott's unpublished letters to Boring, he commented that "Skinner is O.K. I hope that if he doesn't think that we are that he will come to do so."[13]

No other reasons were evident for why the Minnesota psychology faculty may not have wanted Skinner. Most likely, they wanted to see a record before he was hired—uncertain of how he would turn out as a teacher, how his promise would be fulfilled, and if he would accommodate to the department. Harvard did not try to keep him. When Skinner finally did return to Harvard 13 years later, it seemed fortuitous, as he happened to meet Boring at a professional meeting where the process leading to an offer began.

In any case, Skinner did not persevere in trying to gain a Harvard appointment while he was still a fellow there. Perhaps he felt he had lost his welcome. Eventually, he accepted the necessity of finding a job elsewhere and worked at it. Those were not good times for the hiring of psychologists and professors, and Skinner had a hard time. As it turned out, Boring and others attempted to help him, although they probably could have done more. Some may have wanted him off their hands, whereas others might have wanted to retain him.

Skinner had spells of bitterness about Harvard not making him an offer. He wrote his supporter, Leonard Carmichael at Brown University, "I should have appreciated a year's work here at section teaching . . . but although the department here knows of my predicament, it is apparently not interested. My only hope lies in PWA [Public Works Administration] apparently" (Skinner, 1979, n.p.).

What would have happened if the University of Minnesota had not made Skinner the offer is irrelevant now. He might well have fumbled about in a second-rate place, hard as that is to imagine for a person of his promise and conceit. Like Einstein and many other gifted historical figures, Skinner might have had to earn his living in a relatively menial job. Inevitably, however, he would have risen to substantial status somewhere. His research and writing gained him increasingly wide attention. Even the stimulation of other first-rate minds may not have been essential for him. He had already accumulated enough research ideas, general concepts, and good work habits to labor anywhere as he further established his distinction.

When he was loose in his laboratory, Fred was as vital and creative as he had been as a child. True, he was more focused on animal behavior and how to control it, but even that was an extension from childhood. The effort to control the world around him was seldom constrained as in his childhood.

The book that made Skinner's fame was already gestating in him, almost ready for birth. He had powerful supporters when needed, even though he did not particularly cultivate or exploit friendships. He was respected for his intellectual brilliance and dominating presence. He commanded attention when he spoke. He was crisp, sharp, influential as a speaker, and loaded with vitality and fresh ideas. When he finally became a professor, bright students filled his classes. They considered him one of few teachers who was a privilege to listen to. These attributes, which applied to Skinner as he matured as a graduate student and then as a fellow at Harvard, were to reach fruition during the academic career he now embarked on for 10 years at Minnesota.

ENDNOTES

1. B. F. Skinner, personal interview.
2. Ibid.
3. Ibid.
4. Ibid.
5. Ibid.
6. Unpublished correspondence with author.
7. Ibid.
8. F. S. Keller, personal interview.
9. Harvard archives.
10. Ibid.
11. Ibid.
12. Ibid.
13. Ibid.

▶ 4

Becoming an Academician

Minnesota 1936–1941

As his research fellowship at Harvard was soon expiring, in 1936, Skinner showed modest initiative and anxiety about his next job. Then, and for the rest of his life, he left his fate largely up to accident and luck, though at times he worried. When he was a mature scientist, he even proposed methods of doing research that would enhance fortuitous occurrences. Now, however, Skinner was increasingly concerned, for the only time in his life, about whether he would find a good university teaching position from which to begin his academic career.

"I decided almost by accident to go into psychology," he remarked.[1] He did not deliberate in choosing Hamilton College. A fortuitous association with a cultured and science-minded dean and his family there "grafted on to my Susquehanna heritage" (Skinner, 1984, p. 43). Attending Harvard graduate school and advocating behavioral psychology there happened through his haphazard reading. "They were nothing that I planned."[2] Why shouldn't getting his first teaching job also be accidental?

However, at this crucial time in his life when he needed an initial academic position, Skinner found himself poorly prepared by having no teaching experience. He commented that he might not have a job before he "starved to death." Furthermore, he thought that his graduate advisor, Garry Boring, didn't like him. Despite his general appearance of confidence, Skinner occasionally did feel concern and pessimism. He was too proud, however, to ask for favors or otherwise to seek jobs aggressively. He would never promote himself in obvious ways.

Fred loved to argue forcefully for iconoclastic views that could become strong and fixed. He invented clever and dramatic devices, often unconventional, for training and exhibiting animal behavior, rearing babies, dropping bombs, and much else. He attracted attention and publicity for his opinions early on and all of his life. "My wife is always telling me," he once said, 'You're the kind of person who thinks Queen Victoria was a man and that Napoleon didn't die. . . .' I became a big arguer for behaviorism before I knew anything about it."[3] He was usually doing intellectual battle on behalf of new ideas and inventions.

After the first major job offer, which he badly needed, opportunities for other positions came at propitious times. Only the first one came hard, at least in his naive opinion. The move in 1936 from a Harvard research fellow to a Minnesota teaching instructor occurred after the Harvard faculty generated a few outside prospects for him over several weeks. Despite Skinner's apparent willingness to continue his fellowship indefinitely and his relative passivity in searching out an academic job, the transition occurred smoothly and fast.

Academia in the mid-1930s was a relaxed, "old-boy" network of very limited dimensions, compared with today's hugely expanded and keenly competitive market. There were around 5,000 psychologists then; today there are over 75,000 members in the American Psychological Association (plus thousands of other psychologists who are not members). Then, most psychologists were employed by colleges, universities, and other public institutions. Few were in applied and private practice—areas Skinner never considered. He wanted to do only teaching and research.

Skinner was not subjected to interviews, ratings, or votes of department staffs, as he would be today. He was directly offered a few openings that were known to senior faculty at Harvard who regarded his potential highly, and by friends of theirs who were recruiting discreetly. Openings were seldom advertised; there were no "meat-market" employment booths at annual professional meetings as there are today. White male students of white male professors were the clientele who were, for the most part, placed informally and without wide attention.

Even though Skinner had impressed important figures in his field at Harvard, perhaps the most prestigious among 10 or so major centers of psychology then, he nonetheless had trouble getting his first job as quickly as he wanted it. Partly, this was because good academic jobs were always scarce, though the ratio of applicants to openings was far smaller than today. More crucially, he had no teaching experience, and that is what was in demand. Fred also had high aspirations. For example, he dismissed, without comment, a job for which Boring had recommended him at a YMCA college in Springfield, Massachusetts. At the same time, Boring told Skinner that two universities turned him down because his reputation was "too great." His research brilliance was established. His teaching experience was nil.

Skinner wrote, and others confirmed, that he may "have made a grave mistake in taking so much research work rather than teaching. I have lost several jobs . . . because of lack of teaching experience. At the same time I have been turned down for beginning teaching jobs because I have published too much."[4] Yet it is hard to imagine so independent a spirit taking teaching assignments instead of his fellowship at Harvard, solely to get a university job more easily afterwards. More likely, he would have ignored such advice if it had been offered. In the long run, his research that culminated in his famous book in 1938 eventually advanced his reputation and influence far more than teaching would have. But Skinner remarked that contemporaries such as Ernest Hilgard, Donald Marquis, and Gerald Wendt surpassed him in academic status in the short term because they entered the teaching track promptly upon completing their degrees.

By contrast, four years later, Skinner "was groping for the bottom rung" (Skinner, 1979, p. 178). He also reported that he had a terrific advantage. While climbing the ladder, he had five years of freedom to write *The Behavior of Organisms* (1938). Characteristically, he briefly regretted not gaining immediate rewards on his own terms, for research rather than teaching, and not compromising on what he wanted most to do. Long term, he exulted in doing things his own way.

The obstacles encountered in his job hunt did not deter Skinner from continuing to act independently with little regard for making progress conventionally. He persisted in following his personal interests and sustaining his usually confident manner despite his temporary annoyance at not being hired immediately. Generally, he assumed that his livelihood would be taken care of; he never again became as desperate as he did during his "Dark Year" after Hamilton College. Unable then to succeed at various work, he developed the notion of entering Harvard graduate school to become a psychologist. After making that decision, he had the charm, self-confidence, energy, intelligence, and support of faculty, who recognized his great potential, to surmount all other major obstacles in his life.

While job hunting, Fred was merely impatient. Soon, he was told of at least three jobs at major universities and accepted the offer from the University of Minnesota. For it, he had the powerful support of three leading psychologists—Garry Boring, Walter Hunter (who had been a useful critic), and Leonard Carmichael—all of whom carried substantial weight with "Mike" Elliott, chairman of the Psychology Department at Minnesota. After obtained his Ph.D. at Harvard in 1913, Elliott was deeply respectful of the place.

Elliott founded the Psychology Department at the University of Minnesota in 1919. By the time he hired Skinner, he had been in the job of chairman for 17 years. Boring, a contemporary and old friend, wrote to Elliott about his erstwhile student Skinner:

All I can say is that you have there your chance to get a young genius who, under your beneficient protection, would blossom out even more than he has. . . . He has been too much protected . . . [at] Harvard. Now he knows that he should have faced the reality of a teaching job earlier before he got such a reputation as a research man that people would be afraid of him for menial work. . . . Skinner is very anxious to please, and is most exceptionally able.[5]

Skinner certainly did not anticipate Boring's glowing recommendation—this, from his advisor whom Skinner had most especially not tried to please and from whom he expected antagonism at worst and indifference at best. Eventually, Fred concluded that Boring's letter "had turned the trick." Apparently, he never seriously wondered at the time how he did get the job. As usual, he must have assumed the best of his reputation. It is remarkable that Boring, of all people, would write that Skinner was very anxious to please. His own experience with Skinner was certainly the opposite.

Fred pointed out about his research, "I would take whatever I found," always pursuing his own interests, "but not if I must pay the piper."[6] He would not be beholden to anyone; the conclusions would have to be uniquely his. Among other early research, he created an auditory "inkblot" test used at a state hospital, originally named the "verbal summator," then the "tautophone" (Skinner, 1979, p. 180).

Skinner thought that "The Department of Psychology [at Harvard] looked upon me as a deserter."[7] It was a strange comment, considering that he had no choice but to leave there. But he probably felt all of his life that his outspoken opinions and contentiousness offended people who might otherwise have supported him even more than they usually did. Although he could have learned, from popular textbooks, the conventional psychology he needed for teaching, he ended his formal education without, by his account, ever having read one.

In his recommendation letter to Elliott, Carmichael noted that Skinner is "a really original man . . . and . . . [a] genius" and that "something is wrong . . . if he is not recognized."[8] Elliott was an elitist New Englander who acted the part in his manner of speaking, aloofness, and formality. He had insisted that the Minnesota Psychology Department that he initiated be located administratively with the natural sciences rather than with philosophy or education, as was common at that time. He hankered for another Harvard Ph.D. to join his faculty and it was a bonus to gain a brilliant one.

Despite the opposition of some senior members of his department to Skinner's appointment, Elliott went directly to his dean without hesitation. He told his superior that Skinner was a "comer" whom he very much wanted, and he received permission to offer him $160 above the standard instructor's beginning salary of $1,800, plus summer school income if he chose to teach it ("much less than mine," Keller wrote[9] two years later after accepting an instructorship at Columbia for $3,500). The following year, Skinner became an assistant professor, and four years later, an associate professor earning $3,000. He made no note of such fast promotions.

The association between Elliott and Skinner was felicitous from the start and largely remained so throughout Elliott's life—at least superficially. They were always courteous and respectful to each other. This, despite the fact that Elliott consistently confided his criticisms of Skinner's arrogance to Boring, and Skinner confided to friends his criticism of Elliott's deference to the university administration. Their formal politeness clouded only briefly when Skinner left Minnesota in a huff over his salary.

Elliott almost always openly expressed appreciation of Skinner's budding genius. He never seriously crossed Skinner except on promotion when he tried to preserve fairness within his department as well as budgetary limits. He supported almost all other requests, was obviously reluctant to turn any down, and was anxious about editing Skinner's manuscripts for the book series he edited.

Elliott might comment wryly to friends about the bucking bronco whose manuscripts he dared not change for the publisher he represented, but he almost never actively opposed Skinner's opinions. Elliott displayed no personal professional ambitions other than to run the most prestigious department he could assemble, teach his courses on biographical analysis of behavior and human behavior (which Skinner later emulated), and maintain peace and comfort among his faculty.

Skinner did not actively participate in administration at Minnesota (or later at Harvard), even when he opposed their clinical or statistical bent or other inclinations. He rarely spoke against or led opposition to departmental policies. Rather, he reserved his fire for his personal projects and theories, essentially conserving his efforts in order to advance his own field of experimental behaviorism.

A future psychology department chairman at Minnesota, Kenneth Mac-Corquodale (1975), who was at first an undergraduate, then a graduate student when Skinner was there, remarked that although "the rest of the staff never put any impediment in his way . . . I think that they probably suddenly felt like a bunch of draft horses in the midst of which a thoroughbred—a rather twitchy one at that—had been dropped, not on their own invitation" (p. 7).

Skinner often referred to the barrenness of faculty social activity at Minnesota and the richer interactions subsequently at Indiana and Harvard. Whatever the cause—his colleagues' existing connections, his newcomer's discomfort with the place, or a pervasive faculty taciturnity associated with the state's northern European traditions—Skinner felt relatively isolated in the department both professionally and socially.

With the Minnesota department quite open-minded, diverse, and eclectic,

Skinner drew closest to an unlikely colleague, a macho but genial professor of industrial psychology, Howard "Whit" Longstaff. Skinner was next closest to the congenitally aloof but formally respectful, friendly Mike Elliott. Bill Heron, Skinner's colleague in laboratory work, was not sociable and never became a good friend outside the lab. Starke Hathaway befriended him and was also a skilled gadgeteer and inveterate mechanical inventor, but Hathaway was even less sociable than Heron.

Longstaff became his closest colleague in the department probably because he was the most friendly person generally, small-townish and witty, and loaded with memorable rural Ohio sayings. He was also interested in opera music. But Longstaff was an outdoorsman, and he and Skinner shared little culturally or intellectually except for music.

Skinner's best friend, socially and intellectually, at Minnesota was Herbert Feigl, an eminent philosopher and a founder of the philosophical school of "Logical Positivism" with which Skinner was empathetic, although later critical. Its premise was to make philosophy the logic of science, applying the methods of mathematics and natural science. Although Feigl was also educated and strongly interested in psychology, he was careful to speak modestly about it and not to compete with Skinner in that field. But he did have the mind and background to be gently critical and helpful when Skinner chose to use him to test out his ideas.

Like Elliott, Feigl recognized Skinner's failings, particularly his disinterest in and dogmatism about psychology outside his chosen domain of behaviorism. Feigl soon understood that it was useless to argue with Skinner. The Center for the Study of the Philosophy of Science, which Feigl cofounded at Minnesota with Paul Meehl, favored arguing three times on an issue, but if it got nowhere, to quit discussing it. Feigl, in a nursing home at age 85, still had a keen memory and sharp thoughts. He had no communication with Skinner after Skinner left for Indiana. While Skinner was at Minnesota, Feigl considered him to be

> *very stubborn in thinking about the world. He wasn't interested in the mind-body problem. I didn't expect him to be. . . . He was an independent thinker and I learned a lot about psychology from him. I never succeeded in arguing with him. He understood but wasn't interested. I was interested in physics and philosophy; he was not. He never acknowledged Thorndike. He wasn't interested in the physiology, only in stimulus-response.*[10]

Feigl was a congenial, witty, and easy-going companion. Although he wondered at Skinner's lack of scholarliness about disagreements in his field and his inattention to precursors, he was benign in his criticism, and he and Skinner enjoyed each other's company. "He was a very important person to me," Skinner reported of Feigl. "He was the first person to use the words

'Logical Positivism' in print. . . . We had a very good intellectual relationship although he insisted that we always 'cultivated our own gardens.'"[11] In his scientific approach to philosophy, nonmetaphysical and nonemotive, Feigl's views probably influenced Skinner. "As far as I was concerned," Skinner wrote (1979), "there were only minor differences between behaviorism, operationism, and logical positivism" (p. 161). Skinner seldom acknowledged the impact of others on him, however. Still, at the end of his life, he began to analyze ethics behavioristically, as the logical positivists had tried to do.

"I've not had many long-term friends," Skinner said. "If I'd seen more of Feigl, it would have continued as a warm friendship but I didn't correspond with him. . . . I am very busy and my work could find no room for it."[12] He simply didn't value or cultivate close friendships even when he did have the time. Feigl appreciated Skinner's immense and distinctive contributions to behavioral psychology. They enjoyed their intellectual discussions as well as their social camaraderie. They liked to go out "on the town" together without their wives, as hedonistic bachelors. Although neither had a reputation as a lady's man—they appeared to be too serious for that—they did get privately playful after hours with women students. As Feigl put it, "For months we went out together on dates which our wives never knew about."[13]

This type of activity was not uncommon for male faculty and their female students, right up to recent times when it is banned or limited in written ethical codes. But most of Feigl's and Skinner's students at that time had no intimations of such bouts. Skinner's role was certainly not bruited about, at least until several years later, at Indiana and Harvard. Even toward the end of his life, he said that he saw nothing wrong with relationships between professors and students. He believed that he acted like an equal with them, was never forceful, and never took advantage of his superior position. But the times had overtaken him, and his rationale, even if true, would not generally be acceptable today.

Rather isolated at the top of the stairway on the second floor of the Psychology Building at Minnesota, Skinner's office was more accessible to students than were most. The others mainly clustered near the department office on the first floor and had to be approached more formally. Fred was often in his office, with door opened, and with no secretary to screen out visitors. Students dropped in just to talk about mutual interests—in behaviorism, research, utopian communities, the arts.

This was a rare and exciting privilege for bright, interested students—one that they often savored for the rest of their lives. One who later became a distinguished psychology professor spoke for others when he referred to the "extreme stimulation of his teaching. I took everything he offered." Skinner was criticized by a colleague for giving too high grades, and others were envious of the students he attracted. But Elliott encouraged and tapped this rich lode of stimulation for students as no one ever did again. Perhaps because Skinner never again had a superior so interested in his quality as a teacher, he gradually lost his enthusiasm for undergraduate teaching. Soon after leaving Minnesota, he did little teaching, and then on a limited basis with graduate students.

Skinner found teaching and intellectual dialogues with his best students at Minnesota highly rewarding and gathered round him an especially serious group of those who admired him. "I have never again been so richly reinforced as a teacher," he said.[14] Nor did he ever again so avidly pitch into the teaching experience. Ultimately, the rewards of giving of himself that way did not suffice for him. He used his classes and other groups to test out his evolving ideas but the gains for him eventually played out. He was a self-directed and self-centered individual who, in the words of one of his students, wanted to influence the whole of society more than just those who were attached to him.

He initiated an informal seminar of his smartest and most interested graduate students to meet in his home monthly. Most of them eventually became well known and creative psychologists. Skinner took pride in the number who took advanced degrees. Almost all of them earned Ph.D.s and had notable careers: Paul Meehl, Howard Hunt, Norman Guttman, Marian Kruse (Bailey), William Estes, Kay Walker (Estes), and others.

There were also some conspicuous absentees who would have been welcome into that elite group. Most obviously missing was Kenneth MacCorquodale, who became Skinner's leading advocate at Minnesota later as a professor and department chairman. He was put off by Skinner's arrogance and especially resented Skinner's advances to a woman friend of his. He was unstinting, however, in his praise of Skinner's brilliance, creativity, and ground-breaking theory.

At times, colleagues such as Feigl dropped in on the meetings. Seldom, however, was Skinner's wife Yvonne (who became "Eve" at Minnesota and thereafter) in attendance. Typically, she stayed apart and did not participate in (or even listen to) discussions, while she pursued her own interests in literature, art, and travel. She never wanted to bask in reflected glow, even to the end of their life together. Like her husband, she wanted to be her own person and referred questioners about her life to read her diaries—which she ended before marriage and recently placed in the Radcliffe library.

The atmosphere of the department at Minnesota was congenial to a scientist such as Skinner. It was rooted in the empirical, objective, and experimental. It was also one of the earliest departments to require grounding in statistics. Skinner seldom openly expressed his antagonism for that field. The department was fairly free of dogma, with a commitment to science. Doctrinaire or proselytizing psychologists and followers did not flourish there. The faculty was let alone to pursue individual interests.

Department policy assigned senior faculty members to teach the huge classes in introductory psychology that enrolled hundreds, even in 1936 when

Skinner began teaching. From the start, however, Skinner was favored by Elliott with small, select groups of 20 of the brightest students, whom Elliott called "crème de la crème," chosen from the large total enrollment. Initially, he was influenced by Boring's letter to him referring to Skinner as "a young genius."

Previous scholastic standing was the main criterion used in screening for Skinner's select groups. The students also had to ask to get into Skinner's classes, and Skinner interviewed all of them personally. He took pride in them, later calculating that 5 percent had gone on to complete Ph.D.s, probably a high figure for the time. Remarkably, Elliott chose his newest staff member to teach these highly special classes. It was another sign that Skinner was quickly recognized as intellectually and personally exceptional, that bright students were more likely to be attracted to him than to his colleagues, and that he had a firm, broad-ranging, exciting viewpoint about animal behavior and cultural life that he applied in his classes to a wide range of human activity.

One of Skinner's class rolls alone included a future law school dean (Howard Sacks), famous actor (Kevin McCarthy), Harvard dean (Franklin Ford), notable research psychologists, head of an animal-training center (Marian Kruse), state governor (Orville Freeman), and well-known author (Max Shulman). Skinner tried, sometimes successfully, to interest those who came in to talk with him to do research on topics that he was working on, particularly about language and utopian communities. Flattered, the students tried but seldom did they know exactly what Skinner wanted (nor did he follow through to guide them). Rarely did they produce data he used, and, except for William Estes, he never collaborated with them.

Frequently, Fred recorded his lectures through a Dictaphone and re-viewed transcriptions when writing his books and articles—an effort at effi-ciency that he sustained to the end of his life. He would write down almost anything that occurred to him, and from time to time he would examine his notes for ideas to pursue further. Eventually, a graduate student of his at Harvard, Robert Epstein, collaborated with Skinner to select what they con-sidered to be the most provocative of such comments, which they published in a volume called *Notebooks, B. F. Skinner* (Epstein, 1980).

"If I have a human nature," Skinner told me, "it is to want to influence students—without attending to their counter-arguments. . . . I was a teacher [with] a chance to teach a small group. . . . I was talking from the very beginning . . . how you can bring about changes." But Skinner wanted to present his views as plainly and eloquently as he could, and let them go at that. He often seemed not to hear disagreements, simply remaining silent after they were presented. Even with so fierce and notable an opponent as Noam Chomsky on verbal behavior, Skinner preferred to ignore his arguments.

Skinner did not try to tie his students to him nor even to relate closely to them. Even the few who attempted to get graduate degrees through him seldom felt he was personally involved, even when he supported their efforts. Often after taking a class from him, they were stimulated by his new ideas and their broad implications for human behavior. Pumped up by this initiation, they began to think as he did and talked with him to try to elicit his encouragement for their ideas.

A few of Skinner's students readily accepted the limitations he set on any personal relationship with him and grew independently from his stimulation, but many were discouraged by his lack of follow-through support for them. When, in their initial eagerness, they sought a closer connection to him, their road got rough. Skinner practiced on them what he had worked out for himself. He acted as if he could teach them best by leaving them alone. While he never spoke or wrote much about personal reactions to his father, Skinner encountered in him the kind of aloofness that he himself may unwittingly have repeated. The problem probably lay more in his personality than in the benefits students presumably reaped from being left alone.

Fred valued his own autonomy above all else and thought that his students would want the same. Often, however, they did not value it as he did. His personal charm and accessibility raised false expectations in them of his potential friendship many hungered for. He did ask a couple of them at Minnesota, Marian Kruse and John Carroll, to baby-sit for his children, and occasionally they had dinner with Eve and him, but he did not otherwise invite them—or others—into his personal life except for a seminar or playing chamber music.

Students often did not realize that Skinner did not want them to try to please him. To the end, he still prided himself on making no demands of them, on exercising no pressure, on acting as if they were his equals and capable of and wanting to advance entirely on their own. He would not be the "Herr Professor," as he put it. His support for his daughters, however, he called "reinforcement" and did not stint on it.

My early reaction was the common one—excitement then disappointment. From his early years at Minnesota until his last years at Harvard, Fred replied with little more than a brief note of appreciation for my publications that I sent him; when we got to talk about them, he usually agreed with their content, however. He certainly bloomed as a friend when we worked on this biography. But even as we began this book, he remarked that he knew he would gain as much as he would give in doing it—his typical attitude.

He taught idiosyncratic courses at Minnesota, most of which have never been repeated: Psychology of Language, The Psychology of the Fine Arts, The Psychology of Literature, The Psychology of Art, Music, and Literature, Psychology of Thought. All but one of his course descriptions in the University catalogs emphasized experimental data. Eventually, he published articles on these subjects based on his recorded lectures, as in a chapter titled "Creating the Creative Artist" (1970).

Skinner committed himself strongly to the primacy of science and being a scientist. But unlike Freud and many others who merely said so, he proved his commitment with rigorously scientific work. Eventually, he wrote an analysis of his own scientific ways in "A Case History in Scientific Method" (Skinner, 1956), which he thought yielded more creative results than did conventional methods: Deemphasize preconceived hypotheses; digress from original research plans when the data point to new directions; pursue byways suggested by serendipitous findings; and hang loose, growing and changing as you work. He concluded:

> *We have no more reason to say that all psychologists should behave as I have behaved than that they should all behave like R. A. Fisher [eminent statistician]. The scientist, like any organism, is the product of a unique history. The practices which he finds most appropriate will depend in part upon this history. . . . They [personal idiosyncrasies] are important only when we are concerned with the encouragement of scientists and the prosecution of research. When we have at last an adequate empirical account of the behavior of Man Thinking, we shall understand all this. Until then, it may be best not to try to fit all scientists into any single mold. (Skinner, 1956)*

In the summer of 1936, just before moving to Minnesota, Skinner had been introduced to Yvonne Blue through mutual friends from Chicago. A resident of the Chicago suburb of Flossmoor, Blue was genteel and intellectual with no-nonsense ways. Skinner immediately courted her. A major in English at the University of Chicago, she piqued Skinner's interest with her well-informed conversation about literature. They visited each other several times in the East and in Chicago.

Yvonne (later called "Eve") was a voracious and rapid reader and Skinner was impressed with the fact that she could read "exactly twice as fast" as he could. She bought many new books and reinforced his interest in literature, which influenced him to teach a course in the psychology of literature after they were married. He had also begun to consider the development of verbal behavior. It became a major research and theoretical interest for him, which he credited to Eve. Her companionship played sympathetically on his lifelong literary aspirations.

Fred pursued Eve avidly after they met. He paid her to type for him in Boston and took her to visit his friends and family. He had anxious moments on their visits when they had to register at hotels as married. He mentioned nothing in his autobiography about sex between them and neither of them would discuss it for publication. They maintained privacy beyond the ordinary about their personal relationship, although close friends have indicated that later it was strained.

Pictures taken soon after they met show her as rather delicate, dark haired, attractive, with a quiet presence about her. Feigl, with an eye for women, called her beautiful. A picture of Fred and Eve together suggests matching fine features, trim bodies, and poise. Any doubts they may have had about each other, or distractions of other concurrently appealing companions, were not included in his life story or conversations. They were almost always attentive to each other's sensibilities. Skinner quickly became serious about marrying Eve and stopped in Flossmoor on his way to Minnesota to meet her family.

It appealed to Skinner that her family lived an upper middle-class life in a Flossmoor home with gardens and a tennis court, that her father was a busy ophthalmologist, and that her grandfather (Opie Read) was a well-known novelist and lecturer. They had known each other for only six weeks but had spent most of that time together. At his initiative, Fred and Eve decided to get married.

Pleased to have his life in such good order, Skinner now had a satisfactory academic job, a friendly boss, his stuff packed and ready to lay out in a new home, a temporary place to stay at the University of Minnesota Faculty Club—and to cap it all, a wedding scheduled for Christmas time. At this crucial moment in his courtship, just before he settled at Minnesota, Skinner seemed more interested and involved in his prospective professional career than in his fiancée. Their marriage seemed assured. At his invitation, Eve made a weekend trip to Minneapolis. He showed her around campus and they paid a visit to the Elliotts. She did not feel comfortable in the prospective role of a faculty wife, however, and he agreed that they should postpone their wedding. They never described details of this split but his references to her being a "faculty wife" probably galled Eve as rigorously proscribing her life.

His father wrote to Fred, strongly opposing any change in plans in the already announced forthcoming marriage. He disparaged his son's excuse of difficulty in finding a place for them to live. Further, wrote his father, his son was likely to have more difficulty adjusting to marriage as he grew older, given his already "fixed views and strong opinions . . . [with] a life practically free from responsibilities" (Skinner, 1979, p. 193). His parents objected to the postponement also because it would be embarrassing for them to explain the change in plans to their friends. Furthermore, wrote his mother, he should not expect to figure out married life as scientifically as he would a problem with rats, and if he waited, he might never marry anyone. His parents had never intervened so strongly in his life, but such firm opinions about their son's decision, based upon their sense of Fred's intractability, which seemed to take him by surprise, were not likely to have been entirely new.

After continuing correspondence, Eve sent Fred a card, writing that she'd already told friends and family of the cancellation of their engagement and marriage. She was offended when he "seemed to imply" that he "was not sure that she was faculty-wife material" (p. 193). He seemed insensitive to the impact of such a remark. Finally, however, he took hold of the situation, probably more responsive than he would admit to his parents' admonishments as well as his own desire. He invited himself down to Chicago for a weekend, he and Eve checked into a hotel, and they decided to get married immediately. They then invited both sets of parents to attend the ceremony in her parents' home. Immediately after the ceremony, they hurried back by train to Minneapolis, arriving just in time for him to teach his Monday morning class. His lecture was on the topic of emotions. Thus, he quickly and decisively settled one of the few intense albeit short-lived crises in his life.

Skinner's parents had urged him to take Eve's views into account and try to be fair to her. Crediting their advice, he wrote to his friend Fred Keller in the spring following their marriage: "Yvonne is proving the absolutely perfect wife. . . . Not that I get my way, but I don't mind not getting it" (p. 199). Typically, he could get along well with almost anyone when he needed to for a goal he had. It is unclear whether Eve would have agreed that Fred was so amiable. He didn't even speculate on her feelings.

Fred and Eve were reluctant, even late in their lives, to discuss their personal relationship. They seemed content to leave the impression that they had a relatively smooth, companionable marriage, which he was proud had lasted 54 years, about which there was nothing more of importance to remark. In his autobiography, he rarely discussed his feelings about his marriage—or anything else about his most personal life. A dear friend of his, however, cryptically wrote: "Their marriage, though an open one for both at various times, was ultimately serious and mutually devoted."[15]

His views and expressions of emotion would be especially pertinent when he chose and married Eve, the major intimate relationship of his life. Skinner's choice of a lifelong mate, at a near peak time of desire for sex, closeness, and a family of his own, had to involve his most intense feelings. In the Epilogue of his autobiography (1984), he emphasizes, "I have tried to report my life as it was lived. . . . I have seldom mentioned later significances. . . . Only when I recorded how I felt at the time have I accepted it as part of the story" (p. 398). Apparently, he never did express publicly his feelings for his wife, and Eve threatened to leave him if he ever read her diary. He once mentioned that he kept a private sexual diary but he apparently showed it to no one. He also wrote in his autobiography:

> I also do not think feelings are important. Freud is probably responsible for the current extent to which they are taken seriously. Strachey wrote that 'if anyone had asked Voltaire to analyze his feelings accurately he would have replied that he had other things to think about. The notion of paying careful attention to mere feelings would have seemed ridiculous.'
>
> Rather than tell my readers how I felt, I have left them to respond as I

myself may have responded. It is the reader who must be judged warm or cold. (p. 399)

"I am sometimes asked," Skinner continued, "'Do you think of yourself as you think of the organisms you study?' The answer is yes" (1984, p. 401). Of other good friends, he probably would have written as he did of Fred Keller, though less intensely: "It was fun to be with Fred no matter what we were doing. Only with Eve have I shared so many interests and pleasures" (p. 402). The pleasures were expressed coolly and without much emotion.

Of his own demeanor, he wrote, "I do not believe that my life shows a type of personality à la Freud, an archetypal pattern à la Jung, or a schedule of development à la Erikson. There have been a few abiding themes, but they can be traced to environmental sources rather than to traits of character. They became part of my life as I lived it; they were not there at the beginning to determine its course" (p. 401). Skinner attended too little to his genetic inheritance, considering that he acknowledged its importance—physical attributes, mechanical aptitude, intelligence and creativity, sensory sensitivity, and so on. But the fact that he devoted his life's work so determinedly to the influence of environment enriched the field of psychology far more than if he had scattered his attention more widely or conventionally.

He wrote as if personality traits should, if they existed, show themselves at birth and determine one's subsequent life, like genetics. Skinner accepted the fact, however, that his genetics and environment interacted to produce the person he became, his personality gradually stabilizing and becoming clearer and more consistent as he grew older. Indeed, that is the way I found him to change from his young adulthood to the end of his life. What he had begun to show in his childhood, youth, and young adulthood came into ever sharper focus with the passing years.

One can use common expressions to describe Skinner's personality that do not presume a particular theoretical structure. Taken on his own terms, the description of his personality can "be traced to environmental sources." Autonomy, self-confidence, desire to excel, the need to influence others, precision, a cutting creative edge in accomplishments, liberality in relationships, coolness of feelings: These are personality attributes regardless of how they are labeled.

Skinner's closest friend, Keller, in a burst of unusual emotionality, said of Skinner: "He didn't dare to be moved. He closed it off as if he might fall apart. It was too painful. Like he might say, 'My right leg is no good. I must cut it off.'"[16] Keller did not amplify this analysis. There was little evidence of brittleness in Skinner's emotions. He never did fall apart or apparently even come close. Was Keller perhaps projecting his own greater sensitivity onto his friend?

Of course Keller was a unique case. His ambivalence, although similar to that of others toward Skinner, is clearer and more intense. Besides expressing his critical attitudes only sparingly, he also acknowledged: "He's been my hero. I idolize this man. I admired him tremendously for what he could do."[17]

Ultimately, Keller fought off the attraction as it grew in him and Skinner did not reciprocate its intensity. "I've never been a disciple," Keller commented. "He asked me to go to Indiana. It was wrong. I'd have been too influenced by him. I never worshipped him. I never felt I did him any good [except] I promoted his work."[18]

Some of these same reactions occurred in many of Skinner's students—the anguish of being inspired, the high hope of finding an elusive grand relationship, the letdown when they realized that there was nothing more that Skinner was going to give them. In answering the question whether he sustained friendships over the years in any emotional way, Skinner answered:

> *No, I don't. Even with Fred Keller, I was a very close friend. We'd call and have long chats and so on. I wouldn't call it anything like affection. . . . Well, it is in a way. . . . We had a marvelous cooperative relationship . . . warm relations. . . . He got high once and said, "Burrhus and I are friends," to make it clear there was no homosexual involvement.*[19]

The fact that Skinner mentioned the subject may be considered significant, but there is no evidence of anything sexual.

In his marriage, the most intimate, enduring relationship of his life, Skinner's personality surely shows itself. His work came first. But he was also determined to marry Eve, establish a home, have children, and appear as a properly settled professor—in part perhaps to please his parents but adopted as his own objective too. He did establish his permanence as a strong husband and father, and was proud of it.

Skinner had learned from his mother to conform outwardly to conventional standards, however rebelliously and unconventionally he pursued his theories, research, and private life. Living as a bachelor in the Minnesota Faculty Club would not only have thrown him in with a likely minority of unmarried professors but it would also have been a pretty cold milieu for someone who valued family life so highly. In any case, Fred said and wrote little about his marriage—passion, sex, or conflicts. Certainly, there were occasional references to differences between them, as when Eve vehemently opposed moving to Chicago or California, and less strongly, to Indiana, but she seemed determinedly to avoid almost all public connections with Skinner's professional life. She set about constructing an independent way of her own. It is hard to imagine another approach that could have succeeded as well in their marriage. They were both extremely independent-minded.

Was Fred as cool with Eve privately as publicly? He seemed to be with everyone else except his daughters. There is no doubt of his abiding interest and strong feelings for the girls, which showed itself in many ways from direct expressions of affection to concrete support and intervention. He helped them get into schools and obtain jobs, befriended their husbands-to-be, and tried to stay in geographical proximity. Only with Eve and Keller, in earlier times, did he behave in so friendly a fashion, though never as such an interventionist.

Fred did more for his daughters than most fathers do. His daughters reciprocated his feelings, believing that he took more interest in them than did their mother. Deborah called him "soppy"[20] in his feelings for them. Julie called him a "storybook father" (Vargas, 1993). His private life with Eve remained obscure to others except, perhaps, to their children and Fred Keller, in whom Skinner confided some personal difficulties early in their careers. Colleagues such as Feigl, Meehl, other friends, and occasionally acquaintances at his three academic venues knew some facets of it. Talk abounded about his dalliances after his marriage, and continued to the end of his life. Although rumors began at Minnesota soon after he arrived there, they seemed to peak at Indiana and endured at Harvard. Several friends observed a strained relationship between Eve and Fred for many years, which the friends attributed to the likelihood that Eve knew of his affairs (since her sister did).

Why the liaisons and strain with Eve never became more public may be exemplified by Keller's comments: "That was a thing that I studiously . . . avoided. One heard rumors . . . but I avoided completely getting involved or taking any consideration of that."[21] Still, students at Radcliffe seemed to circulate rumors about his affairs. Early in our discussions, Skinner wrote me: "It is hard to say . . . about Eve's and my personal lives. Minnesota was very puritanical. There was scarcely any drinking. I remember being surprised . . . that . . . [W. L.] drank a shot of whiskey every night . . . Indiana was wide open. There was a much stronger wall between academy and town life."

If Elliott had any intimations about Skinner's personal relationships with his students, they may have been obliquely reflected when Elliott reviewed his own professional life in 1952 for *A History of Psychology in Autobiography— Volume IV*. He made only passing reference to Skinner, although by then Skinner had stayed a decade at Minnesota, spent three years at Indiana, and returned to Harvard. Skinner had already published the basic research and theory that clearly established his enduring fame in psychology. In his retrospection, Elliott almost ignored his most famous protégé and ex-faculty member.

The occasional ambivalence in their relationship was evident, as might be expected between so unbridled a creature as Skinner and so formal and conventional a one as Elliott. More remarkable was the courteous and respectful interaction they maintained with rare exceptions, such as when Skinner ignored Elliott's request that he further edit his master work, and when they discussed the Indiana job offer.

In his autobiography, Elliott paid generous tribute to a number of his faculty, especially Karl Lashley in neuropsychology and Donald Paterson in applied psychology, for their major contributions to their fields. About Skinner, however, all Elliott mentioned was how inspirationally he had taught his select introductory classes in psychology, probably his least remembered claim to lasting professional fame. Why Elliott omitted Skinner's notable creation of the dominant science of behavior during this century seems inexplicable, given his often stated high regard for Skinner. In many other less memorable places, Elliott did pay generous tribute to Skinner's genius—but not in his autobiography written six years after Skinner had left Minnesota.

Yet Elliott mattered a good deal to Skinner. He appreciated the start Elliott gave to his academic career, and he and his wife were grateful for Elliott's personal friendliness and that of his cultured wife. Skinner seldom openly criticized or stood aloof from Elliott as he did from other paternal figures such as Boring. But he did treat Elliott curtly when he (Skinner) left Minnesota and he made snide remarks about Elliott's administrative conservatism, which Skinner believed retarded his progress. Elliott, in turn, derogated Indiana. Through his mother's eyes, Skinner would have respected Elliott as upper class, at the same time perhaps resenting such superior status.

Elliott was quite capable of understanding, tolerating, and exploiting Skinner's idiosyncrasies. Although there is no evidence that he dared counsel with Skinner on what Elliott considered his self-centered behavior, or some deficiencies he might want to edit in Skinner's manuscripts, Elliott did write this to a student at that time in a way that he might well have spoken to Skinner:

> *One thing I gather from your autobiography—you will never be completely satisfied either with yourself or your future prospects. It will be up to you to harvest the gains in life that come from such an attitude and to fight off the curse that it also carries with it.*[22]

Neither Elliott nor Boring abided intense iconoclasts well. At times, Elliott was peeved with Skinner's invariable criticism of nonbehaviorists, even though he himself was largely a behaviorist. Elliott was also grossly biased against women pursuing careers in psychology, retarded the promotion of a colleague who divorced, and participated wholeheartedly in the "old-boy" network. Skinner's brashness against such conventions would upset him. Elliott valued peace among his faculty, and although Skinner had the manners he admired, he was irritated by Skinner's stubbornness in pursuing his own theories and his brusqueness with others' views.

Skinner's disappointments and dissatisfactions were not usually clear to others nor openly expressed, but they did contribute to the larger moves he made in his life. He was at various times unhappy with his pay and promotions at Minnesota, for example, but generally kept such reactions to himself even after he took action on them. He was not satisfied that Elliott had done all he could to keep him at Minnesota when Indiana offered him 50 percent more money and the department chairmanship. But Elliott felt he had reached the end of his tether in advancing Skinner faster than other faculty members—faster than anyone except Lashley—and was annoyed with Skinner's indifference to that favor.

Except when he was unsure of a vocation when he needed one, and occasionally when under other stress, Skinner was generally contented with his life, even when working hard and aloof from others. He moved rapidly from promising fellow and researcher at Harvard to fresh faculty member at the University of Minnesota. There, he taught more avidly than ever again. He also conducted basic research in animal learning, invented crucial new equipment, wrote the manuscripts of several of his most important articles and books, and delved into verbal behavior in a novel way, applying his behavioral theory. The "Skinner box," which he refined for his rat experiments at Minnesota, is listed in the *Random House Dictionary* (1987), as used "especially in operant conditioning . . . that gives the animal . . . reward or permits escape." It was a term that Skinner did not use, however; it was first popularized by Clark Hull, and remains in widespread use today (Skinner, 1984, p. 164).

With his small select classes, Skinner was surrounded with highly motivated students "through the appeal of his originality," as Elliott put it. As Skinner (1979) described it, "Much of what was 'original' about me was due to the fact that I was wholly unprepared for teaching and had no idea what to choose as a textbook" (p. 191). As a consequence, he spoke more spontaneously. He was far more animated, colorful, and stimulating to bright students than more formal lecturers. The fact that he attracted and held good students was more a tribute to his vocally fluent intelligence, his commanding yet congenial presence, the novelty and sense of his perspective, and his clear, confident presentations than to his knowledge of basic psychology. He had never read the texts he was asked to use and then found to be too pedestrian to recommend.

Fred would probably have chosen none of the textbooks even if he had been more knowledgeable about introductory psychology books. Most likely, he would have used no conventional textbooks but would have had students dipping into original sources for what he considered to be the most important research and concepts. That is what Elliott did for the courses he taught on Human Behavior and Biographical Psychology. In addition, Skinner was supposed to counsel with graduate students wanting to work in areas of his interest. It was this latter task that gave him the most trouble in academia at Minnesota and for the rest of his life, although there were always students eager to work with him. He simply did not support his students with the warmth and persistence for which many of them yearned.

Skinner was, however, proud of those students he attracted. Of his first student, John Carroll, he wrote to Keller: "I've got a grand graduate student coming. . . . I snared him away from Yale and . . . Indiana. Has a brilliant record and sounds as mature as a Harvard Professor" (Skinner, 1979, p. 213). Later, he wrote: "I stole W. K. Estes from engineering and Norman Guttman from philosophy" (Skinner, 1979, n.p.). But most of them had trouble primarily in understanding what Skinner wanted them to do—if anything—at his behest. Some did not complete their degrees with him because he was not available or forthcoming when they needed or wanted his support and encouragement.

Years later at Harvard, he missed the final examinations of some of his students, which they remembered and which he says was unavoidable. At Minnesota and Indiana, he got as far as such exams with only two graduate students. Even his first student had a hard time of it. Now an eminent scholar in linguistics and statistics, John Carroll recollected that Skinner was friendly and appealing to him. Upon becoming "Skinner's student," however, Carroll found himself discouraged by faculty member Donald Paterson from taking his (Paterson's) basic class in individual differences. Paterson told Carroll that he didn't need the course because he was a Skinner "experimentalist." Skinner had never heard of this episode.

Though he liked Skinner, Carroll never hit it off with him. Skinner's version was that he gave Carroll a project to analyze verbal behavior, but "he preferred a statistical approach." So, Skinner (1979) says, "I arranged for him to work with . . . Thurstone's people at Chicago" (p. 213) in statistics. Skinner never did like to work with many subjects nor with statistical analysis. "Statistics," he wrote, "encouraged psychologists to continue with poor methods" (p. 213). Carroll took the criticism personally. He didn't understand what Skinner wanted him to do with verbal behavior, and found a more congenial home at Chicago where he cultivated what became a lifelong interest in linguistics and statistics.

Carroll and Estes were Skinner's only Ph.D. students at Minnesota who completed their degrees with Skinner alone. No students finished during his three years at Indiana, although several began their work with him, which they had to complete with Estes and others after Skinner moved to Harvard. Incidentally, Carroll was a skilled pianist and composer, and had played Skinner's harpsichord in his home. Even so, he didn't know until recently that Skinner invited musicians into his home regularly to play classical music. Carroll was never invited to play with them even though he baby-sat there at times.

Most students who started graduate work with Skinner did eventually complete Ph.D.s but seldom by working closely or exclusively with him. One referred to him as more "distant" than "cold." Skinner seldom volunteered to help, although he would often provide it if asked directly. One devoted ex-student, however, has always remembered that when he asked Skinner to review a professional paper for him, Skinner totally rewrote and vastly improved it, for which the student was ever grateful.[23]

Skinner's seminal work was almost ready for publication soon after he began teaching at Minnesota. Elliott wanted to publish it in the Century Psychology Series for which he was editor. The major thrust of *The Behavior of Organisms* (1938) was its clean advocacy of a rigorously defined behavioral psychology, supported by extensive original research. It was subtitled *An Experimental Analysis*. Throughout his research as a fellow at Harvard, which undergirded his memorable and now classic first book, he struggled with the reflex, distinguishing between two types. First was the classical one that was established and elicited by a stimulus associated with it, such as the salivary response to a tone in Pavlov's experiment. But he observed another kind of reflex that was chained to a stimulus by being associated with reward.

Skinner raged silently when his former mentor, Boring, insisted that humans could, by introspection, observe events of the brain. Skinner was too focused on, too excited by the prospects of controlling the reflex with food, strengthening or weakening it by providing or withholding the reinforcement, to tolerate Boring's conventionality. Skinner took the word *reinforcement* from a translation of Pavlov's work.

Keller first used the word *operant*, which was the term Skinner applied in *The Behavior of Organisms* to actions that could be shaped by reinforcement. It contrasted with "respondent" behavior, which was a simple correlation of a stimulus and a response. In the book, he was still bound, however, to the "reflex," which he regretted ever after. His later research and writing would be devoted to operant conditioning, which he extended to the shaping of all forms of animal behavior.

Unlike other research on animal behavior, Skinner's did not include a lot of experiments, the results of which were averaged together. He considered each rat's results separately, despite not only the growing emphasis on statistics throughout psychology but also the specific emphasis on them at the University of Minnesota.

Skinner's book was part of the Century Psychology series that Elliott edited. Skinner had to raise $500 from the Society of Fellows at Harvard to include all the figures he wanted in the book. It sold poorly: 800 copies were published, some of which were not bound. The first printing did not sell out until after World War II—125 copies were still available four years after publication, in 1942. Hardly anyone realized that it would eventually be acknowledged as the most important experimental psychology book of the century.

Early on, Keller wrote: "The book is great. . . . It comes up to, and goes beyond everything I had anticipated, and I had Great Expectations. In my humble opinion, it is the most important single contribution that this century has seen in the field of psychology" (Skinner, 1979, p. 220). Thereafter, Keller became the book's greatest promoter and made his department at Columbia University a center for research in Skinner's image.

Skinner himself said, "*The Behavior of Organisms* represented my work at Harvard. At Minnesota, my work was on the application of the book; it had not included any."[24] Especially, he observed:

> If you use a hand switch to operate the dispenser of food you can shape behavior. That's something very different, with the switch in your hand, through successive stages to get what you want. We were stunned by that. . . . With a switch in your hand you just carve behavior up.
>
> I think it was that success and my beginning to talk about practical things in Utopia and the control of behavior I was talking about with Castell [philosophy professor at Minnesota and major figure in Walden Two] et al all came pouring out when I wrote Walden Two. So I think you could take the Minnesota years . . . [as] precisely the years of application, and that includes . . . applications of verbal behavior. . . . I think I was reaching out to new things. That would be partly the influences I met at Minnesota.[25]

Skinner's main animal experimentalist colleague at Minnesota, William Heron, contributed in the Minnesota tradition by combining as many experiments and subjects as possible to build up numbers. In the last project they discussed, Heron proposed that he and Skinner collaborate on a Ford Foundation grant he had obtained for an experiment running 24 rats simultaneously in as many "Skinner boxes." Skinner agreed, although he had doubts based on his intensifying view that the ideal experiment would consist of one animal whose behavior could be almost completely controlled. The crucial matter to him was to understand so fully what determined the course of behavior that the predicted behavior of one subject would suffice to substantiate the theory.

Heron and Skinner shared a similar viewpoint about the determination of behavior and were logical collaborators except on the issue of numbers of cases. Heron conventionally opted for the largest practical numbers and respected statistical analysis while Skinner aimed for the conclusively explained single case.

They started to work together in the department's laboratory almost immediately after Skinner's arrival. While Heron used rats, Skinner turned increasingly to pigeons. Heron recalled various forms of Skinner's genius. He thought the invention of the lever that animals could press to obtain food was perhaps his most crucial discovery for the research that underlay his theory. With it, the experimenter could provide an immediate reward for animal behavior partly or completely as the researcher chose. Heron also greatly admired Skinner's capacity to "take junk lying around the lab and make effective apparatuses from it."[26]

Skinner walked away from this project with Heron without discussing or even stating his reason. Until I interviewed Heron over 40 years later, Skinner thought that Heron must have been antagonized, and Skinner was apologetic. As it turned out, however, Heron claimed to have been and to have remained neutral about it, remarking that he understood and accepted Skinner's rejection of the project. He thought it was because Skinner was pursuing other interests, including a course he taught on the radio. At any rate, they had both long ago forgiven, even forgotten, whatever resentment either may have harbored.

Echoing the wistful longing of students, Heron also "wished I could be closer to Fred"[27] in their research, especially the last proposed collaboration. But Fred did "kind of skip out on me."[28] Even to a reluctant Skinner, their plan to run 24 Skinner boxes simultaneously was "certainly impressive." Despite their many problems in getting the complicated structure to work consistently, Skinner (1979) seemed at one point to agree with Heron that the approach "greatly improves upon the method as previously reported [in *The Behavior of Organisms*] since tests of significance are provided and properties of behavior not apparent in single cases may be more easily . . . studied" (n.p.).

Skinner's interest in running so many rats at the same time did not last long, if indeed he ever sincerely shared Heron's enthusiasm. Soon, he walked away from the project, dropped down to four rats for an experiment of his own, and his commitment then returned to the one well-studied and controlled subject.

With a droll wit and an acerbic tongue, Heron thought the project Skinner developed toward the end of his Minnesota tenure—the pigeon bombsight—"was a kind of crazy idea, and I still do [at age 91]."[29] He himself wrote up what he thought was a better idea and sent it to the War Department. He proposed attaching fire bombs to rats where they could chew through the ties and be dropped in coops over Japan. He believed the department tried it with bats over New Mexico and burned down some barracks. He also thought Skinner should have used homing pigeons in his bombsight so they could be easily retrieved.

While Skinner complained of the sparse social life at Minnesota, Heron and his wife chose not to socialize much with colleagues. Unlike Skinner, Heron had no regrets. He did once visit the Skinners, observed the "baby box," and scratched the head of its occupant.

When he heard of the Indiana offer, Heron, like Elliott and Boring, thought that Skinner was "too valuable to be head of a department," that he had "more important things to do." Nonetheless, he opposed concrete incentives to keep Skinner at Minnesota. After meeting with his dean, Heron wrote the dean a letter in which he objected to "adjustments" for Skinner ahead of a more senior department member.

Heron was also critical of Skinner's laboratory habits. Noting that he had been in charge of the psychology laboratory and apparatus shop where Skinner also worked, Heron commented that "[Skinner] is quite ruthless in his disregard of the rights of other persons . . . he has . . . more important things to do than to replace a tool . . . [and thus] encourages similar behavior in his students. Therefore, if Dr. Skinner remains here, I would appreciate being relieved of the responsibility . . . [for the lab]."[30] A lab assistant at the time, later a distinguished research physician, echoed Heron's criticisms. But Skinner's experimental laboratory work at the university had already peaked and he worked thereafter mostly in his own settings. Heron did not take the threatened action.

Nothing more seems to have happened between Heron and Skinner. In fact, Skinner never knew until late in life about the letter Heron wrote to the dean about him. They remained on agreeable terms after they no longer worked together. Skinner was soon off to other research. As his career progressed, he constantly pursued his own diverse and innovative notions freely without regard to financial reward, security, or the activities of others. Meanwhile he continued to consider application of his theory to verbal behavior—a combination of his sensitivity to language, his never relinquished literary aspirations, and Eve's constant interest in literature. To free himself for a year of full-time research on verbal behavior, he applied for and obtained a Guggenheim award. However, when he got his notion about a bomb sight operated by pigeons he could train, patriotic zeal [for World War II] took priority. He obtained a grant for military research through the General Mills Company to develop his superficially whimsical, yet potentially crucial, weapon. The Army had no precision bomb sight yet. He postponed the Guggenheim to develop one.

Fred's thrust was always to pursue his own behavioral animal research wherever it was leading him at the moment. Except for this military venture, he avoided any review or supervision. Only for the Army project, which he designed partly out of a sense of duty, did he accept inspection as the War Department required. While he bent to no imposed pressures, and he loafed at times with music, baseball games, and other recreation, he was highly productive and zestful in pursuing his numerous interests. Bursting with new ideas, inventions, devices, and applications, he was constantly moving into new territory, broadening the applications of his research and theory to manage animal (including human) activity.

A former graduate student of this period, William Estes, a notable psychologist who became a colleague of Skinner's at Harvard, vividly described Skinner's effect on him. He was first hired by Skinner at Indiana because of a "need for hands" to teach sections of beginning experimental laboratory. Both alone and in collaboration, he did research with Skinner using *The Behavior of Organisms* as his inspiration, even though it gave "skimpy treatment to the emotions" which interested Estes.

As a graduate student, however, Estes acted neutral on the subject. The research resulted in a publication that carried his name as co-author with Skinner. He, the student, presented it at an American Psychological Association convention. Because of Skinner's negative attitude, they didn't call the reaction a Conditioned Emotional Response (CER)—but everyone else did.

Estes rarely disagreed or argued with Skinner, and Skinner was very supportive of him. Only when he began to work independently did Estes display interest in mathematics, which grew rapidly even while Skinner was attacking the mathematical approach. To the end of his life, Skinner deplored the leisure time his ex-student had in the Navy to study mathematics. "He did brilliant work," said Skinner, "as a graduate student . . . by himself . . . but I think this mathematical psychology is a dream . . . but an impossible dream."[31]

Estes would not argue with Skinner. As adept as Skinner in avoiding unpleasant confrontations, he remained friendly to the end, though they pursued different kinds of research and were committed to different methods. He retained his admiration for the Skinner of his student days, the charisma of his teaching, and the richly stimulating content of his courses. Whatever else they thought of Skinner's theory, most of his serious students were indelibly marked by his inspired teaching. But despite his respect for them and his desire to see his students function independently, Skinner was almost always dismayed when they did studies involving "mentalism," cognition, introspection, or sophisticated statistical methods, or seriously digressed from his views in any other way.

On the final day of 1938, Skinner wrote to Keller: "The last day of my best and happiest year!" He had not yet, however, "made over the entire field to suit myself," and "the damn science is folding up" (Skinner, 1979, p. 226).

These would be persisting themes for the rest of his life: Happy times with his work to which he was totally devoted. The desire to make over psychology in the image of his behavioral science. His annoyance—at times, anger—that psychology kept entangling itself with introspection, mind, cognition, instead of concerning itself with the control of animal behavior through the powerful concepts he had devised.

ENDNOTES

1. B. F. Skinner, personal interview.
2. Ibid.
3. Ibid.
4. Harvard archives.

5. Ibid.

6. B. F. Skinner, personal interview.

7 Ibid.

8. University of Minnesota archives.

9. Harvard archives.

10. H. Feigl, personal interview. (Incidentally, eventually, Skinner did acknowledge Thorndike.)

11. B. F. Skinner, personal interview.

12. Ibid.

13. H. Feigl, personal interview.

14. B. F. Skinner, personal interview.

15. Harry Levin, unpublished correspondence with author.

16. F. S. Keller, personal interview.

17. Ibid.

18. Ibid.

19. B. F. Skinner, personal interview.

20. Unpublished correspondence with author.

21. F. S. Keller, personal interview.

22. Unpublished correspondence.

23. Wells Hively, unpublished correspondence with author.

24. B. F. Skinner, personal interview.

25. Ibid.

26. W. Heron, personal interview.

27. Ibid.

28. Ibid.

29. Ibid.

30. Ibid.

31. B. F. Skinner, personal interview.

▶ 5

Inventiveness and Dissatisfaction

Minnesota 1941–1945

Although Skinner is associated mainly with Harvard, where he earned his Ph.D. and spent his last 26 academic years on the faculty, his first teaching position was at the University of Minnesota for the decade from 1936 to 1945. They were the years of his most successful teaching and greatest creativity and applications of his theory. For his last several years at Minnesota, Skinner had special grants and awards to do his own research and writing with little connection to the University or to teaching. He was to sustain this kind of autonomy for the rest of his life, at Indiana and Harvard Universities, and after retirement when he remained professionally productive until his death. He always worked in a major university academic position with funding for personal research and writing. It is hard to imagine him flourishing any other way, nor did he ever seriously consider any other course after he obtained his Ph.D. and used up his fellowship time.

To make both ends meet early in his career, Skinner had to teach summer school and extension courses at Minnesota. Harvard also invited him to teach in the summer of 1939 but that did not fit his schedule until a year later, when he did take the offer. But in 1939, his father offered to replace his summer school salary if he'd bring his family to stay with his parents instead. Fred accepted his father's invitation but never did comment on how they all got along. He mentioned only that he tried to write a book on verbal behavior based on his radio course on the psychology of literature at Minnesota. For private work space he fixed up the basement of his parents' home—as far as possible from the attic where he had wasted a year between college and graduate school trying to write literature.

What Fred managed to write in his basement office, however, turned out to be a mishmash of his various ideas. Eve commented that Fred was not happy surrounded by four women, including his mother who was "crochety." After reviewing with Keller what he wrote, he decided he had at least the outline of a book on a science of verbal behavior based on his theory of behaviorism, but that it would have to wait to be completed.

Skinner used teaching largely as a way to organize his data and ideas for publication to a wider audience. Teaching for itself never was Skinner's primary interest, although he was a superb performer. His lectures were free flowing, intellectually stimulating, often personalized with firsthand observations from his current reading and research, well organized, and eloquently delivered. Many bright students avidly took whatever he taught and vividly remembered that exciting experience.

Although he enjoyed having students who admired him and his lectures, Skinner was not content to bask in their esteem. Throughout his life, he tried continually to enlarge his areas of influence. He began by controlling and shaping the behavior of rats and pigeons, then worked to influence students, then expanded his scope to address his profession, and finally extended his impact to the public and the structure and institutions of society. He published not only professional books and articles but also trade books and articles in popular magazines.

He had a flair for publicity and got lots of it, what with dogs that climbed walls at his instigation, chickens that played baseball, the baby-tender, the pigeon bombsight, the utopian communities, teaching machines, and so on. All worked by means of his basic position in shaping behavior: positive reinforcement for operant conditioning. He also gained a large audience—in the millions—for two of his books in which he discussed important basic issues in human behavior: the conflict between individual freedom and social effectiveness, and communal living versus individualism. They contained both popular appeal and professional and philosophical challenges.

During his most vigorous period at Minnesota, Skinner "could think clearly for about four hours a day," he told me. He referred to generating original ideas, writing, devising experiments, and originating applications of his work. By contrast, in his last year of life at age 86, he could "think clearly for only about one hour a day."[1] That, he said, was the main difference in his mental behavior at his fertile peak compared with his old age—a sharp decrement in quantity but not, he thought, in quality. Actually, quality did seem to enter in toward the end, as he aborted his attempt to write a book on ethics because he could not probe the subject as intellectually as he wanted to.

As well as being Skinner's closest friend, Fred Keller became a notable contributing researcher and cheerleader for Skinner after they finished graduate school at Harvard. Keller's ascendancy as a fellow student diminished quickly as Skinner acclimated to the Harvard graduate school. After graduate school, Keller became more of a supporter and admirer of Skinner's behavioristic views, especially after Skinner's *The Behavior of Organisms* was published in 1938. Keller was less aggressive and pursued the theory less ostentatiously than his friend.

Although Skinner apologized for not giving Keller the original manuscript of his masterwork to review immediately, Keller read it soon after publication and thereafter became an unabashed follower of Skinner's. Keller didn't seem to mind taking second place in the field; in fact, he made Columbia University a hotbed of research on Skinnerian behaviorism. Skinner had supported Keller's transfer from Colgate to Columbia, where Keller remained for many years deeply attached to Skinnerian theories without any hint of competitiveness with his comrade. He willingly acknowledged his debt to Skinner and recognized that some of his fame came to rest on their close friendship. When he was at Columbia, Keller tried to get Skinner an appointment there but Skinner saw no major advantages to leaving Minnesota at the time.

With Minnesota "off the beaten path," Skinner relished the occasional notable who visited there. One was Bertrand Russell, who taught at the University of Chicago during the 1938–39 school year. During Russell's side trip to Minneapolis, Skinner told him that, despite Russell's critical view of behaviorism, he had excited Skinner's interest in this explosive new development in psychology before Skinner entered graduate school.

With his continuing attraction to literature, writing, and the analysis of language, Skinner became interested in Shakespeare's sonnets. The sonnets particularly intrigued him as he noted that the use of a particular word was more likely to produce another one related to it in some way, often by sound or some other unintended relationship. The connection was not through alliteration, however, as was the general belief. Skinner found no greater occurrence of alliteration in Shakespeare than by chance. Wordsworth's alliteration was far below chance, perhaps because he was "self-conscious about ornament" (Skinner, 1979, p. 237), whereas in Swinburne, alliteration occurred far beyond chance.

The outstanding Shakespearean scholar at Minnesota at that time was E. E. Stoll. He rebuffed an invitation from Skinner to discuss Skinner's theory with him, writing, "I frankly have no faith in your undertaking so far as I understand it."[2] Such a comment was typical of criticisms Skinner experienced for his views on many subjects but especially on language where he did word counts to demonstrate relationships. Such critical comments often were balanced by fervid praise for his exciting new hypotheses. The same conflict continues today over the behaviorist view that language develops through positive reinforcement.

Skinner's lifelong literary interest led him to teach the first University of

Minnesota courses in the psychology of literature. He also taught one of the first statewide courses on the radio, on verbal behavior. He hoped his transcribed notes would suffice to provide a book on verbal behavior. They did not, though they provided a skeleton for it. Included was a way of counting the relationships in the uses of certain words so he could track how one led to another. He also assigned word count studies to interested students.

Skinner was strongly tempted to criticize the conduct of world affairs for not applying positive reinforcement to achieve goals. However, he made the deliberate choice to pursue his narrower psychological research rather than "spend all my time on the Depression at home and Nazism abroad" (Skinner, 1979, p. 230). His only directly political incursion was to offer his services as a speech consultant to Wendell Willkie by writing the then Minnesota governor Harold Stassen, a Willkie adviser. He accompanied his offer with an illustrative rewrite of a paragraph in a recent Willkie speech. He was ignored and Stassen does not remember receiving such a letter.[3] It was the only time Skinner described when he apparently agreed with his father's Republican politics.

Fred gradually realized that he had little chance of affecting major world events except through expanding his reputation as a behaviorist and proposing applications of behavior shaping methods to national and international activities. He wanted to achieve such influence and deliberately reserved his efforts for where he could have the greatest impact on influential people. Thus, he tried at various times personally to influence such business leaders as the head of Polaroid, an executive of IBM, and others.

Eventually, Fred would apply his theory to improve society in structure and function through books describing an invented utopian community (*Walden Two*), and making a case for controlling the forces in society that shape individuals (*Beyond Freedom and Dignity*). These two of his many books would have huge sales, generate sharp controversy, and broadly influence social thinking. *Walden Two*, his novel describing a behavioristically based utopia, written while he was still at Minnesota, used thinly disguised colleagues there to argue his views. Several publishers rejected *Walden Two* as too pedantic, stilted, and dull. Eventually, to get it published, he had to promise another manuscript—a potentially more salable basic psychology textbook.

Skinner was not active at mundane levels of community or national action, although later in his life he did contribute to ads for the anti-Viet Nam War movement. He did not throw himself into political campaigns, propagandize for legislation, or try to initiate community programs. He seldom worked with groups. He chose either a less conspicuous voice via group ads or a more individual voice in the form of personal publications and lectures propagandizing for his own views. He almost always remained aloof from direct earthy connections with people, the bargaining give-and-take of political activity, and the vehemence of social agitation. He stood apart. His life proceeded through the turmoil of his times without his being sucked into or joining it. He chose his own ways and times—rather detached, fastidious, relatively pure, and precise. He was a well-controlled intellectual individualist.

For example, in 1943, a group of 13 notable psychologists sought support for a statement of psychological principles that they considered essential for a sound peace—such as that war is built into, not born in, humans, and that the trend of human relationships is toward broader collective security—all well-intentioned and humane. But in answer to the group's request for his support, Skinner wrote, "While I subscribe wholeheartedly to every one of your ten points as a citizen, I will not put my name to them as a psychologist. It is a plain question of intellectual honesty. I do not believe we have the slightest scientific evidence of the truth of at least nine of these propositions" (Skinner, 1979, p. 276). He took most seriously his role as a scientist.

Consistently, he insisted on scientific support for assertions about improving the world. Although he did publish in areas where his data were thin (*Verbal Behavior, Walden Two*), he tried to base his books on his theory of learning founded on his laboratory research, and most of his books and articles depended on those data. Sometimes, however, the data were based upon objective descriptions from his own behavior alone.

Psychologists are still claiming expertise and authoritatively expressing opinions on current issues ranging from child care to feminism, early memories, AIDS, homosexuality, and so on. Skinner would demur that where there were no data to support such opinions, only attitudes and values could legitimately be expressed, and they should be labeled as such. They are not scientific psychology. This is not to say that Skinner never drew conclusions going beyond his data, nor did he object to that being done provided the limits are clearly stated. He did, however, demand more rigor from those who disagreed with his basic principles.

Fred ignored most of his critics, although he sometimes acknowledged and then might attack or try to answer them. His rebuttals were seldom successful; they didn't eliminate objections or fend off movements. His critics seldom changed nor did he. His work spoke for itself with widespread and growing influence. If he had simply insisted on playing an idiosyncratic role in psychology by formulating a theory of behavior, a technology of shaping it, and brilliant insights into methods of enhancing its science, his originality would have stood out clearly. But he went beyond these specifics to insist that alternatives, exceptions, and additions to his views usually were worthless or already incorporated into his principles.

Early on, for example, Skinner declared and sustained for the rest of his life a dim view of mathematical analysis. Drawn to his theory and experimental approach, his first students, John Carroll and William Estes at Minnesota, and others such as Herrnstein at Harvard, grew interested in and developed sophisticated statistical methods to analyze their research despite Skinner's antipathy.

Skinner did apply simple mathematical techniques he could manipulate logically more as clever improvisations than for statistical precision. This was his bent in all his research—to do simple handwork. He approvingly quoted Thorndike on animal research where the animal was held by hand while being studied instead of being kept in a mechanical device. Some students moved away from him because of his disinterest in statistics. The field has now almost universally incorporated more advanced statistical methods than he used. Most research has also come to depend on groups of subjects and correlations rather than control of the single case. Skinner's distaste for the study of groups did not reduce the importance of his creative views. But others found and still find statistics and large experimental groups useful. He did occasionally contradict himself when he discussed rate of learning as proportional to the "reserve," and also with an equation to obtain the height of the cumulative record.

His opposition to large numbers of experimental subjects and to mathematical analysis of data dates from his graduate student days when statistical methods were primitive and his inventiveness with individual lab experiments sufficed to support his conclusions. Still compelling is his view that controlling and predicting the one case is more significant than detecting a small even though statistically significant tendency among many cases. Statistical techniques, however, even in Skinner's early academic years, were becoming recognized as a major scientific tool, with Minnesota among the leaders in this trend. Nonetheless, his views about how science progresses emphasized direct, close, sensitive, intelligent observation of animal behavior at firsthand and as continuously as possible, one or a few subjects at a time. He tried to avoid elaborate statistics and large numbers that explained differences among groups rather than the control and prediction of individual behavior.

Skinner also wanted to maximize accidental insights by operating as free as possible of preconceived hypotheses that might limit keen on-the-spot observations. To him, crucial results often appeared serendipitously, and he believed that one should enhance the opportunity for their occurrence and observation. That possibility was increased by working firsthand with just one or a few animals at a time.

The "Tom Swift" traits of Skinner's childhood and youth—inventiveness, independence, and desire for personal mastery and control—remained deeply seated in his adult personality and only became more subtle, more powerful, and more pervasive with time. At first, he was delighted to start work with his Minnesota laboratory colleague William Heron on Heron's grant from the Ford Foundation. They were to operate "a monster of an apparatus" (Skinner, 1979, p. 222) of 24 boxes. He quickly grew impatient, however, with the numerous mechanical problems that kept intruding and the complexity introduced by the sheer numbers. Typically, he simplified and smoothed the graphs by inventing a "summarizer" that averaged the recording pens at least by smaller groups of 4. Soon, he walked away from the "monster" altogether. He had simpler, more direct research in mind, and he also wanted to explore his expanding interest in verbal behavior.

At the time, Skinner was becoming increasingly disgruntled with Minnesota. He "saw no way to the top" (Skinner, 1979, p. 236). He knew Heron was disgruntled with him for what Heron considered poor habits in the laboratory and he resented the jealousy he sensed in colleagues for his appeal to graduate students and his growing professional stardom. He was also sensitive to minor criticism, such his tendency to give too may high grades for a normal curve. What he expected at Minnesota is difficult to discern. He had been promoted faster than anyone except an earlier star, Karl Lashley; he had Elliott's support and encouragement; and he could pursue his own interests in teaching, research, and writing. In a relatively short time, he had many capable, admiring students. He did, however, live penuriously in rather poor quarters and was offended by limits on his promotions and status.

In any case, Elliott discouraged Skinner from leaving Minnesota and played up the notion of a sabbatical in two more years. In time, however, Skinner's resentment grew strong enough so that an offer elsewhere with better status and pay would find him ready to leave Minnesota. In addition, Minnesota was his first academic position and it was a kind of apprenticeship where he first became acquainted with some of the unpleasantries of faculty life, especially administrative, which were more universal than he realized. It was not unusual for new faculty to feel excluded at Minnesota, left to work out social activities on their own. He and Eve cultivated their own activities, especially in the arts. Both his father and mother were sensitive to their social acceptance, and that probably had an effect on Fred. His mother usually tried to ingratiate herself, and his father struggled to be popular, at least politically, while still wanting to be his own man.

Fred Keller told him of a job opening at Columbia. Skinner, in his disgruntled mood, at first said he was interested, although he finally decided it had little to commend it. He then began to get nibbles from other good universities, though not for the best jobs in rank, pay, and duties. Offers came from the University of Chicago, Columbia, Louisiana State, Indiana, and Illinois, among others. His connections and reputation were good and growing and he was considered a "comer" who would eventually be offered and ready to take a first-class position.

Skinner's interest in verbal behavior was intensifying. Instead of The Psychology of Literature, he began teaching a course entitled The Psychology of Language. He had transformed himself into a behavioral scientist, and the specificity and rigor in research on language appealed to his always lively interest in literature. He talked to his friends and colleagues about this growing focus and they encouraged him. Thorndike told him to "waste no time on Korzybski [famed linguist]. He is learned, but not in linguistics, and seems to me definitely insane."[4] Many experts in literature and language became openly critical of his unconventional views. The shaping of behavior—including language—by the environment was very different from the conventional view of verbal development. He inspired some strong support. But the conventional view remained that language emerged in a predetermined sequence from within the child as it matured, similarly in all societies.

The ideas of others sometimes did infiltrate his own, even if slowly and unacknowledged. Two graduate students, for example, in class pinned Skinner down on his statement that a word one has difficulty recalling is pronounced more forcefully when eventually expressed. They demonstrated that he had to get more specific about the social situation that would give rise to such behavior. It had to be in conversation when the parties were expected to respond. He accepted that modification.

Along with most other faculty without independent means, Skinner lived on campus in a genteel near-poverty existence in the usual shabby housing available there. His original quarters, an apartment duplex, were small, old, and ungracious. In fact, without his father's financial help, Skinner would have been even more cramped economically until the distant day when two of his books became best-sellers. At best, even as a full professor at Harvard, his salary was never munificent.

Skinner seldom complained of lack of money, though he was certainly aware of it. He mentioned running short at times and being unable to take trips even to professional meetings. Many well-known professors did live rather poorly. Skinner's father now offered to help them buy a home. Although his father said that he had financed his son's education, Fred believed that he himself had earned most of the money for it with their collaborative book on workmen's compensation. Fred considered he had done most of the work as a donation to his father. Fred was ambivalent about acknowledging financial dependence on his father, although while his father was alive, Fred readily accepted his largess. Simultaneously, Fred did not hesitate in giving whatever he could to his own children, including private schools, travel, and ultimately the royalties from his books.

Comfortable modern houses were available to Minnesota faculty members in an attractive section of land owned by the University and leased to faculty either to build on or to purchase with already completed houses. With his father's financial help, Skinner was able to buy one of those homes and his family lived there for the rest of its time in Minneapolis. The house has since passed through the hands of three more professors at Minnesota. Upon moving into a hotel, his parents even gave their son's family their grand piano.

Over the years, Skinner pursued—part seriously and part recreationally—the debunking of pseudoscientific phenomena. He was a board member of *The Skeptic* magazine, which liked to deflate mystical concepts trying to pass as scientific. His iconoclastic postures began in high school. He also noted sarcastically any bombast in the town newspaper. Now that he was a scientist, Fred took to attacking a wide range of quasi-scientific claims, including J. B. Rhine's popular extrasensory demonstrations that Skinner showed could be affected by subtle cues.

Rhine's contentions and demonstrations for telepathy were funded on radio by the Zenith Foundation. Skinner believed that the calls of "heads" or "tails" on coins were determined by prior calls, that guesses could be explained as a form of verbal behavior decided by the individual's associations. There was a general tendency, for example, to name "heads" oftener than "tails" because, he thought, the game is called "heads or tails" with "heads" being named first.

Skinner smoked cigarettes occasionally in college, and in the years at home between college and graduate school he became a heavy pipe smoker. He continued the habit in graduate school and at Minnesota, making his own pipes and buying special tobacco mixtures. In 1941, he quit smoking for a week, then a month, then gave away and threw away his pipes. One reason was because he had read the original long-term research on smoking and mortality rates by Raymond Pearl published in 1938. The original study linking premature death to smoking is now over 57 years old! Skinner also attributed his quitting to a fundamentalist preacher in Minneapolis, Luke Rader, who denounced various sins on his radio show. "What do you mean you can't control it? Isn't it your arm that raises the glass to your lips? Do you mean to tell me you can't control your arm?" Skinner has often had such unlikely allies who might agree with him only on the value of self-management via practical behavioral control.

Skinner acknowledged and exploited many accidental events in his life and considered that they had always played a major role in shaping him. While traveling on a train in the spring of 1940, he observed a flock of birds flying by and idly wondered whether they might be used to home in on enemy planes on bombing missions. He didn't daydream for long. In a few days, he had bought some pigeons from a restaurant poultry store in Minneapolis, fixed them in harnesses, and began to train them to peck grain from the bull's eye of a target.

His major independent research project at Minnesota then became to develop a pigeon guidance device for the military. It was his most colorful creation. At the beginning, he thought the device could aim a missile system—before discovering that the military had no missiles to direct. He then changed his goal to a bombsight and trained his birds to peck at a ground target. Incidentally, Paul Meehl recalls seeing one of Skinner's collaborators, Norman Guttman, gyrating a crow before they completely switched over to pigeons because they were less "emotional."

The other major project he planned at Minnesota was the Guggenheim Foundation award to write his long contemplated analysis of verbal behavior.

In a patriotic impulse, Fred postponed the Guggenheim in order to work on the pigeon bombsight. He opened what proved to be a long campaign for military acceptance by presenting the idea to a professor of aeronautical engineering at the University and then to a dean involved in military research. He convinced them of the value of such a system for planes and gained their support for research funding from national agencies.

The day after the attack on Pearl Harbor, Skinner resumed work on his pigeon target pecking device, enlisting graduate students Keller Breland, Norman Guttman, and others to join the effort. He trained his pigeons to release darts to hit targets on the floor. Although he did gain hearings from research administrators, his efforts to obtain official approval and support for the project continued to be frustrated. He wrote up his proposal at great length in the effort to obtain backing. It is still labeled "Restricted" in the University of Minnesota file, although details of it were published long ago.

One director turned down Skinner's project for World War II, commenting that it might be used in the next war. Another administrator liked and supported the project but was backing two other troubled "outrageous" proposals and wouldn't add Skinner's to them. After six months, General Mills finally backed the research financially and provided quarters for it at the top of a flour mill in downtown Minneapolis. There, as one of his student-employees described it, "Our operation was in a single, large room. We had shop facilities . . . experimental equipment, bird cages . . . all around. . . . In general everyone was free to proceed on a course he felt would contribute most. . . . Fred produced more ideas than the rest of us, but we all furnished a great deal of feed-back for his efforts."[5]

Skinner used his sabbatical for the military project. The bombsight design was refined by having the pigeons peck a translucent plate upon seeing an image of the target. This was rewarded intermittently with grain on the plate. The process was automated electrically. Six more months passed before the device was given another hearing, following which more data were requested. In another six months, they received from General Mills a contract for $25,000 "to develop a homing device" designated "Project Pigeon." Skinner found that three pigeons could be accommodated in the space available for sighting in the nose of the plane. He then refined his method to involve a rule of three for greater accuracy—one more of many serendipitous events that often guided his experiments. They used hemp seed (marijuana) instead of ordinary grain to reinforce the birds and also acclimated them to distracting noises that were likely to occur.

Other refinements were made continually. All the time, Skinner was also extending his basic research on behavior shaping via this experiment for a bombsight. He and his coworkers even trained a bird to play a simple tune on a primitive piano. Skinner considered the "most impressive" experiment to be one on "successive approximation," where the researchers reinforced each

Father as General Counsel
for Hudson Coal Company

Mother as a young woman

Skinner at age nineteen

Wife, Eve, with daughters,
Julie and Deborah

movement the pigeon made toward knocking a ball until the bird was batting it about avidly. He was impressed with the ease of directing behavior by a hand switch rather than by another mechanical device.

The pigeon project continued to be plagued by administrative changes in specifications the military demanded. Reviewers constantly suspected deficiencies and needed reassurance. At what Skinner thought was their final inspection, scientific observers recommended an additional developmental contract of $50,000. Nonetheless, the project was then abruptly canceled. In his last year of life, Skinner mentioned that one consultant whom he thought had strongly supported it was really undermining it.

After having exercised considerable self-control for many months, Skinner turned bitter. He was still resentful that the United States not only had no method to guide a missile but it also had no missile to home in on enemy targets. The Germans were already using them on American troop landings. The Russians had dogs carrying bombs to enemy tanks. The Swedes had taught seals to blow up mines. Churchill's scientific adviser was said to have regretted the failure to put Skinner's pigeons to effective use.

As might be expected, Skinner then began to write a book to describe the history of the bombsight research but the records available to him were inadequate and restricted. Despite the frustration, Skinner recognized that he had in this study managed to apply his research for *The Behavior of Organisms* (1938) as a useful technology. More than any other outcome, he enjoyed creating such applications of his theory. Ultimately, he did publish an account of the pigeon enterprise in the *American Psychologist* (January, 1960) under the title "Pigeons in a Pelican." As with this title, he never lost his touch or delight with apt phrasing.

Meanwhile, Skinner was growing ever more emotionally attached to his daughters, the primary area in which his feelings developed throughout his adult life. His daughter Julie had always delighted him and he was more involved with her from her birth than was Eve. He had stayed with Eve in the delivery room, which was almost always forbidden in those days. Eve anxiously called her physician when Julie first cried but generally Fred was the more concerned. He wrote that "we [sic] eventually abandoned breast feeding" (Skinner, 1979, p. 217) and he weighed Julie frequently throughout the early weeks.

He also set an early deadline on another baby: "One of the first things I made [at Minnesota] . . ." (Skinner, 1979, p. 275). Yvonne agreed but told Fred that she dreaded the first couple of years with a second child after her burdensome early experiences with Julie, their first. He proposed easing Yvonne's work with what came to be called the "baby-tender." (It was sometimes miscalled the "Skinner box," a laboratory device that was perhaps his most important invention for the progress of behavioral science. Created for lab research primarily with rats, then pigeons, it was an entirely different project from the container for babies.) The "baby box," as the tender was also called, was what made him most famous and infamous to the public. Asked to recall Skinner's contributions, most educated people who recall him cite the baby box—although he, sensitive to public criticism of boxes for humans, avoided the word *box*, preferring to call it the "air crib."

The air crib was a roughly double bathtub-sized box with sound-proofed walls; a large window with a darkening curtain; warmed, filtered air; and a strip of sheeting that could be cranked to obtain a clean section to replace a dirty one. The first box barely fitted through the Skinners' house doors. Neither its size nor its construction was ever standardized. Different builders introduced variations—the last one Skinner visited, for example, was built of fine wood by a skilled furniture maker. In any case, it was less spartan than conditions often were for babies left outside it. There was plenty of room for exercise and for toys to engage hands and feet, and it was used only when the baby did not need personalized care.

Almost immediately upon arriving home from the hospital, the new Skinner baby, named Deborah, thrived in the baby-tender, to the pleasure of her parents. She was very healthy and contented and did not even have a cold until she was 7 years old. Despite dire predictions and widespread myths about how she turned out, Deborah is now a skilled artist and writer living in London with her husband and is devoted to her family and pleased with her upbringing and her father. Most dramatic was the mistake anti-behaviorist Bruno Bettelheim made in referring to her suicide for which he later apologized.[6]

Skinner often acted as a behavioral scientist in rearing his children. Positive reinforcement was constantly applied to affect behavior he and Eve thought needed to be shaped. They ignored Julie's religious education as a child but she experimented on her own with the religious rituals of her friends, going with them to various churches and Sunday schools. She never found a denomination that sustained her interest. Incidentally, Skinner criticized Julie when she was a parent for doing too much for her kids (just as he did with his daughters, although he claimed he "let them alone"). She drove one to college and was "too indulgent with her younger daughter. I criticize that,"[7] he said, while denying that he had done the same with his children.

Fred and Eve had occasionally punished Julie when she was very young in emergency situations, such as when she grabbed a breakable object. But when Skinner's student, William Estes, concluded from his research that punishment did not have a reliably salutary effect, Fred and Eve agreed to stop punishing Julie and told her so. They made positive reinforcement work almost alone. They also roamed the house nude until the girls' adolescence, but Skinner claimed never to have felt "erotic impulses" toward his daughters.

The baby-tender gave Skinner special opportunities to observe and shape Deborah's behavior. He plotted her movements in it. He made special toys she could work inside it. He put to use the unpleasant clamminess wetting the "bed" produced to help her gain better bladder control. Deborah thrived and Eve appreciated the tender's convenience as a place to park her when Eve wanted to do something else.

Noticing that when the parent stood by until the child on the toilet urinated, Skinner realized that such attention might be welcome, thus rewarding retention instead of letting go. This became an extremely important principle in child rearing: Parents must be sensitive to the rewards they may unwittingly provide for unwanted behavior by their mere presence or smile. Skinner found that he could shorten and reward the process of urination by having the moisture, upon reaching a strip of paper under the seat, set off a music box.

Warmth, cleanliness, noise, light, and health could be controlled by the baby-tender. Challenges to the baby could be introduced when desired and could be modified at the parent's wish. The child could be picked up and held whenever the parent wanted to. Disadvantages were minimal.

Deborah was exceptionally healthy. She developed normal resistance to infection, she kept remarkably clean, she developed highly regular sleeping habits, she was congenial socially, and she seldom cried. Skinner hoped that he could study how children raised in so controlled an environment would benefit but he never got around to such research. He was reluctant to treat children as he did his laboratory animals and was sensitive to criticism on that score.

Incidentally, Eve thought that throughout her life Deborah most closely resembled her in looks, interests, and responsiveness while Julie was more like Fred. Certainly, the two girls looked and acted quite differently. Julie ended up as a colleague of her father's, pursuing the same theory and applying it to the education of children, whereas Deborah pursued the arts like her mother, especially, but also her father. Yet it is hard to discern any preference or affinity Skinner had for one daughter over the other, except that he made Julie his literary executor, since as an educational psychologist, she did share his professional interest in behavior, and attended some of the same professional meetings. Also, Julie lived nearer the family home than Deborah after the two daughters married.

Intermittently from then on through the rest of his life, Skinner encouraged anyone who wanted to build the baby-tender commercially or for personal use. Despite attempts, no one ever successfully tapped a mass market. One developer took orders and money but never produced the product. Many have been built by hand, however, right up to the present. At one time, Skinner wanted to recruit twins, one of whom could be raised in the tender, the other not, but he never did initiate such research.

Nonetheless, Skinner gained great notoriety for the baby-tender. His biggest publicity coup was a long article he wrote while at Minnesota. Eventually, it was printed with illustrations in *The Ladies' Home Journal* in October, 1945, shortly after he and his family had settled at Indiana. The article was entitled "Baby in a Box." Newspapers, radio, and news films picked up the story and Skinner received hundreds of letters. Misconceptions began immediately and persist to this day. They came from people who believed that the box was cruel, unfeeling, and parent depriving. People sometimes confused it with the "Skinner box" for studying animals. Rumors spread that Deborah had been institutionalized, psychotic, suicidal, hated her father, and so on. Truth never overtook the myths, even though parents continue to build or borrow tenders for their babies.

How did it happen that Skinner was so solicitous and protective of his daughters when he did not show such attitudes toward his wife, students, or friends? Perhaps he was acting as if the girls were an extension of himself and interposed no barriers between them. They also began life with his cooperation and were totally dependent on him and Eve. He never did like to exercise authority, and although he sought privileges when they enhanced his independence, he seldom if ever gave orders or invited deference.

Kay Walker, one of Skinner's students at Minnesota (who later married William Estes), studied verbal behavior in children with Skinner as a co-adviser along with a more helpful co-adviser Florence Goodenough. She found Skinner "distant" rather than "cold." Julie was one of Walker's subjects and for a time Skinner consulted with her daily on Julie's developing speech. Estes considered him paternal with his daughters but not with students.[8]

Skinner's attitude toward children generally was illustrated by the reaction of the son of Herbert Feigl, Skinner's closest friend at Minnesota. Now a research physician in Seattle, Eric Feigl moved to Minnesota with his family at age 7. He remembers visiting Skinner's home occasionally over a period of five years, being impressed by sets of chessman in glass cases adorning the place and being treated as an adult. Skinner asked him questions "intensely, seriously," and Eric found him "an impressive person, self-confident and with an analytic demeanor with me."[9] He asked the child for his opinions about this and that as if he were an adult and Skinner wanted to confirm his existing views of children.

Because it might bear on Skinner's relationship with Eve, Eric Feigl discussed his father's interaction with his own wife. Since his father and Skinner had been best friends at Minnesota and went out together like bachelors, one might infer some similarity in their marital relations. Eric thought his father pretty much ignored his wife intellectually, even though she had taken philosophy at the university in Vienna along side her husband-to-be. Feigl went out mostly without his wife, with male cronies he liked to talk with and with whom he "ogled waitresses." Eric remembered his father's arguing with Skinner about his research and considering him too self-centered. They did not socialize much together with their wives.

Although retaining a bitterness to his death about the failure of his project with the military, Skinner eventually laid the pigeon project to rest. At last, he was free to take up the Guggenheim grant for which he was committed to work on a theory of verbal behavior. He "hoped to do the work at Minnesota because of 'less congestion' there [from the war effort]."[10] He built himself an office in the basement of his home, which was also fitted as a workshop.

In the Psychology Department laboratory, Skinner continued to work a while on pigeons. They lived much longer than rats (decades instead of months) and he wanted to determine how long their memories were. They proved to be very long. Skinner would work primarily with pigeons for the rest of his animal research on various problems, including the study of how hunger affected problem solving, and the defintion of behavioral terms. For the remainder of his time at Minnesota, however, verbal behavior—and his only novel, about a utopia based on his behavior theory—occupied most of his working time.

Skinner's Guggenheim grant called for him to study "the actual behavior of the individual in emitting speech" (Skinner, 1979, p. 281). Traditional material on grammar, syntax, classical rhetoric, he said, would not be useful. In short order, he found his empirical data from early experiments on language to be inadequate to explain the complexities he wanted to deal with. While still at Harvard, Skinner had studied nonsense sounds emitted by a device he invented, which he first called a "verbal summator" then a "tautophone" (p. 180). Subjects would interpret the sounds as they wished. But Skinner's data were and remained thin gruel for his theory and he could not readily collect more satisfactory material. So he decided for the first time to skip research for a publication.

Could Skinner be satisfied with a book that was theoretical, without research data that always before had been available to support his writing? He tried to justify himself. What reinforcement, he asked, could a scientist find in producing a book without data? And could a scientist find it rewarding to read such a publication? "I knew nothing about linguistics," he told Keller. "Somebody ought to do it—and it seems to be up to me. But what a field! Almost all the professional linguists are all wet psychologically" (Skinner, 1979, p. 150).

Skinner decided that he need not find and publish confirmation for his theory; rather, he could aim for "the discovery of uniformities, the ordering of confusing data, the resolution of puzzlement" (Skinner, 1979, p. 282). With initial reluctance, he did produce his book without basing it on language research. Toward the end of his life, Skinner said that he considered *Verbal Behavior* (1957) his most important contribution to psychology.[11] It was not published for 23 years after he began work on it in 1934. It was an unusually long gestation period for him, much longer than for any other of his books. He had always been far more efficient and direct about producing his publications than this time.

"All this material," he wrote in its Preface, "was used in courses on Literary and Verbal Behavior at the University of Minnesota in the late thirties, at Harvard University in the summer of 1938, and at the University of Chicago in . . . 1939. A manuscript . . . was to have been completed under a Guggenheim Fellowship in 1941 . . . and a version nearly completed [in 1944–45]" (Skinner, 1957). It was largely written during his tenure at Minnesota.

Kenneth MacCorquodale as assistant editor of the Century Psychology Series under R. M. Elliott (publisher of *The Behavior of Organisms*) corresponded with Elliott about Skinner's proposed book on verbal behavior. They were trying to make a more remunerative deal by packaging with it a book on education "that the educators couldn't possibly understand." Further, "As for Fred's writing, I am in total agreement with you, let us publish anything we can get our hands on, Science and Human Dignity if necessary, Technology of Teaching if possible. . . . As for demilitarizing him he is, as I know, completely intractable and will not change a comma so don't waste your breath."[12] After all, Elliott had long ago argued strenuously, but without effect, with Skinner about his great first book—that it was too dense, it ignored other people too much, it wouldn't sell, and he should "make more concessions" to readers.

Science and Human Behavior (1953), Skinner's only basic textbook, published much later by Macmillan, became a bargaining chip for *Walden Two* (1948, 1976) instead of for *Verbal Behavior* (1957), which was published by Prentice-Hall instead of Elliott's Appleton-Century. As it turned out, the supposedly profitable textbook was neither conventional nor popular and sold nowhere near as many copies as the presumably risky *Walden Two*, which became a best-seller. In any case, the furor over Skinner's long-standing views of verbal behavior was largely delayed until the book was finally published.

Skinner's student at Minnesota, Marian Kruse (who later married Keller Breland [who died], then Bailey), who helped care for Julie and did light housework for the family, also transcribed a draft of *Verbal Behavior* mainly from the Dictaphone. Skinner then rewrote it many times to tighten it up. Throughout the work, Kruse found Skinner to be an amiable employer who paid her personally. "Skinner came across as having the whole world in his hand,"[13] she observed. But earlier, trying at his suggestion to do research to support his views of verbal behavior, she never understood what he wanted. One of her tasks was to try to define Thoreau's style in *Walden*, its "psychological essence," and for a year she struggled inconclusively to classify Thoreau's words, clauses, and other parts of speech.

Kruse did not consider Skinner to be aloof and she never observed any serious problems between him and Eve, except that he persistently wanted Eve to develop more interests and activities outside the home. Eve, however, was satisfied to spend most of her spare time reading. Although Kruse was the student closest to him at Minnesota, when Skinner wrote his autobiography, he asked her only about her work with Keller Breland (on animal behavior).

Married, Kruse and Breland left Minnesota to organize their own business as "Animal Behavior Enterprises" in Hot Springs, Arkansas. There, they trained animals for commercial use at fairs and for TV ads and not for further basic research on behavior theory.

Recalling Skinner as her teacher, Kruse thought he did not easily tolerate objections to his views and usually "overrode" the students who met with him at his home. She never saw him get angry in intellectual debate, however. The most upset she ever saw him was regarding "social injustice," especially in the classroom, and Julie's treatment at school. Nor did he take well, she thought, to criticism of his understanding of animal behavior. She and Breland wrote *The Misbehavior of Organisms* to enlarge on Skinner's concept of animal behavior to include species differences. But Skinner was annoyed with their criticism and took years to reconcile with them.

Opinions of Skinner in the classroom varied greatly, except for almost universal agreement that he was a brilliant and stimulating teacher, one of the best his students had experienced. They were impressed with different facets of his behavior. Another member of the seminar in his home at Minnesota, Lloyd George Everest (and his wife) wrote that his "most vivid impression . . . is the flexibility of his [Skinner's] enthusiasm. It could instantly race from profound concern with verbal behavior to what he needed to do to make a child's toy. . . . I could never guess which venture he judged more important."[14] Others were sharply critical of his refusal to deal with arguments and logical inconsistencies.

Although Skinner had been asked as early as 1940 by the chairman of the Psychology Department at the University of Indiana whether he would be interested in coming there, it was not until 1944 that he received a concrete proposal. It was an offer of the chairmanship, with an assistant, a much higher salary (he was asked to suggest the amount), and freedom to do his own research. Indiana so readily agreed to the $7,500 he asked for that he regretted he had not requested more.

Immediately after arriving at the University of Indiana, he liked the atmosphere—the friendliness of the prior chairman and the faculty, the small-town environment, and the behavioral orientation. Eve had not wanted to leave Minnesota, and Skinner talked to Elliott about what Minnesota could offer. He could be promoted to associate professor with a salary of $5,000. "Elliott seemed to think it was an unheard of salary for a psychologist—$7,500,"[15] Skinner commented. Referring to Indiana, Elliott uncharacteristically said, "I think it is a dump." "It was then," said Skinner, "that I decided to go" (Skinner, 1979, p. 285).

Skinner had always felt left out at Minnesota. He lacked the status of the full professors whose intellectual equal he easily was, he was not looked up to by the faculty, and he was essentially a loner. It was Skinner himself, however, who gave the impression of being indifferent to competitive feelings, of being content to be let alone to shape his own life, and of wanting to pursue single-mindedly his own professional projects.

Skinner had not achieved fame as fast as he thought he would with his first book, which strikingly emphasized and amplified his form of behaviorism at the forefront of experimental psychology along with Guthrie, Tolman, and Hull. He was open to a job change because of his dissatisfaction with his status at Minnesota, as well as his salary. He also sensed unfriendliness in his colleagues, which probably reflected their general reticence and independence more than a rejection of him personally. Aside from Heron's complaint about his untidy lab habits, the only criticism on record was that he gave too high grades and was aloof and arrogant. Even so, Skinner found his students rewarding and his enthusiasm was unbridled for the brightest ones. He considered his years at Minnesota to have been the best of his teaching career.

Ambivalence about Minnesota persisted for the rest of Skinner's life. Among many other statements he made about his experience there, he told me late in life, "They brought me out of the Harvard cocoon, there's no doubt about that. I loved Minnesota, a liberal state, I loved it—but Elliott wouldn't move me up. . . . I would have stayed at Minnesota if they had boosted my salary. Whether that would have been the best thing I don't know."[16]

Skinner thought that at Indiana he would have national stature academically as head of a major department, that he could build himself a new laboratory, that he could study just one pigeon at a time (nobody had ever insisted that he study more!), that he could have more of his own graduate students. "Elliott," he said, "ran the [Minnesota] department very well, but entirely from the University's point of view which I tried to correct when I got to Indiana . . . from the department's point of view and fighting with the Administration."[17]

Autonomy, prestige, and money appeared to be Skinner's main considerations, in addition to that edge of being warmly received, especially by both the eager president of the university and the retiring department chairman, and then being welcomed socially. Still, he said, "I didn't like being chairman, I didn't want to be . . . but I felt that Minnesota was a dead end for me."[18] Meanwhile, Boring and Elliott, without Skinner's knowledge, were corresponding about his future and agreeing that to take an administrative job was a sign of intellectual deterioration for Skinner, so committed a scientist and researcher. They themselves both were administrators! After accepting the new job but while still at Minnesota, Skinner began to write down his goals for an ideal department: reduced teaching load, improved library, discussion groups, practical courses, and maximum support of research.

Was his heart in the acceptance of the departmental chairmanship at Indiana? It is doubtful. Within a year, Skinner had turned over the chairmanship to a colleague so he could pursue his own work. He initiated no major changes, except to try to get more behaviorist friends on the faculty. He never did express any pleasure in the exercise of power. He never acknowledged any importance to him of prestige. It seems clear that he took the position because of his pique at Minnesota socially and his frustrated desire for quicker promotion in rank and salary. He acted as if he bore the university some grudge, especially as Eve seemed not to have as much say as usual about a move.

What does seem inevitable is that Skinner should eventually end up at Harvard where as a student he had shaped his lifelong theory, where he had made his best friends among both fellow students and faculty, and where academic prestige was the greatest. Although he never indicated it in any way, Indiana seemed to function merely as a way station between Minnesota and Harvard.

ENDNOTES

1. B. F. Skinner, personal interview.
2. University of Minnesota archives.
3. H. Stassen, unpublished correspondence with author.
4. Harvard archives.
5. Unpublished correspondence with author.
6. Unpublished correspondence with author.
7. B. F. Skinner, personal interview. See also Skinner, 1979.
8. Kay Walker Estes, personal interview.
9. Eric Feigl, personal interview.
10. B. F. Skinner, personal interview. See also Skinner, 1979, p. 274.
11. B. F. Skinner, personal interview.
12. University of Minnesota archives.
13. Marian Bailey, personal interview.
14. L. G. Everest, unpublished correspondence with author.
15. B. F. Skinner, personal interview.
16. Ibid.
17. Ibid.
18. Ibid.

▶ 6

Interim at Indiana
1945–1948

Skinner's annoyance over his mediocre status at the University of Minnesota broke loose once he had a firm offer from the University of Indiana. R. M. Elliott, despite his efforts to keep Skinner at Minnesota, made uncharacteristically caustic comments about Indiana, skeptical remarks about Skinner's potential as an administrator, and amazement at the Indiana salary offer, which was 50 percent more than his best counteroffer. Skinner ignored Elliott's arguments and simply repeated that he was leaving.

Elliott's letter to Garry Boring in January 1946, concerning Skinner's self-centered and arrogant attitudes, was more candid than usual for him. It concluded: "Can't you manage somehow to keep it [this letter] entirely to yourself? I could not have written it to any other person living and I should be happiest if you could forget what I have said. If you want another Minnesota opinion and want a favorable one, write to Feigl."[1]

Reviewing Skinner's tenure at Minnesota just after it ended, Elliott wrote that despite Skinner's indifference to Elliott's strong desire to retain him, "my loyalty to him and what he stood for did not weaken, especially since our most able graduate students gathered around him like flies around honey."[2] Elliott then reflected on Skinner's inspired experimentation with his pigeon bombsight and the small dedicated research group he assembled to develop it. At that time, Elliott remarked, Skinner seemed to become "exalted" and the University's pedestrian work "just didn't count."[3]

With the long-considered but eventual rejection of his military project after his uncharacteristically laborious attempts to please his military reviewers, Skinner reacted "very badly, cursing the brass hats and damning all psychology," Elliott wrote.[4] Skinner acknowledged in his autobiography that he did lose his temper on that rare occasion.

When Skinner first received the posh offer from Indiana, Elliott observed that the pay was so much above regular scale at Indiana that Skinner was required to put in 11 months for it instead of the usual 9 to avoid offending his prospective colleagues there. Further, Elliott wrote, he "warned" the dean of the Graduate School at Indiana that "Fred's brilliance . . . would have to be taken in compensation for his egotistic traits and that what I feared would prove to be a lack of administrative talent."[5] When, Elliott wrote, "Fred tossed his head and declared that he would go [anyway, despite Elliott's objections] . . . [it] convinced me that the time had come when Minnesota should for its own peace be glad that he was going."[6]

Toward the end of his time at Minnesota, Skinner invited Feigl and Elliott to visit his home to hear him read from a small book called *Walden Two*. Displaying a detailed relief model of the community that he had built of wood, Skinner invited critical discussion of the manuscript of the utopian town founded on his behavior principles. Elliott declared "I don't think the book will have any success and possibly no publisher."[7] It was a terribly wrong, though widely shared, prediction about a volume that was to sell over two million copies.

In further correspondence with Boring, Elliott commented that Skinner had written him from Indiana that, contrary to Elliott's predictions, he had got his research well organized and that his life there was highly enjoyable, partly for social reasons. "The Skinners were not particularly social here," Elliott remarked, perhaps because the department seemed set in its ways. "I wonder, I wonder,"[8] Elliott ended. He continued in his letter to Boring: "My own judgment would be that you should not consider Skinner in his present mood."[9] (Was Boring already thinking of Skinner for Harvard?) "I definitely answer in the affirmative your question whether his willingness to become head of a department is a sign of 'mental deterioration'. . . . If he can get control of his emotions . . . I will still predict only the best from his cerebrum . . . [which] has always fascinated me."[10]

It is noteworthy that Elliott remarks about Skinner's need to get "control of his emotions," since Skinner seldom displayed them and denied their importance. But Elliott encountered him in an especially bitter period of job dissatisfaction, which never recurred as intensely. He was up against severe financial constraints and saw little opportunity to improve his lot substantially at Minnesota, his first book for years sold few copies, and his practical progress was stymied.

Although soured by losing Skinner, Elliott's assessment is probably as informed as can be obtained about Skinner at the end of his Minnesota years. He recognized that Skinner was likely to have a brilliant career and devoted students. Elliott also saw that Skinner, at that point, was impatient to hurdle the limits of being a junior staff member and felt ready to assume the mantle of a senior, respected professor nearing the top of his field. Skinner's competitive sense at that time was as acute and overt as it ever was. It took only a visit to Minnesota from Ernest Hilgard, a dean at Stanford, to accentuate his "feeling rather out of things" at Minnesota. Skinner noted that Hilgard, a contemporary exactly the same age who gained his Ph.D. from Yale about the same time as Skinner won his at Harvard, had moved steadily to the top in academia. The difference was that Hilgard had not luxuriated as a research fellow for several postdoctoral years but had begun on the academic track even before he got his Ph.D., and continued right along afterwards.

The Elliott-Boring correspondence suggests that Boring was already considering Skinner for Harvard and did not believe his appointment at Indiana to be a serious impediment. Nor were Elliott's reservations likely to dissuade a faculty power such as Boring, attracted to Skinner's growing importance, even star quality, from acting for a university seeking outstanding professors. Boring would probably assume he could get anyone he wanted. This was so, despite the fact that Boring had even more intense reasons than Elliott to be critical of Skinner.

That Skinner had proven more ambitious for rank and salary than Minnesota could or would fulfill did not discourage Boring. He knew that Harvard represented the apogee of academic prestige, including in psychology. Harvard was more accustomed than Minnesota to departmental jealousies and to flexibility in hiring and promotion. Moreover, it was used to accommodating prima donnas.

For the celebration of the centennial anniversary at the University of Indiana in the late 1980s, Skinner wrote a statement for a commemorative booklet. Because of his recent brain concussion, he could not attend the ceremony to deliver his paper in person. In the brief written narration he substituted, Skinner recalled his happy time at Indiana. He appreciated the warmth and support of the prior chairman, Robert Kantor, who hired Skinner to replace himself. Kantor was a "humane, scholarly man, helpful . . . in every possible way . . . [and] wonderful with our children."[11] Skinner never wrote so glowingly about anyone at Minnesota.

He did little teaching at Indiana, which he had limited as a condition of his appointment, and concentrated on his own research and writing. "In many ways, I was starting anew" he noted.[12] He had discovered pigeons as superior research subjects, he had invented an automatic shocking device for rats, and he was blessed with "one of the best" Ph.D. students—the most productive he'd ever had—Norman Guttman. Guttman had become his student at Minnesota, moved with him to Indiana, and transferred to William Estes as his Ph.D. advisor when Skinner left Indiana. As another provision of his appointment, Skinner was to have an administrative assistant, and after a year he obtained one: William Verplanck. Nonetheless, Skinner took a year off from his administrative position the year after beginning his brief two-and-a-half-year stint at Indiana.

In contrast to Minnesota, Skinner wrote, Indiana was generous with travel money, which contributed to the brevity of his stay there. At Minnesota, he had no money to go to conventions and other meetings, whereas Indiana paid his way. It was at a meeting in New York that he inadvertently met with Garry Boring, who invited him to lecture at Harvard University. Skinner took a term off from Indiana for that purpose the year after he got there. It led to a sharp turn in his life.

William Estes, who had received his Ph.D. from Minnesota in 1943 as a student of Skinner's, had then gone into the army. He was hired by Skinner at Indiana to teach beginning experimental lab because of a "need for hands," as Estes put it. He had begun doing research with Skinner's theory while a graduate student and soon noted that Skinner ignored the role of emotions in learning behavior. Growing more interested in them, Estes began to do research on emotions with Skinner's unenthusiastic assent.

Estes and Skinner never overtly disagreed or argued despite the fact that they had differences and were associated throughout their academic lives. Working with Skinner at Minnesota and Indiana, Estes later became a colleague at Harvard. Their lack of overt disagreements was partly because of Estes's extreme social shyness and laconic speech, traits that almost got him rejected for graduate work (and teaching) at Minnesota when he began there. He was also too slow a chess partner for Skinner's taste.

Skinner wrote ironically of Estes's "service connected disability" from his military tenure. "His brilliant career as an experimentalist soon yielded to mathematical model-building, from which he suffered for many years" (Skinner, 1979, p. 318). Part humorous, part cutting, such a remark should have tried Estes's good will toward his mentor. Nonetheless, he continued to express the highest respect for Skinner.

In his autobiography, Skinner mentioned Estes's work on emotions only once, and then briefly. Still, Estes always referred to Skinner as "very supportive" despite the fact that he generally ignored Estes's later work. Skinner especially attacked Estes's mathematical approach, remarking that it represented "flight from the lab."

At Indiana, Skinner ignored his juniors, spending most of his time with peers. Having been personally recruited by Skinner for Indiana, Estes may have sensed some rebuff. With his general charm and vitality, and the intellectual excitement he generated, Skinner unwittingly aroused more hope for friendship than he would fulfill. According to Paul Meehl (1989) in *A History of Psychology in Autobiography*, Skinner precipitated many "identity crises" among his students. After high expectations, many felt rejected by Skinner's apparent neutrality toward them. Skinner "explained" it as the advantage of "leaving them alone." His students could grow best without his interference, he thought, as he himself had sought to be let alone. Some of his students did appreciate this hands-off policy. Wells Hively, for example, thought it was just right that Skinner let him complete his thesis on his own, then strongly supported it at the oral exam.[13]

By the time Skinner reached Indiana, Boring was writing to "Fred" and signing as "Garry." From their new-found friendship, which surprised and pleased Skinner, Boring wrote his former student:

> *The differences between you and me always were, I think, that you had a strong cathexis for your ideas, seeming a fanatic to me, and that you were definitely aware of differences from yourself and constantly directing your invective against them. . . . I thought they probably lay within the [realm] of human fallibility, although when your invective was directed against me, I tended to reply crisply.*[14]

In a 1945 article in the *Psychological Review*, Skinner commented that "I am interested in Boring from within" (n.p.).[15]

There's little doubt that Skinner flourished emotionally at Indiana as he had not at Minnesota—despite the fact that his work at Minnesota, over its much longer span, was far more impressive and indeed represented the height of his inventiveness. Substantial offers continued to come to him (including one from Louisiana State for which he recommended Keller), all of which fell short of his aspirations in some significant respect. He denied that he was awaiting a Harvard offer, but when it came, he showed little doubt about accepting it.

Skinner had been discontent at Minnesota. One of his biggest disappointments was the paltry sale of and attention given to his magnum opus, *The Behavior of Organisms*. He was not automatically heeded when he talked, and although the campus and community publications gave attention to his ideas about reinforcement, training animals, the baby-tender, and so on, he was not acknowledged as much as he thought he deserved.

Skinner's father continued to subsidize his major living expenses, furnishing money for his home in Bloomington, for cars, for vacations, and for the children's private education. His father considered it appropriate that the older generation should help the younger, even though his father contributed to both his parents and his son. In a 1991 interview, Eve Skinner remarked that her husband's parents had always been generous to them; there is no evidence that hers were.

Although Skinner was discontented with his colleagues and chairman at Minnesota, they generaly respected him. Donald Paterson, for example, spontaneously wrote the dean to ask that every effort be extended to retain Skinner, while also recognizing "the contributions of other members of the department who antedate him in length of service."[16] But Skinner had no ambivalence about his place at Indiana.

There's another factor about Indiana that Skinner did not mention, pointed out by a student, later a long-time faculty member at Indiana, James Dinsmoor. Dinsmoor (1987) wrote about visiting Bloomington for the first time for an early conference of behaviorists. Dinsmoor observed its "Green walls of foliage," "A shallow stream rippling over a rocky bed" alongside the highway, and "a ravine between two steeply sloping hillsides." "The center of Bloomington looked very much like the downtown area of any other sleepy county seat in southern Indiana," with "commercial establishments, mostly housed in buildings that revealed their 19th-century origins" (p. 441).

It was a pastoral setting and Skinner probably found comfort in its similarities to the small town of his childhood and youth. Even the department staff had the congeniality and social interaction of small-town people. Furthermore, the department was Skinner oriented. His was not a new theory for them to absorb but a lively source of interest and research they appreciated, similar to his students' attitude at Minnesota—but not to the faculty there. It was at Indiana that the first conference on the Experimental Analysis of Behavior was convened. Variously dated as 1946 and 1948, Dinsmoor clearly places it in 1947 (1987, p. 441). "There is no question," he writes, "that Skinner was the dominant figure. He was a youngish-looking 43 at the time, with a high 'intellectual' forehead" (p. 444). Increasingly, it became "his" organization in its devotion to his theory, its applications, and research.

Dinsmoor continued:

Although Skinner was at the height of his creativity as an experimental scientist and was well known among his fellow psychologists . . . he was not as yet a major figure. As I recall the spirit of the conference, we regarded him more as an especially shrewd and resourceful member of our expedition into the unknown . . . than as an authority whose thoughts were to be treasured. . . . No one, I believe, would have cited him in the almost scriptural way that is sometimes done today. . . .

From my notes, it is clear that Skinner was by far the most active contributor to the proceedings. He devoted quite a bit of time to the formulation of a standard set of definitions (theoretical concepts), classifying behavioral functions in terms that were ultimately reducible to physical description. Whenever there was an empty spot in the program, he offered some more definitions or treated his audience to selected tidbits from his large store of unpublished research. (Dinsmoor, 1987, p. 444)

While at Indiana, Skinner offered help after Dinsmoor's arrest for picketing Lyndon Johnson over the Vietnam war. "Despite the claims of various literary figures that Skinner is some kind of fascist, he has always struck me as well to the left of center" Dinsmoor wrote. "Note, for example, his treatment of gender discrimination in *Walden Two*."[17]

Dinsmoor's is probably the most vivid statement of Skinner's presence and interaction with colleagues near his professional maturity. This conference was the precursor of organizations that were the most Skinnerian of any: The Society for the Experimental Analysis of Behavior, Division 25 of the American Psychological Association, and the Association for Behavior Analysis. This period also marked the beginning of the continuing publication most vital for Skinnerian behaviorism, the *Journal of the Experimental Analysis of Behavior*.

Skinner's commemorative paper on Indiana notes that "I am afraid I did very little for the department at Indiana. After meeting with Boring, we resolved our many differences," and he was soon off to Harvard after only two and a half years in the Indiana setting he found so idyllic. Despite his fondness for the place, he seemed to refer to it most often in contrast to Minnesota, as when he wrote of Indiana: "With *Walden Two*, the Baby Tender, and especially with the pigeon as a new subject of experiment, I was on my way to something new."

Actually, *Walden Two* was written at Minnesota, in a "white heat" of somewhere between 7 and 12 weeks, much faster and with more emotion and less revision than anything else he ever wrote. Also created at Minnesota was the baby-tender, first used with his second daughter. It was also there that he began working with pigeons. He wrote about his time at Indiana when he was in his eighties and not as rigorous about following firsthand factual material he tried to depend on exclusively when he wrote his autobiography, or he would have acknowledged Minnesota as the birthplace of these innovations.

In the beginning at Indiana, he tried to act like a department chairman. He gradually got over his awkwardness in using his secretary, and he stood behind his faculty to raise their salaries, as if to make up for Elliott's deference to the administration at Minnesota. He proposed, unsuccessfully, that curriculum changes be made only after scientific study of student behavior. He also initiated lunch-hour discussions between faculty and students, open house on Sunday afternoons, and informal seminars in which Skinnerians argued with students of different orientations.

Skinner had trouble getting on with his own research, however. Because of the war, some materials were hard to obtain, but he did resume his old habit of using single apparatuses rather than working with the larger numbers he tried to accommodate to at Minnesota. Free to do just as he wished in his teaching, he used no textbooks and no reading lists. His students did not need to memorize material for tests. They were to learn how to control behavior and convey their mastery of their methods on his exams.

About his graduate course, the Analysis of Behavior, he wrote to Elliott after two months at Indiana, "The students merely keep an exhaustive notebook of their research and their ideas and they are learning more about behavior than was ever gotten out of the longest reading list . . . in the world. . . . We are, I believe, really going to turn the elementary teaching in psychology upside down."[18] Elliott's similar course depended on reading rather than research, but both required keeping a personal notebook.

Skinner's friend, Fred Keller, at Columbia, described by letter a textbook that he was coauthoring to use in his classes, based on Skinner's views. Skinner replied, "I wish I had the same freedom and backing here, but I don't feel like jamming what looks like my own stuff down the throat of this Department" (Skinner, 1979, n.p.). This was the department of which he was chair. His reluctance to exercise power outweighed his desire to have his way.

Skinner considered the town of Bloomington to be a "backward community." For example, blacks could sit only in the theater balcony. The Skinners led a social life limited to the academy. "The Indiana years," he remarked,

> . . . *were dry years intellectually. We never got into the social swim in Minneapolis and it was quite a swim [at Indiana]. There were a lot of people who did a lot of almost Junior League partying. There were difficult people there [Minnesota]. I think I handled it pretty well. Eve never liked it. I never liked it. . . . We never have been social. We were invited to all kinds of things when we got there [Indiana]. . . .*
>
> *There was a regular weekly dance club. . . . There was a great deal of drinking. I've never drunk as much as I did at Indiana. There were people . . . in town and on the faculty who thought we were a pretty wild young crowd. . . . It was an entirely new kind of social life. . . . Cocktail parties . . . nobody gave dinner parties.*[19]

Eve and Fred started a play reading group that they continued at Harvard.

It was at Indiana that Skinner gained the reputation of being a roué. He had courted young women at Minnesota but discreetly and not in public. But at Indiana, perhaps as result of his drinking, he was more overt in making overtures to the wives of colleagues and others, and his encounters became widely known. Never, it seems, did he sustain an affair or mislead women about his superficial intentions. But it seems likely that his wife became aware of his peccadilloes, since the many friends with knowledge about them included her sister.

In reply to my direct question about his sexual behavior at Indiana, Skinner replied,

> *Oh yes, of course, that was a very high life there. I don't see any harm done at all. I greatly admire the different attitude toward these things now. . . . When I was a graduate student here [Harvard] at first . . . the police . . . would break into a house or apartment and arrest people for fornication. . . .*
>
> *Well, yes, [at Minnesota and Indiana] I violated the taboo about faculty and students. I think that's because I started teaching at a time when no one was raising this question at all, when it was pretty rampant, as it was in*

English colleges with homosexuals. . . . There were no standards of ethics of that kind. . . . I have always regarded my students as equals . . . going to a first name basis right away, and treated them as equals. So it was much easier then to behave as one behaves with other people who were not students.[20]

In a letter to me, Skinner remarked that "it is hard to say what I should say about Eve's and my personal lives. Minnesota was very puritanical. There was scarcely any drinking. . . . There was a much stronger wall between academy and town life. [At Indiana] the academy was suspected of having orgies. They weren't that bad, but there was a lot of drinking and playing around, and that was our first indoctrination, if that is the word."[21]

While Skinner was at Indiana, there was more action on the variously named baby box, baby-tender, air crib, and Heir Conditioner. His second daughter, for whom the baby-tender was built, is sure that its inhumane reputation came from its original designation as the "baby box" by the famed *Ladies' Home Journal* article, confusing its name with the "Skinner box" in which he trained his rats and pigeons. Although Elliott wrote, "The only time that human beings are subject to boxes is when they are dead,"[22] articles followed the *Journal* story in publications all over the world. Skinner received hundreds of letters, most of them asking how to obtain a baby-tender, but some were virulently antagonistic to what they considered to be a barbarous practice. One referred to "caging this baby up like an animal just to relieve the Mother of a little more work." And "If you don't care what happens to your baby, why have one?"

The name "Heir Conditioner" was proposed by one J. J. Weste, with a plan to mass produce the baby-tender, the first of several such proposals, all unsuccessful. The man planned to distribute them by direct mail and to charge no more than $100. At first, he wrote to Skinner about supply problems, then made estimates of proceeds, then quit writing or replying to others who ordered. When Skinner finally saw models, he was dismayed at their bulkiness. There were design defects and shipping problems, production was on a financial shoestring, and orders were taken and paid for but never filled. Finally, the entrepreneur disappeared. With Skinner's approval, a furniture manufacturer took over the manufacturing but he too made serious design errors, boosted the price to $420, and never succeeded in constructing the baby-tender efficiently. Although it has still never been successfully mass produced, it continues to be homemade in numbers, probably in the thousands by now.

In the spring of 1946, Indiana paid Skinner's way to attend a meeting of experimental psychologists at the Harvard Club in New York, where he delivered a paper. Fortuitously seated next to Boring, the next day they had their first long talk since Skinner had been a graduate student and fellow at

Harvard. It was an accident of proximity Skinner later cited as one of many that had changed his life.

A few months later, Boring wrote to Skinner and asked if he would give the William James Lectures at Harvard for a term. Skinner agreed to give 10 lectures and a seminar on verbal behavior during the fall. He would base them on his notes for his stalled book on the subject, hoping in this way to restore it to life. Not knowing about these James lectures, Keller wrote, "Report reaches me that you are doing too goddam many things. . . . I want from you, sir, a book on language . . . but I'm not interested in Ethics, children's books, chess, baby-tenders, cryptanalysis, or what have you."[23] At Keller's invitation, Skinner taught at Columbia the summer before lecturing at Harvard.

How relatively simple it was to make faculty appointments at that time! During Skinner's William James lectures at Harvard, Boring dropped by his office one day and casually remarked, "Smitty [S. Smith Stevens] and I would like to have you in the department" (Skinner, 1979, p. 339). If Skinner agreed, they would put up his name and the administration would ask an ad hoc committee of outsiders to evaluate him. The Department of Psychology at Harvard had split, with the personality part joining sociologists and social anthropologists as a new Department of Social Relations. The experimental psychologists were left with the old department and needed Skinner for the learning field. Skinner warned them that he would make it over in his own theoretical image with a laboratory and students. He managed to get their original salary offer of $9,000 raised to $10,000 plus research funding for five years until he could find other sources of support.

Despite some past carping about Harvard, Skinner commented that "there was really no question that I should accept. . . . I felt that I belonged at Harvard" (1979, p. 340). He said nothing about the rest of his family's opinions. "Yvonne[24] and I had enjoyed our life in Bloomington," he commented, "and professionally I had learned a few lessons. I had seen the political side of university administration and resolved never to see it at close range again" (p. 341). He never had become intensely involved with it nor had he been burned by any such activity. He also recognized that he "could not say much for my teaching" and "the laboratory I had dreamed of . . . never came into existence. . . . I was in the mood for a clean sweep."

The notable "Shakow Report" (Shakow, 1947) on the reshaping of clinical training programs in psychology was being circulated for reactions. It eventually became the model for the education of clinical psychologists. "It struck me as definitely a sell-out to the medical profession," Skinner wrote,[25] "and as heralding a generation of clinical psychologists with no greater understanding of a science of behavior than the psychiatrists now have."[26] Not only did he desperately want psychology to concentrate on becoming a science but he wanted it to concern itself with changing observable behavior rather than depending on introspection. If it would not meet those two criteria, he would leave the field.[27]

Shortly before he left Indiana, Skinner wrote to Elliott on a theme that was to rile him for the rest of his life. It was his disappointment with psychology as a science. Eventually, he would even try to shed the word *psychologist* as his professional designation in favor of *behavioral analyst*. To the end of his life, Skinner was still threatening to resign from psychology and the American Psychological Association. He repeatedly wrote out resignations for publication; he never publicly printed them, however. In his last year, he spoke of writing an article entitled "Why I Am Not and Never Have Been a Psychologist." When a new organization of psychologists was formed in 1988 to focus on psychology as a science, he was an enthusiastic early supporter whose statement was quoted in recruitment ads. Then the new organization, the American Psychological Society, also disappointed him in its actual function: It accepted the study of "cognitive behavior" as science and concerned itself heavily with the practice as well as the science of psychology. He turned against it also and was sorry it had used his endorsement.

Skinner made no apologies for departing Indiana so soon, despite leaving several students beached, as well as some faculty members he had brought there and who had come because of him. Estes took over Skinner's students, none of whom had completed their doctorates by the time Skinner left. Although Skinner was asked in his eighties to talk at the Indiana centennial commemorative celebration, there are few signs of his time there. There are no archives recalling his tenure. Unintentionally, Indiana served mainly as a way station to Harvard, marking Skinner's elevation to full professorship and the privilege of paid travel, which he believed at least facilitated his advancement to Harvard.

By 1948, Skinner and his family were off to Harvard and looking for a house within walking distance of the university. They found one built for an artist early in the century, bought it for temporary use until they could build their own, and moved into it just before school started in the fall of 1948. It turned out that he and Eve were settling in at Harvard for the rest of his life.

ENDNOTES

1. University of Minnesota archives.
2. Ibid.
3. Ibid.
4. Ibid.
5. Ibid.
6. Ibid.
7. Ibid.

8. Ibid.

9. Ibid.

10. Ibid.

11. B. F. Skinner, personal interview. See also Skinner, 1979, p. 284.

12. B. F. Skinner, personal interview.

13. Unpublished correspondence with author.

14. Harvard archives.

15. Skinner reiterated this remark in his autobiography (Skinner, 1979, p. 295).

16. University of Minnesota archives.

17. Unpublished correspondence with author.

18. Ibid.

19. Unpublished correspondence with author.

20. B. F. Skinner, personal interview.

21. Unpublished correspondence with author.

22. University of Minnesota archives.

23. Harvard archives.

24. Skinner's wife, Yvonne, was also called Eve.

25. Unpublished correspondence with author.

26. Ibid.

27. At the American Psychological Association convention of 1989, an editor, George Zimmar, at Greenwood-Praeger, excitedly told me his latest news: Skinner had resigned from the APA and no longer considered himself a psychologist. But as always, Skinner had simply told it to someone and not published it.

▶ 7

Walden Two, from the Heart

1948

Although *Walden Two* was written quickly toward the end of his stay at Minnesota, Skinner could not get it published until he was about to leave Indiana three years later. Although most of his writing is idiosyncratic and recognizable both for the ideas and for personal references, this one was written from the heart, with more emotional display than any other of his sustained pieces.

Writing at "white heat" was the way a novel should be written, he believed, especially if one were a member of the literati, as he had hoped to become when he graduated from college. Since then, however, after becoming a psychologist, he adopted a cooler scientific stance, both in sticking close to whatever data he had and to the conventional format for professional publication.

In the *American Psychologist* (1981), Alan Elms analyzed "Skinner's Dark Year and *Walden Two.*" Elms extended his notion of a crisis year between college and graduate school, to describe as another crisis year the time preceding *Walden Two* from which Skinner emerged the architect of a community based on behavioral principles. By this latter "identity crisis," Elms must have referred to Skinner's growing unhappiness with Minnesota and a prospective move elsewhere. The book became an icon for youthful post-World War II idealists. Most of them would not know that what became their model of a utopia was a logical application of Skinner's first book, *The Behavior of Organisms* (1938).

Indeed, aside from his lifelong yearning to be a literary writer, Skinner led a remarkably consistent and progressive professional career. Beginning with the basic research leading to his theory of operant behavior and positive reinforcement, he explicated and expanded his ideas directly over the years in a variety of forms. He wrote popular treatises and participated in interviews explaining his theory to beginning students and the public, published a textbook based on his theory, made films, and participated in formal discussions of his views. He applied his theory practically and widely, and most specifically, in *Walden Two,* to social living. His theory was deliberately invented and tried to cover the most important facets of community behavior.

With *Walden Two,* Skinner cut away from professional conventions and wrote more as an extension of his spontaneous notebooks rather than his scientific publications. Although it is not like an ordinary fictional best-seller, Skinner nonetheless lets himself go as never before for publication. He included literary references, metaphors, and other poetic and literary devices; used wit and introspection to describe interpersonal relationships; and poked fun at the academic and salvational pretensions of his main characters.

Comparing *Walden Two* and Bellamy's *Looking Backward,* Margaret Ziemba in "Contrasting Social Theories of Utopia: An Analysis of Looking Backward and *Walden Two,*" (Ziemba, 1977) interpreted Edward Bellamy as believing in the essential goodness of human nature and trusting in intellectual and moral capacities. Skinner, on the other hand, viewed humans as constantly exposed to environmental shaping that could be willy-nilly or purposefully applied for salutary personal and social goals.

Post-World War II youths, including those returning from military service, were searching for a more value-oriented way of social living than was conventional. In national politics, remaking the postwar world was a popular pursuit, taking various forms such as world government and rehabilitating former enemies. More young people than usual were pursuing alternative life-styles.

Skinner was ready to lay out a vision of community living for these youths who were the kind he had as students both before and after the war. He built in rewards for individuals and groups with social behavior controls that would satisfy individual human needs with the fewest restrictions. He could unleash his imagination, eloquence, and ideas in applying his principles of positive reinforcement to all aspects of life. For the first time in his professional life, Skinner could cut loose with all of his best practical ideas and persuasive eloquence.

Employing in *Walden Two* three major characters he knew well from the University of Minnesota, Skinner argued for and against his own ideas for perfecting human communities. Frazier was a professor who had abandoned the university (as Skinner never did, despite his criticisms) to organize and participate in the utopia and to articulate Skinner's concepts. A professor of philosophy, A. Castle (really University of Minnesota's Alburey Castell) argued conventionally against it as powerfully as he possibly could. Burris, the narrator and an open-minded current professor of psychology, obviously Skinner himself (Skinner's mother's maiden name was Burrhus, as was Fred's real first name), mediated between the two adversaries to try to determine the truth for the visitors being shown the place—and for himself to decide whether to move there.

Even before World War II, Skinner had been testing out ideas of utopia on his students and colleagues, discussing and reading from his manuscript. He put students (including Gladys Aronsohn) to work studying past utopias and reporting on them. Shortly before he left Minnesota, he completed the manuscript in seven weeks by his last report to me (although he mentions three months in another place). In any case, it was written far faster than anything else he wrote, partly because it was a novel and needn't be as carefully scientific and close to his research, and partly because he had yearned since college to write a novel but had never before been able to find a consuming theme that would sweep him along as this one did.

Skinner noted that "the fact that I was moving into an unpredictable new environment [Indiana] may well have had something to do with my dreaming of a better world. But I just started writing and wrote the whole thing out not really knowing in advance where I was going."[1] At last, he had written at least a quasi-literary work with the emotion of an artist. Even by 1967, it was, so far as he knew, the only novel in 30 years to be written by a trained psychologist.

Published finally in 1948, 10 years after his basic book on his seminal theory, *Walden Two* was the broadest specific application of behavior shaping Skinner was to write. He had no intention of founding or participating in any concrete enactment of the utopian community. Neither he nor Eve wanted to live communally and never did live even briefly in any of the communes that were found on his model—even though he could not have been more persuasive or eloquent about why one should do so. Originally, he did not envision that others might create the model community he had described.

Skinner had his own agenda. After completing the manuscript for *Walden Two,* he tried for three years to get it published before succeeding. Without success, he tried the title *The Sun Is But a Morning Star* (Skinner, 1979, p. 299), taken from the last paragraph of Thoreau's *Walden.* Resuming the original title, he continued to have more trouble getting it into print that any of his other manuscripts. Encouragement came from the most likely quarter, old friend Keller, who wrote that it "ought to be the most talked about book in the country when you finally release it" (p. 329) (to *release* it was hardly Skinner's problem), and that it was the most "upsetting and inspiring thing" he had ever read.

The editors who reviewed the manuscript thought it was too talky, the prose creaked, it was much too long, and the story was badly organized. All that was probably true; Skinner didn't deny it. He became desperate. Finally, Skinner managed to get the book accepted by offering also to write an introductory textbook for the publisher. The title reverted to *Walden Two* because, wrote Skinner, there was another book with *Star* in its title (Skinner, 1979, p. 330). The book was published in 1948 as Skinner was about to leave Indiana, by Macmillan, whose Free Press also published the promised compensatory textbook *Science and Human Behavior* in 1953.

Although the later book did not sell nearly as well as *Walden Two*, late in his life Skinner was proud to report that nearly 40 years after publication it was still being used as a textbook without any revision. Along with *The Behavior of Organisms, Science and Human Behavior* had become a "citation classic" used as a reference in thousands of other publications. The text of *Walden Two* was rather stilted, uneven, and more argumentative than narrative; there were a few moments of eloquence, however. Mainly, it was a reasoned presentation of some of the most exciting ideas of the century about how behavioral technology could be applied to produce a community of happy and fulfilled human beings.

Sales started slowly but accelerated, moving up from a total of 9,000 during its first 12 years to 8,000 in its 13th year and to 40,000 in its 16th year. At present, it totals over three million and is still selling. Many people suggested additional ideas. Timothy Leary urged Skinner to try psychotropic drugs "to guarantee brotherly love." A man named Huntington visited Skinner to recommend nudism. A venture capitalist and an architect vented their opinions. The CIA called on him to request a report on Russian planned communities. Skinner attracted large audiences whenever he talked on the subject.

The idea of a utopian society has produced widely read books for centuries and is likely always to be welcome by youths and idealists. Skinner updated the subject with detailed behavioral engineering that was to him "more revolutionary than splitting the atom." It was a logical extension of his ever-lasting efforts to change society through his ideas. In *Walden Two*, Skinner's principle of positive reinforcement seemed to have no limits in shaping human behavior. It was to be exercised benignly over people choosing to live in the settlement and able to leave at any time.

The plot is simple. Two American military officers on a Pacific Island read an old magazine article describing plans for founding a community named "Walden Two." Skinner had already written a sketch ("Cincinatus 1946") about a young biologist who returns from war service to teach and "to turn swords into plowshares and it's very dull, very boring, and he's terribly unhappy."[2] It was the same mood as that of the two veterans in *Walden Two*. Returning to the university, they discuss the idea with Burris, the teacher of one of them, who had discussed a utopian community in his class, though he denied having any deep interest in the subject. They then decide to visit Walden Two with their girlfriends if Burris can arrange for that.

T. E. Frazier, the founder of Walden Two, "is a self-proclaimed genius who has deserted academic psychology for behavioral engineering, the new discipline upon which the community is based" (Skinner, 1979, p. 296). Burris looks him up in his professional yearbook where he finds his address listed as "Walden Two, R.D. 1, Canton" (Skinner 1976b, p. 6).[3] Burris promises his two visitors to write to Frazier to discover whether Walden Two still exists.

Frazier replies immediately, inviting them all to visit. Burris also meets a colleague from the philosophy department, Augustine Castle, who had been fascinated with Burris's comments about Walden Two, had himself taught a course on utopias, and accepts an invitation to come along.

Frazier and Castle are the major adversaries on Skinner's views for his model community and they argue continuously. While very empathetic with Frazier, Burris pretends to be impartial but is easily convinced by Frazier. In the suspenseful final scene, after leaving the place, he walks back 60 miles to enlist in the community. One of the two couples had already joined the place, the other didn't because the woman "loathes" it.

Skinner poured his ideas and attitudes about all facets of social living into *Walden Two,* including his personal preferences about the arts, sexual liberty, personal autonomy, and the elimination of punishment, force, and the exercise of power. Commercials were deleted from radio. There were no heroes, professional titles were omitted, and leadership was unostentatious and objective—like good engineering. Life was a continuous experiment and when conflicts arose, ways were found to make reason prevail.

Through careful planning, no one had to work more than four hours daily and less desirable tasks required fewer hours of labor. Cleaning sewers, for example, required only two hours to constitute a day's work. Skinner justified most of this as being scientifically based, although connections to research data were often tenuous.

Children were trained in ethics by age 4 and a culturally enriched life included good music and early sex. No one drank alcohol because "we gratify the needs which are responsible for the habit in the world at large" (p. 55). Residents lived in plain buildings made of "rammed earth" (p. 18), ate when and where they wished, and didn't have cars. Crowds seldom gathered because a wide range of activities was available for small groups. Everyone was satisfied because the work was equitable and there was plenty of time for painting, singing, reading, and playing music—and making love without promiscuity because "we encourage simple friendship between the sexes" (p. 129).

Numerous other clever ideas were freely incorporated into the place, some trivial and some provocative. One was to maintain a front lawn by enclosing a flock of sheep inside a moving electrified fence to keep the grass cropped. Eventually, a string was substituted for the fence and new lambs adapted to habits they had been born into. Following Bellamy's *Looking Backward,* streets were enclosed as connecting walkways between buildings. Tea was taken in a large glass and a swinging handle reduced spillage. Dress styles changed slowly and were unrelated to status. Dishwashers, not generally in houses then, were used like those already in restaurants. Concerts were short, informal, and uncrowded since they could be held almost anytime and any place. The arts flourished because everyone had leisure time to learn and produce them, appreciative audiences were at hand, competitiveness didn't sour the interest, and the community enlarged its appreciation from being constantly exposed to them.

For their first year, babies were raised in air-conditioned cubicles like Skinner's baby-tender and everyone, not just parents, enjoyed the kids. Babies were then moved into group spaces gradually until they were eventually living three and four in small rooms with frequent changes of roommates. At age 13, they moved into adult buildings. "The school is the family . . . the child advances as rapidly he likes in any field" (pp. 109–110). There was no fixed education system; it mixed with work. There were no breaks between levels of schooling. "Are there any natural breaks in a child's development?" (p. 111) Frazier asked.

But "What are your substitutes for our 'standard motives' [for education]?" (p. 113), Castle asked. Frazier answered that "our substitute is simply the absence of" what Castle cites: "fear of one's family . . . [of] low grades or expulsion . . . grades and honors" (p. 114). He added, "I can't believe you can really get spontaneity and freedom through a system of tyrannical control" (p. 118).

Marriage often occurred early and mothers averaged age 18 at the birth of their first children. "There's no economic obstacle to marriage at any age. . . . Sex is no problem in itself. Here the adolescent finds an immediate and satisfying expression of his natural impulses. . . . They will never have the same capacity for love again. . . . Our boys and girls know each other very well" (p. 121, 124). The extended family operated pervasively and there was less promiscuity because there was more loyalty to the group and wide friendships.

There was also a "Walden Code" that changed "from time to time as experience suggests. . . . Each member agrees to abide by the Code . . . [which] acts as a memory aid until good behavior becomes habitual" (p. 150). One example: "Don't gossip about the personal relations of members" (p. 151). Also barred: "The delicate expression of thanks" (p. 158) to one person because it excludes the rest of the group. Encouraged was "the ready expression of boredom" (p. 151). Skinner called this "experimental ethics" (p. 161), since the process discovered what worked to achieve group goals and what needed to be changed. (For Skinner to take so seriously the matter of discouraging gossip and encouraging the expression of boredom stand out since such trivia may distract the reader from more important problems. But they do bespeak his own personality: He hated gossip about his affairs and he also hated boredom.)

Children were trained to endure small frustrations in order to gain longer-term gratification. When they returned, for example, from a long hot hike, they had to stand for five minutes before steaming bowls of soup before they could eat it. "Unhappiness in doses that could be swallowed," was the way Skinner described it (through the character of Frazier, p. 104). "The traditional use of adversity is to select the strong. We control adversity to build strength" (p. 105).

Castle expressed the problem with feelings: "We all know that emotions are useless and bad for our peace of mind and our blood pressure. . . . But how arrange things otherwise?" (p. 92). Frazier answered, "Some [emotions are] . . . productive and strengthening . . . joy and love. But sorrow and hate . . . anger, fear, and rage—are out of proportion with the needs of modern life, and they're wasteful and dangerous" (p. 92). One learned instead "by studying the great works on morals and ethics—Plato, Aristotle, Confucius, New Testament. . . . Looking for any . . . method of shaping human behavior by imparting techniques of self control" (p. 96). Frazier concluded that Jesus discovered the successful principle of changing behavior without force or other negative emotions by preaching "love your enemies." This not only eased the lot of the oppressed but it also made them less miserable by precluding negative thoughts.

> *Jesus, who was apparently the first to discover the power of refusing to punish, must have hit upon the principle by accident. He certainly had none of the experimental evidence which is available to us today. . . . You avoid the torture of your own rage. . . . What an astonishing discovery . . . to find that in the long run you could control the stronger man in the same way! (pp. 245, 246)*

"The actual achievement is beside the point" (p. 25), Frazier pointed out.

> *The main thing is, we encourage our people to view every habit and custom with an eye to possible improvement. A constantly experimental attitude toward everything. . . . Solutions to problems of every sort follow almost miraculously. (p. 25). . . . This is the freest place on earth. . . . It's not planning which infringes upon freedom, but planning which uses force. . . . We can't leave mankind to an accidental or biased control. (pp. 247, 248)*

Skinner never did speak up for the mechanisms of democracy to decide or challenge the community structure. He thought that he had found a way to reconcile scientific validity and satisfaction in communal members. "It doesn't matter whether they know why those things have been set up. . . . It all depends upon whether it will be best for the culture and for those living [there]. . . . That's why I don't argue about religion" (n.p.).

In a democracy, voting had little direct relationship to how governing proceeded, Skinner thought. In *Walden Two,* it was the wisdom of "Planners" and "Managers" that governed. They were designated initially by some undescribed means. After serving a maximum of 10 years, they picked their own successors. What prevented them from becoming despots was the fact that they could not acquire monies or goods beyond what every community member possessed, there was no power to be exercised autocratically, and there was no force to be employed to impose arbitrary decisions. Soviet Russia had begun with some good ideas, thought Frazier, but became offensively mired in dogmatism and propaganda, and in leadership and force.

In the original *Walden,* Thoreau wanted only to be left alone to solve his problems by searching his inner self and learning to live apart in harmony with nature. The simplest ways of living would generate the fewest demands on society for material satisfactions. Thoreau would change what he didn't like through control of his own life and if necessary through personal civil disobedience.

Although Skinner was also a thorough rebel and chose to think and work independently (even though he lived conventionally), he wanted to apply the most advanced behavioral technology to community living. Yet Skinner might have lived somewhat like Thoreau had he not become a scientist and married. He might have tried harder at a writing career. He loved to visit Thoreau's pond. He had the spirit of a small-town independent boy who tried to control his environment; he personally never did take to communal living.

After he became a scientist, however, Skinner sought to reconcile communal living with personal satisfaction—for others—rather than content himself with shaping only his own life. He never did envision the whole world living as in *Walden Two.* He clearly chose to remain outside of it and viewed it as an ideal that he would not extend universally.

Early reviews referred to the book as including "some ingenious new psychological twists, . . . a brisk and thoughtful foray in search of peace of mind, security, and a certain amount of balm . . . , a sunlit hill with an extensive view in many directions . . . , and . . . an extremely interesting discourse on the possibilities of social organization" (Skinner, 1979, pp. 346–347). There were also the attacks that fed on the carcass of "authoritarianism" and "fascism." *Life* magazine declared that "such a triumph of . . . the dead hand, has not been envisaged since the days of Sparta. . . . *Walden Two* . . . [is] a slur upon a name, a corruption of an impulse" (p. 348). It gratuitiously attacked as well the "glass-walled cage" of the baby tender. The media identified behavioral engineering with enforced controls imposed by a dictator rather than, as Skinner described it, with a voluntary association which people agreed to and from which they could withdraw at any time.

The book is still occasionally attacked—and continues to sell well to youngish, idealistic students and others who dream and still organize "Walden

Two" communities around the world. They exist now from Los Horcones, originally on the Baja peninsula of Mexico, to a version in the north woods of Minnesota near the Canadian border where a canoe outfitter, Frank Hansen, for decades scheduled his employees' work by "Walden Two" principles. Also from Twin Oaks in rural Virginia to the Dandelion Community in Ontario, Canada, which incorporated a detailed behavior code. Apparently, none has ever been corrupted by a despot or a despotic group; members have come and gone usually because they lost interest or chose to pursue other goals that required moving away.

A good narration of one of the more successful and sustained "Walden Two" communities is *A Walden Two Experiment: The First Five Years of Twin Oaks Community* by Kathleen Kinkade (1973). Twin Oaks was founded in 1967 in Louisa, Virginia. As Skinner himself observed in his Foreword,

> *The life portrayed in Walden Two was the goal of Twin Oaks, but it was not approached through the application of scientific principles. . . . [They] simply muddled through. . . . If Twin Oaks is now on its way to something close to Walden Two . . . it is because certain principles have stood the test. . . . Now . . . Twin Oaks is ready to raise children. (p. x)*

In 1978, 30 years after *Walden Two* was published, the television show NOVA invited Skinner to visit Twin Oaks, a rural, then 11-year old cooperative community based on *Walden Two* and filmed him doing so. It had grown from 8 members to 85 of whom "most newcomers leave after only a year or two. The basic problem is the constant turnover." Twin Oaks also varied from Skinner's plan by basing its living on making hammocks, which required a 45-hour work week. When asked why he didn't live in such a community, at age 74, Skinner replied, "Well, I'd have to divorce my wife . . . who doesn't believe in the community. . . . And the practical problems are more difficult than I realized" (*Detroit News*, January 18, 1979).

What is most impressive about this and other accounts is how down to earth the Twin Oaks residents were in describing problems and solutions, as if they were inventing the utopia as they go along. They were not imposing it as rigidly as Skinner described; rather, they applied their own humanitarian and common-sense solutions to the problems of living closely together. They did so without the crazy quilt of improvised and frequently inconsistent solutions that were usually inherited in conventional communities imposed on residents and against which Skinner and most of the "Walden Two" residents were rebelling.

In 1972, a version of "Walden Two" was founded near Hermosillo, Mexico, for 20 retarded and autistic children by a young middle-class Mexican couple. ("If I were to rewrite *Walden Two*," Skinner told me in 1990, "I would have a few mild psychotics wandering around. . . . It's an ideal environment.") Unlike

Twin Oaks, these residents began with a 41-page "Code of Adult Behavior" prescribing the relationship between adults and children that emphasized the community welfare and minimized competition. In 1980, the people moved Los Horcones ("the pillars"—of a new society) to a barren 250 acres 100 miles south of the Arizona border.

There, unlike "Walden Two," which housed 1,000 people, 28 adults and 11 children, whose composition changed slowly over time, residents tried hard to live by the 24 behavioral objectives, 150 specific acts, and 30 classes of behavior specified by their code. This code gradually dwindled; what remained was automatically maintained by its natural consequences. They interacted with Skinner, though he never visited the place.

"They do a wonderful job with their children," Skinner remarked after some residents had visited him in the United States. "They make an effort not to punish . . . and it shows. I've never seen a group of kids who so genuinely loved each other and were so cooperative." When introduced to the game Monopoly, "instead of trying to drive each other into bankruptcy, the young players offered to lend money to each other so everyone could be wealthy" (*New York Times,* November 7, 1989). This community, said Skinner, which comes closest to the "engineered utopia" of *Walden Two,* has published several professional articles.

In a 1989 article in *Behavior Analysis and Social Action,* they described their "personalized system of government" (Comunidad Los Horcones, 1989). It revised Skinner's management plan by having managers teach others their organizational skills, having all members participate in governmental decisions, and encouraging face-to-face control. Modifying Skinner's antagonism to daily participatory government, this little community encouraged all members to participate in governing.

Like New England town meetings, this form of participation probably requires a smaller group than the fictional *Walden Two.* Yet it had trouble, which one of its leaders attributed to its small size. While the population hovered around 25 to 30, 60 people had come and gone during 17 years. Some believe that a larger number would help it stabilize and attract returnees. Departures have been attributed to the desire for more individualism and family time. "I just didn't want to change for what the community was offering me," one member said.

Noting how little encouragement Skinner had received to initiate the ideal community, Spencer Klaw (*Harpers,* April 1963) nonetheless wrote that Skinner "is confident that there will be no lack of volunteers." Many wrote offering to help "if Skinner should ever decide to start an experimental community." He never did, though he continued to speak about it in "a sort of recruiting talk."

For years after the book was published, Skinner continued to make notes about details of his ideal community. "At times," observes Klaw, *one gets the impression that Skinner wants to build a Utopia mainly to prove, once and for all, that he is right about human nature, and his critics wrong. . . . He tends, for example, to dismiss his critics by remarking sarcastically that "a lot of psychologists just aren't very bright." . . . He feels that he must do what he can to set right the times into which he was born. (Klaw, 1963, n.p.)*

"An enclave of misery elsewhere in the world may not affect me or my children," Skinner observed, "but I may feel guilty about it. . . . It is the fact that so little is being done about it! Is it up to me?" A "lifeguild" (Skinner's name for the community) should be run by an elite of managers and planners.

In conversation with Burris, Frazier declares, "You think I'm conceited, aggressive, tactless, selfish" (accusations leveled against Skinner). "But God damn it, Burris! Can't you see?" he asks, "I'm—not—a—product—of—Walden—Two!" (Skinner 1976b, p. 233) ("a very moving scene," Skinner told me). "Give me credit for what I've done or not. . . . Isn't it enough that I've made other men likable and happy and productive? Why expect me to resemble them. . . . There's never a complete rebirth" (p. 234).

Incidentally, Skinner asked Elliott what the attitude of Alburey Castell, head of the Philosophy Department at Minnesota, was toward *Walden Two*, since he was the model for Castle, the ascerbic philosopher-critic. Castell was one of his colleagues with whom Skinner had discussed *Walden Two* at length. Castell's expressed attitude was neutral, bordering on indifferent—or else he wouldn't talk candidly about it.

Regarding management of the enterprise, Skinner said, "I would want them to know exactly what would happen to them if they joined. It doesn't matter whether they know why those things have been set up. . . . It all depends upon whether it will be best for the culture and for those living in the culture."[4] Once again, asked whether he might ever live in a "Walden Two," Skinner wrote: "Why expect me to resemble them? Must I possess the virtues which I've proved to be best suited to a well-ordered society?"[5]

While Skinner was still at Minnesota, his ever-growing notebooks were including comments on the control of specific human behavior. By the time he moved to Indiana, his application of controls had become so pervasive in his lectures and conversations that the annual staff skit at Indiana included student Norman Guttman's parody of Skinner repeating little more than the word *control*. Skinner considered softening the word *control* to *influence* or *effect* but was reluctant to abandon the power of the concept that human behavior could be molded benignly according to Skinnerian learning theory, without punishment. He believed that he had solved the major problems inherent in the control of human behavior for "the good life."

What he had not solved, at least to the satisfaction of civil libertarians and committed democrats, was a way of modifying the structure and controls

Baby Tender,
early version

Teaching Machine

With Marian Anderson, receiving honorary degree at Hobart and
William Smith Colleges

Skinner in basement study-bedroom, circa 1988

according to the expressed wishes of the governed. Paul Meehl said that Skinner just shrugged when asked if he would approve of slavery if it improved the lot of society and slaves did not suffer. (He may have shrugged only because he thought the question demeaned his well-known commitment to democracy and humanitarianism.) In commenting in his *Notebooks* on the Swedish law requiring worker participation in industrial management, Skinner wrote, "In democracy, the people are authorities on how policies work . . . and they keep policy makers in power or throw them out. But they are not qualified to design policies" (Skinner, 1980, pp. 188, 189).

According to *Walden Two* (1976 edition), to organize the community:

What you need is a sort of Non-Political Action Committee . . . government means . . . mainly the power to compel obedience (p. 180). . . . We want a government based upon a science of human behavior. . . . We have no truck with philosophies of innate goodness—or evil, either. . . . But we do have faith in our power to change human behavior [declares Frazier]. "We're using the only technique of conquest which has ever given permanent results: we set an example. We offer a full and happy life. (p. 182)

Frazier asks Castle what he would do if he suddenly found it possible to control human behavior. "I would dump your science of behavior in the ocean" (p. 240) is the reply. "But," answers Frazier, "you would only be leaving the control in other hands. . . . The charlatan, the demagogue, the salesman, the ward heeler . . . all who are now in possession of the techniques of behavioral engineering" (p. 240).

Frazier denies that he is, as Burris claims, a genius:

I'm no more distinguished as an intellect than I am as a person. . . . You can hear my mind creak in the pompous cadences of my prose. . . . I have only one important characteristic. . . . I'm stubborn. I've had only one idea in my life . . . the idea of having my own way. "Control" expresses it . . . a frenzied, selfish desire to dominate. I remember the rage I used to feel when a prediction went awry. I could have shouted at the subjects . . . "Behave, damn you!" . . . Eventually I realized that the subjects were always right. (pp. 270, 271)

(It is a touching commentary by Skinner on a profound view of himself: his desire to dominate and his noteworthy stubborness.)

When Burris says he thinks Frazier's work must be finished, Frazier flares up:

Do you think I'd be content with a set of cultural conditions in which mankind was in equilibrium . . .? . . . You will shake off the pessimism which fills the abysmal depths to which we've sunk, and you will begin to see the potentialities of man. You will begin to expect great things . . . what do you say to the design of personalities? . . . The control of temperament . . . the control of motivation. . . . Think of . . . a society in which there is no failure, no boredom. . . . If we can't solve a problem, we can create men who can. (p. 274)

An address by the president of his university is reviewed in the newspaper and Burris agrees with its high-flown goals but adds "it was obvious that no one . . . had any notion of how to set to work to attain them" (p. 293).

Skinner did—with more heart than he ever sustained on any other subject. It was his lifelong subject as an adult—the broadest social application of his early creative research that he was to apply for the rest of his life—and it was a novel to boot. In most of his other publications, Skinner was acerbic toward his profession and critics in both psychology and academia. But the utopian communities were more like his children, thoroughly his and not competitive with or challenging him. He was invariably kindly and supportive with them—as with his daughters.

ENDNOTES

1. B. F. Skinner, personal interview.
2. B. F. Skinner, personal interview, unpublished. See also Skinner, 1979, p. 296.
3. *Walden Two* was originally published in 1948. A paperback edition was issued in 1976. The locations of the excerpts from *Walden Two* used herein will vary from the 1948 edition to the 1976 paperback edition. Page numbers used herein to document these excerpts refer to the 1976 paperback edition.
4. B. F. Skinner, personal interview.
5. Here, Skinner is mimicking a comment Frazier made to Burris in *Walden Two* (p. 234). See also Skinner, 1979.

▶ 8

Settling in at Harvard

1948–1964

By the fall of 1948, in time for Harvard's new term, the Skinners were moving to Cambridge, Massachusetts, where they relocated into an older house within walking distance of Fred's office. They considered it temporary until they could find a lot and build to their own taste. Although they had never lived as a family outside of the midwest, in Minnesota and Indiana, Cambridge felt comfortable, immediately like home, as it was to be for the rest of his and Eve's life together.

The decade at Minnesota was Skinner's major period of experimentation in establishing the pattern of his adult life as a teacher and scientist. His move to Indiana provided a quick boost in fame, fortune, and independence. Bloomington, Indiana, also proved to be a quietly satisfying return to a pastoral setting with warm and ample social connections.

Skinner's stay in Indiana would be short-lived, however. Casually, at a professional meeting in New York, his old advisor Edwin Boring asked if he would deliver a lecture series at Harvard. Skinner agreed, and the following term he was asked to join the faculty. Despite his productive, even distinguished, career at Minnesota and Indiana, it was Harvard University with which he will be forever associated. He arrived there at age 44, near the height of his intellectual power and vitality, and with a reputation and status that opened most doors to him. "I think it's quite wrong," he told me, "[to say] that I was anxious to get back. I did find that people who had been exiled from Harvard to Minnesota often speak very roughly of Harvard. I don't think I ever did any climbing."[1] As recently as 1995, even a couple of Harvard professors were surprised to hear that Skinner had ever been anywhere else.

Harvard provided the spaciousness for almost anything Skinner wanted to do for the rest of his life, lasting for 42 years after his arrival. He had bright students, he taught what he wanted to about controlling behavior, he enjoyed stimulating colleagues in a wide variety of fields, and he met famous people at the university, in the community, and around the nation and world. He also occupied a prestigious and readily publicized pulpit from which to deliver his messages about how to control behavior—and how to change the world.

In addition, Skinner's wife could develop her sense of independence through new activities, especially in literature and art, displaying more autonomy than she had elsewhere. Pursuing an education in art, Eve eventually worked as a docent at the Boston Museum of Fine Arts, which proved deeply satisfying to her. Their daughters were able to attend good private schools nearby, where Skinner could visit them and observe their education. And he could tap responsive sources of support for his individual projects.

What Harvard did not do was pay him generously, even though it started him at more than Indiana. They offered him $9,000, he asked for more, and they raised it to $10,000, which he accepted. Even in 1948, that was not princely. Harvard's pay scale generally was surprisingly modest, considering its prestige—but it could afford to pay relatively low because its prestige compensated for mediocre salaries. Except for a few stars, faculty members were financially comfortable only if they shared family wealth, earned private income from consulting or writing books, or found other outside sources of additional income. Skinner earned a large income only when two of his books, *Walden Two* and *Beyond Freedom and Dignity*, became best-sellers. From the proceeds, he installed a swimming pool in his new yard.

From Cambridge in 1951, Skinner revisited Hamilton College for his 25th class reunion, where he received an honorary degree. The festivities "drew me again into a conflict" of his undergraduate years. What the conflict was about is not clear; what is memorable about his reaction is that he "had not known how painful it would be to relive." He hoped to "never have to go through an emotional wringer like that again. . . . Perhaps one can't . . . just walk off and leave such a batch of mistakes behind. Jesus, what an experience."[2] So strong a reaction with such flimsy specifics! Skinner was suffering a long belated emotion that he seemed to have suppressed for many years—an embarrassment long past that he had not sloughed off as casually as he appeared to at the time. More of his life than he would admit had this quality about it, of feelings that had occurred, been curbed, but not disappeared.

That "batch of mistakes" included "the Chaplin hoax, the Class Day [where he and friends sold parodic drawings of their teachers], the Clark Prize Orration (sic) [when Skinner alone presented a travesty of a class speech that his co-speakers had originally also agreed to do]—These were the kind of intellectual vandalism that I never stopped to analyze" (Skinner, 1979, p. 256). Yet, seeing good wherever he could, he concluded that "my college education proved to be surprisingly useful."

All this followed 25 years after he had graduated from Hamilton College. Skinner expressed no such reaction when he was there. It may have related to his attitude toward student rebelliousness during his early years on the faculty at Harvard, which he likened to "anarchy"—and hated, even while he evidently envied it. He reflected:

> *I had spent four years under moderately irksome conditions [at Hamilton], such as compulsory attendance. . . . Today I should no doubt be protesting . . . storming the President's office carrying placards. . . . But that was not the fashion, and I was to leave the college without ever trying to tell myself or anyone else what was wrong with it. (Skinner, 1976a, p. 256)*

Skinner was terribly ambivalent about how frivolously he had protested his servitude as an undergraduate, and regretful that he had not then known enough to attack it more effectively.

His ambivalence was even clearer when he described his last visit, in 1952, with his Hamilton mentor and friend, Dean Saunders, when Saunders was dying. This is one of four touchingly described death scenes in Skinner's autobiography, the others involving his high school teacher, Ms. Graves; his brother; and his ex-student, Sister Annette Walters.

The point is that the anger and conflict that Skinner expressed much later about his years at Hamilton were, at the time, ameliorated by his affection for the Saunders family who embraced him in their home and life. This kind of ambivalence often made him forget his sense of being put upon in his college life. "I was one of his hybrids too. The way of life I found in the Saunders household had been grafted onto the life I had known in Susquehanna and Scranton" (Skinner, 1984, p. 43).

His first office and laboratory at Harvard were in old Memorial Hall, which encompassed a mishmash of activities, including Boston Symphony Orchestra concerts, the ROTC, and a rifle range. He took pride in the building's history, even while annoyed with its inconvenient structure that leaked in bad weather and its poor space arrangement that could not be modified much.

Skinner was back with his old advisor, Garry Boring, who conducted daily luncheons at the faculty club, which psychology professors felt compelled to attend. Skinner suggested meeting only one noon a week so that he could eat at the Club with colleagues outside of his department. Presumptuous as it might seem, he must have made a sympathetic case and was, as usual, obliged.

"We didn't see many people outside the department until '55," he noted. After that, "the department was no longer important to us socially"[3] and they quit giving parties. They started their own play reading group, which expanded their friendships outside the department, met eight or nine times annually, and continued for years as their most important shared social activity.

From the beginning at Harvard, Skinner was sensitive to the symbols of status, even though he often denied it. Their first home in Cambridge was a simple old place, but they considered themselves fortunate to be able to rent it during the postwar housing shortage. It was "on the wrong side of the Harvard Yard." In 1950, they found land a mile and a half from the university, which they bought and hired an architect to build on. The home they built is still occupied by Eve, alone following his death. It is a trim, one-story, flat-roofed modern looking place on a cul-de-sac, the basement of which Skinner outfitted as his office and workshop—and later, also his bedroom.

Skinner's parents continued to send substantial funds for major items such as vacations, private schooling for the girls, cars, and home things. Only once did either of them (his mother after she was widowed) exact a price from them: She asked to travel with Fred's family in Europe where he was lecturing at an international congress. Skinner described their time together as miserable, including the children's misbehavior. An acquaintance of theirs who was on the same ship returning to New York said that she thought the children were "spoiled" and "a pain in the neck."[4] Meanwhile, Fred acquired extra money in the easiest way open to him—teaching summer school.

The family also enjoyed vacationing in New England, spending summers on Monhegan Island in Maine. Skinner had fled there 20 years earlier, seeking a haven from hay fever from which he suffered much of his life. He began to use antihistamines when they were first introduced but had a miserable experience when they sedated him during the day. He invented a hood for over his half of the bed to filter the air, but it did not help.

Harvard's cultural advantages meant more to Skinner because of his culturally impoverished and rural background compared to many other faculty members from more affluent, sophisticated families. As a college student, he had smoothed out his most awkward manners. He further refined them in graduate school, and by the time he returned to Harvard's faculty, he fit the environment as if born to it. He had a natural elegance of bearing, speech, and manners that fit the setting well. However, as he had done elsewhere, he kept a distance between himself and others and seldom became close with colleagues except for a few good friends.

Skinner possessed enough charm and competence to have become a social and administrative leader had he chosen to. But inside himself, hidden from most colleagues, he was hypercritical of his working conditions and his co-workers, and acerbic in thought, even occasionally in speech when he let himself go. Several acquaintances agreed with the wife of a colleague who remarked, "I never liked him. He was terribly arrogant."[5]

Nonetheless, Skinner was highly honored by his profession and colleagues, was elected to honorary societies, and acquired friends and acquaintances who supported him and his proposals. And most did like him personally. Those repelled by his self-absorption and indifference to others were more than balanced by those who found him charming and humane. There were also those who were puzzled by their ambivalence. Even his generally admiring friend and mentor, Richard Elliott, dispassionately and thoughtfully said both, "Have you ever seen such a solipsist?" and "You have there a genius,"[6] and sought to be his friend.

Richard Herrnstein, who was inheritor of Skinner's laboratory, office, and endowed chair on the faculty, and for a time was Skinner's literary executor, articulated an objective position with reticence similar to that of Boring, Estes, Feigl, Elliott, and others who had known him well. Herrnstein had enrolled at Harvard as a graduate student in the early 1950s to study with Karl Lashley, a neuropsychologist. Initially, Herrnstein knew nothing about Skinner but slowly became acquainted with him as one of the two "stars" in the department along with S. S. Stevens. In his second year, Herrnstein had to choose between the two and he chose Skinner who gave a "marvelous" seminar. He also attended Skinner's "Pigeon" meetings—which continued long after Skinner's initial retirement.

Herrnstein found Skinner to take little interest in his students or their research. He summed up Skinner, his Ph.D. adviser, often disinterested in advising his students: "His career is an exploration of his own wonderfully fertile mind."[7] Gradually, Herrnstein developed his own views on learning, had disagreements with Skinner though not with his basic theory, and, to Skinner's dismay, explicated the reinforcing power of punishment.

When Herrnstein returned to Harvard in 1958 from the University of Maryland, Skinner thought that he had changed. He probably acted more independent of his mentor. Herrnstein noted that he "didn't want to be swallowed up"[8] in Skinner's laboratory. He obtained his own space and grants, then inherited Skinner's lab when Skinner first retired in 1964. Herrnstein commented that he "sheltered" Skinner from the university administration to help retain Skinner's Harvard appointment when he took a federal career award. They never did argue intensely.

Eventually, Herrnstein published a paper entitled "The Evolution of Behaviorism" (1977). After reading an early draft, Skinner told Herrnstein that he (Herrnstein) would be sorry if he published it—which Herrnstein did anyway, with few changes. After it was published, Skinner wrote a reply denying that he had ignored the multificity of drives and the ethological significance of animal reactions, or concealed "flaws."

"Fortunately, we remained friends,"[9] Skinner wrote, attributing Herrnstein's criticism to his stress while under attack as racist for his published genetic view of intelligence. Currently, after Herrnstein's death, this view is again under attack because of his coauthorship of *The Bell Curve*. Incidentally, they never discussed the earlier event in Herrnstein's life. Considering himself a loyal friend, Herrnstein recounted his defense of Skinner's prerogatives at Harvard after he retired, and continued to extend courtesies to Skinner. He considered simply that he, like Estes and other ex-students of Skinner's, had naturally reached their own maturity and independent views. As usual, Skinner kept his adversarial—and hurt—feelings under control, though they occasionally showed through.

Meanwhile, Skinner's father's reinvigoration following his professional advancement to Scranton faded, his disappointment with his life grew as he aged, and his depression became intransigent. His wife was not tolerant of his frailties and mistakes, which increased as his hearing failed. Finally, his father retired, embittered about personal failure as well as the undermining of his rock-ribbed Republican world under the New Deal and the dominance of the Democratic Party. His faith in family progress remained, however, as he noted how his son had risen beyond him as he had risen above his father.

Skinner's father and mother together visited their son's family for the last time in 1949 in Cambridge for Thanksgiving. Suffering from what his doctor told him was digestive trouble, his father died on New Year's Day of a heart attack. When Fred visited his mother for the funeral, she told him to say nothing bad about his father—even though he had no intention of doing so. In retrospect, Fred thought that his father had generally offered him sound advice.

Because of the fact that his father's mother had impossibly high expectations for her son, Fred thought as result his father had a chronic sense of failure. Fred himself seemed to suffer few doubts about his own competence and success. While his parents apparently did not try either to inflate or deflate his expectations of himself, he might also have insulated himself from being influenced by his parents. They even seemed somewhat guarded with Fred and avoided trying to influence him. Although Fred's mother would disapprove of his behavior at times because others might frown on it, his father kept hands off almost entirely. After his father's death, his mother remarked, "It is all over." Fred took it to mean that the labor of her life was completed, as if she had been shaping up her husband all of their time together.

At rock bottom, Fred seemed to have deep empathy for his father and for the fact that he had suffered from the domination first of his mother, then of his wife, both of whom pushed him to achieve beyond where he was comfortable. Fred, when asked while he was a fellow at Harvard whether he had written his autobiography yet, replied. "Only the first sentence, 'My grandmother was a fool'" (Skinner, 1984, p. 409). When finally he did write a short version of his life, he began, "My Grandmother Skinner was an uneducated farmer's daughter who put on airs" (p. 409). But it was only after his father's death that he fully vented his empathy and reflected his father's concern that he (Fred) also might be considered "bumpy" and "conceited."

For the next 16 years, Skinner developed, worked in—then turned over to gifted students—his experimental laboratory. He abandoned further major research in favor of consulting with students and colleagues who performed important work on his theory while he did small experiments, lectured, and wrote. Mostly, he published for a broadening audience of fellow professionals, educators, and the public. He took on as his most important task the improvement of education at all levels, applying his methods of reinforcement. Toward the end of this period, as he tired of teaching and laboratory research, he applied for a federal career grant that would free him of all academic duties.

The second most important objective for him after learning how to shape human behavior was to enjoy simple pleasures in his life: play reading, music, travel, reading, talking with his daughters, and conversing with bright students and colleagues. The student who became his successor in the lab, and eventually his prestigious endowed professorship, Richard Herrnstein, remembers also that "when I was a graduate student Fred Skinner . . . [would] stick his head into the graduate student office and say, 'Who'd like to go to Fenway (the Red Sox baseball park)?'"[10]

Following his friend Keller's example at Columbia, Skinner acted on the belief that a behaving organism, even a rat, was a better subject for study than any textbook could be. There was no textbook available that satisfied him. It would have had to be one he wrote. He initiated a small graduate seminar at Harvard where he showed each student how to make a cardboard box into a cage within which the student could reinforce a pigeon for specified behavior. He planned to publish a book on conducting such a class, but abandoned that notion when the student with whom he had planned to collaborate left the university.

After teaching undergraduate courses at Minnesota enthusiastically because of the intelligence and interest of the students he could choose, and not teaching introductory courses at Indiana because the undergraduate program was well established before he arrived. Skinner decided once again to teach an introductory class. Boring taught the basic course—with a textbook he and friends had written—so Skinner decided to create a new class, "Psychology 7," which he named "Human Behavior."

Curiously, Skinner never acknowledged that Elliott had taught a course under the same name at Minnesota when Skinner was there. Although Elliott's class was not as directly related to Skinnerian theory as Skinner's was, it nonetheless focused on similar material: theories of animal behavior, how human behavior was shaped, and how it might be controlled. Students were required to keep a journal of readings and observations. In the course prospectus, Skinner described his new Harvard class as "a critical review of theories of human behavior underlying government, education, religion, art and therapy . . . relevant scientific knowledge, with emphasis on the practical prediction and control of behavior" (Skinner, 1979, p. 7).

Skinner had imagined a small intimate group but found himself confronted instead by 438 students from Harvard and Radcliffe who totally occupied his time. He had no materials prepared, but did manage to hand out summaries of his lectures in advance. The class size forced him to use multiple-choice tests. Despite gaining a reputation as a "gut" course, soon his class was in near revolt partly because of lack of structure, partly because Skinner gave grades on a tough curve, and partly because what he taught was so unconventional (Skinner, 1984, p. 23).

Skinner simply had not organized his ideas well enough to explain his conviction about the need for a unified theory of human behavior, without the "explanatory fictions" that students were used to. He tried, unsuccessfully at first, to convey his belief that explanations should be found "not in our stars nor in ourselves, but in the world in which we lived" (Skinner, 1984, p. 17). Meanwhile, he was demonstrating his belief with research on the power of reinforcing behavior. He reached a point, for example, where he thought he could design gambling machines that would maximize gambling behavior, but he had scruples about describing it for fear it might be used to exploit an addiction.

He also discussed with a psychologist from India the possibility of exposing children to robots who would raise them and then observe how their language, government, religion, and other attitudes developed. Again, Skinner derived the notion from unacknowledged others in his life—J. B. Watson and Mike Elliott. The latter had proposed (while Skinner was still at Minnesota) to use children in China to study shaping behavior.

As president of the Midwestern Psychological Association in 1948, Skinner had delivered his formal address on "Are Theories of Learning Necessary?" He concluded that they were not. In his terms, the behavior of individuals showed "a reasonable order" by itself. It needed no reference to a more distant interpretation through a theory, no invention of explanatory "intervening variables" to place the behavior in a broader perspective.

Skinner was called "antitheoretical," but what he really sought was an observable way to interpret the data most directly—and that's what he taught. Theory, as he saw it, should refer not to "events taking place somewhere else . . . and measured, if at all, in different dimensions," but "a formal representation of the data reduced to a minimum of terms, yielding a greater generality than any assemblage of facts" (Skinner, 1984, p. 12).

Meanwhile, his other interests persisted. For his first year there, Harvard granted Skinner $10,000 for research and $5,000 for each of the next five years. After that, he would need to raise his research funds elsewhere. Project Pigeon reappeared when an Air Force psychologist wanted to publish its history and the *Atlantic Monthly* announced that it was planning an article on it. Despite Skinner's warning to the magazine that the data were still classified as secret, the article was printed somewhat inaccurately and without his name. He remained a consultant to the military, hoping to gain funds for further behavioral research. Harvard, however, had banned classified projects from campus. Following a university uproar, it was revealed that its faculty had secretly experimented with psychotropic drugs under military contract. Worst of all, the students who were subjects had not been told of the hazards.

Although deeply involved in determining rules for analyzing behavior such as who controls whom, how best to exercise control, and ignoring the "minds of men," Skinner was invited soon after he settled at Harvard to apply for a personal psychoanalysis. Its circumstances were prestigious, intended to influence Harvard faculty favorably toward psychoanalysis. Its heavy costs would be paid for by a foundation that hoped to gain support from notable faculty members in psychology, sociology, and anthropology for the psychoanalytic movement.

Skinner treated the offer lightly as if it were a passing diversion. But a personal analysis was so antithetical to all he believed about science, self-control and direction (through one's chosen and controlled environment), personal autonomy, and the superiority of his theory to those of other psychologists and psychiatrists, that it is hard to imagine him as a compliant analysand. Yet he, along with colleagues in his and other behavior sciences, did consider the generous offer. Many accepted it. They had to apply to the Boston Psychoanalytic Society and Institute and promise not to practice psychoanalysis afterwards. After submitting his application, Skinner was interviewed by three well-known analysts, including Helene Deutsch and one of the Bibrings, probably Edward. Fred was interested in learning about analysis as an intellectual project with rich new concepts. A year or so later, he was asked to withdraw his application. He requested that he be officially rejected and given reasons, but he was not given an explanation. He never did know why he was turned away.

Had Skinner been accepted, there would probably have been an explosive mismatch between him and almost any analyst. It is likely that he would soon have become adversarial and an acerbic critic, as Jeffrey Masson had after a welcome as a brilliant convert. A creative Sanskrit scholar and professor at Berkeley, Masson, upon entering analytic training, dazzled colleagues with his quick intelligence, especially their acknowledged mentor, Kurt Eissler. As a quickly favored "son," Masson was hired to study Freud's secret archives in London with Freud's daughter, Anna. His career in the analytic field ended abruptly when he published *The Assault on Truth: Freud's Suppression of the Seduction Theory* (Masson, 1984), an attack on Freud's change from his original view that real trauma of childhood rather than fantasies produced their adult problems.

Skinner was likely to have been welcome in the field—so long as he favored it. He would probably have been affronted, however, by any analyst who acted superior to him in interpreting his personality and by the required frequency and intimacy of sessions. He would certainly have challenged the validity of analytic interpretations about himself.

Karl Lashley, a neuropsychologist who was a brilliant predecessor of

Skinner's at Minnesota and then at Harvard, while at Chicago had "started an analysis with Franz Alexander but had quit in a rage after a few sessions. . . . He had tried to get Alexander fired from . . . the university and had become a bitter and outspoken opponent of psychoanalysis" (Skinner, 1979, p. 155). Lashley also became the "chief antagonist" to Murray's appointment at Harvard because of Murray's affinity for analysis. Incidentally, Skinner wrote to support Murray's appointment (*Studying Persons and Lives*, Rabin et al., 1990).

After his rejection, Skinner apparently never again seriously considered being analyzed, though he remained remarkably favorable toward Freud. He mentioned psychoanalytic interpretations in his work, speculating about or dismissing them for not considering operant conditioning as the way neuroses developed. Referring in his *Notebooks* (Skinner, 1980), for example, to superego functions, he said, "Punishment is the source of the problems which psychoanalysis tries to solve" (p. 243). When he commented about Freud, it was more like a friend would about a kindred spirit than an adversary; he regarded Freud as a pioneer, unconventional and under attack for it, as was Skinner. Skinner was not nearly as annoyed by Freud's lack of a vigorous scientific viewpoint or emphasis on introspection as he was by unscientific colleagues.

Further on, Skinner notes that some analysts capitalize on predicting the course of an analysis, but "if the reasons for making a prediction are not given . . . then the effect borders on soothsaying, and the accuracy of prediction need be no greater to be effective" (Skinner, 1980, p. 254). In discussing invented dreams that might be randomly assigned to a client for research purposes, he asked, "Is the value of the interpretation . . . simply in the interpretation, not in the dream itself?" as with a projective test. And "Freud built a picture out of historical or fantasized fragments; he had no interest in reconstructing a complete account" (p. 254). Skinner continued, "I have been writing about my grandparents and my father and mother. . . . There are 'things inside me' I had thought had long ago vanished. And I now see them in two ways—more or less as I saw them then and as I see them now. . . . Did Freud simply discover the value of getting his patients to write or speak their autobiographies?" (p. 312).

Obviously, Skinner was affected by Freud and psychoanalysis, yet his references to them are far more frequent in his informal notebooks than in his more formal books, where they are sparse. In his book on verbal behavior (1957), about language which so occupied Freud, Skinner mentions Freud far more than elsewhere, pointing out how Freud's comments about associations and identifications can be best explained by reinforcement and punishment, per Skinner. But in Skinner's autobiography, neither psychoanalysis nor Freud played much part.

In 1954, Skinner published an article in *Scientific Monthly* entitled "A Critique of Psychoanalytic Concepts and Theories." In it, he is remarkably benign toward Freud and psychoanalysis, and only mildly critical of its loose theories, broad interpretations, and lack of scientific method. Skinner gave Freud credit for attempting a scientific attitude and credibility. He wrote that Freud was a

> *thoroughgoing determinist . . . pointing to hitherto unnoticed external causes in the environmental and generic history of the individual . . . [accepting] the traditional fiction of a mental life . . . whose eventual physiological counterparts would be discovered.*
>
> *It was Freud himself who pointed out that not all of one's mental life was accessible to direct observation—that many events in the mental apparatus were necessarily inferred. Great as this discovery was, it would have been still greater if Freud had taken the next step, advocated a little later by the American movement called Behaviorism, and insisted that conscious, as well as unconscious, events were inferences from the facts. . . . The cogency of these [environmental] variables was frequently missed because the variables were transformed and obscured in the course of being represented in mental life.*
>
> *Freud appears never to have considered the possibility of bringing the concepts and theories of a psychological science into contact with the rest of physical and biological science by the simple expedient of an operational definition of terms. This would have placed the mental apparatus in jeopardy as a life goal, but it would have brought him back to the observable, manipulable, and preeminently physical variables with which he was in the last analysis dealing.*

Obviously, Skinner admired Freud and regretted that Freud had not concentrated more on what went on outside the body and less on delving inside the mind. Skinner perceived Freud as a friendly father figure trying hard to be a scientist and not afraid to think innovatively. As with his close friend, Herbert Feigl, Skinner seemed to have esteemed Freud as highly cultured, sophisticated, Viennese, very bright, alert, articulate, and an excellent literary writer.

Skinner was much less sympathetic to the conventional practices of psychoanalysis (which Freud himself often did not apply in therapy, substituting direct advice), of endlessly probing the mind. Skinner thought it was a terribly inefficient way of trying to change behavior. But he never did become an out-and-out opponent of psychoanalysis, as he did of cognitive psychology and conventional linguistics in their concentration on what might happen inside the head. In fact, in 1958, when he considered revising his volume *Science and Human Behavior* as a introductory textbook in psychology, Skinner wrote that "in an ecumenical move I would add something about traits and attitudes and spend more time on Freud" (1984, p. 228).

After his early teaching at Harvard, Skinner sensed the possible competition of his course with Boring's "Introductory Psychology," which was losing students. He also was bothered by rivalry with "Social Relations" courses (Psychology and Social Relations were separate departments albeit eventually under one administrator). Perhaps because he wanted to gain greater freedom to teach as he wished, and could also get an assistant, he gained approval to move his course to General Education, renaming it "Natural Sciences 114."

In addition, Skinner asked if his faculty appointment could be moved to the Graduate School of Education, but its Dean Keppel said he "didn't think I [Skinner] would like it" (Skinner, 1984, p. 72), possibly because it might diminish his status as a scientist. With the new title, the course also qualified as a requirement in natural science. He added firsthand observation of behavior shaping with demonstrations of pigeons being reinforced to walk in a figure 8, peck a key by color, and pull hard against a weight. He was emulating what his friend Keller did with his class in introductory psychology at Columbia.

In arranging to reinforce pigeons for cooperation or competition, he attracted the attention of the Harvard newspaper, Boston and other major newspapers, magazines such as *Life*, and television shows such as *The Arthur Godfrey Show*. The trained pigeons proved irresistible attractions to the media. As usual, Skinner encouraged the publicity, even though it emphasized the pigeons' entertaining performance rather than the way he trained them. Nonetheless, Skinner gained fame as an animal trainer.

Students called Skinner's course simply "Pigeons." The graduate students who met informally with him weekly called themselves the "Pigeon Staff." They studied various forms of operant conditioning, which included teaching the pigeons superstition by getting them to associate unrelated events with gaining food. "'Superstition in the Pigeon' was recently reprinted as a 'landmark article' in the *American Psychologist*" (1992, pp. 272–274). It was, as usual, a clever interpretation which commanded attention but which further research suggested was overly simplified.

Consonant with Boring's criticism of his thesis, Skinner often riled colleagues with what they considered superficial explanations of his data. Early in his tenure at Harvard, a psychologist, Gerald Wendt, wrote that "all cults have that advantage . . . that simplification introduced into confusion has high acceptance value" (Skinner, 1984, p. 28). Skinner denied representing a cult, and Fred Keller wrote, "Of course, our colleagues will continue to find fault with us, but we are having a wonderful time and I wonder what *they* are giving their kids that is so much better" (p. 29). Keller and Skinner excited their students with live experiments that demonstrated how animal behavior could truly be controlled.

Skinner's textbook, *Science and Human Behavior* (1953), was finally published as a trade-off for the publisher's acceptance of *Walden Two*. He had not dawdled writing it. He had shut himself up in his office for two hours daily, shielded by his secretary from any interruptions until it was finished. He then mailed it to Fred Keller to review. Atypical for a textbook, it had no charts, figures, or pictures, nor any chapter summaries; in fact, in no way did it resemble a text—as his editor vainly pointed out to him. Skinner described personal events, such as how he came to favor Pavlov over G. B. Shaw.

Meanwhile, his ex-students, Marian (Kruse) and Keller Breland, continued to work for General Mills after Skinner left Minneapolis, training animals for commercial purposes such as advertising and state fairs. They found pigs to be easier and more entertaining subjects than birds and rats. They taught them to eat at a table, put dirty clothes in a hamper, run a vacuum cleaner, and choose to eat General Mills products over others. They established their own training center in Hot Springs, Arkansas, where it still exists, though under different ownership. They received much publicity for the "IQ Zoo" where they applied Skinner's training methods.

Entitled "The Misbehavior of Organisms," the Brelands published an article in the *American Psychologist* (1961)—a play on the title of Skinner's first book, *The Behavior of Organisms*. In it, they maintained that animals had innate tendencies that could complicate Skinnerian efforts to condition them operantly. The rooting behavior of pigs, for example, distracted their behavior as it was being shaped. Taking it as personal criticism, Skinner for years felt alienated from the Brelands.

Long after Keller Breland's death, Marian (Kruse-Breland) Bailey apologized to Skinner, touched by his comment that he had been hurt by the title of their article, for their insensitivity, though not for their substance. In his autobiography, Skinner denied that he had ever doubted the importance of innate tendencies in animals.

Toward the end of his life, Skinner systematically sought to soothe strained relationships and to diminish hurts he caused by bridling about criticism of his views. He acted somewhat as his father had during his bouts of depression, though Skinner never admitted nor appeared to be seriously depressed. He did, however, mellow with age, and sometimes tried to undo the effects of his alienation.

Skinner continued to flirt with politics, discussing, for example, the (mis)practices of government as part of his course, "Psychology 7." His major thrust was to advocate the use of reward instead of punishment and to apply experimental science instead of rigid moral or presumably natural laws. Addressing an institute on the United Nations, he recommended that the American government reinforce with financial aid any of its former enemies' moves toward friendship rather than indiscriminately punishing them. Aversive behavior he would limit to national defense, police work, and other emergency situations.

Meanwhile, his mundane university work with students continued. Skinner obtained his first full-time assistant at Harvard through Fred Keller at

Columbia in 1951 just before the student, Charles Ferster, had received his Ph.D. from Columbia. Obtaining a capable assistant was not only rewarding for the person hired. The faculty member also gained from the experience since not only could the professor help the assistant substantially with research and publications, but the assistant also might reflect glory on the professor he or she worked for.

Ferster was an exceptionally good assistant. He described those subsequent, productive years working with Skinner eloquently and in detail in his article "Schedules of Reinforcement with Skinner," included in *Festschrift for B. F. Skinner* (1970), which honored Skinner's early first retirement at age 60 to take his federal career appointment. Skinner almost always attracted bright, hard-working, devoted students, but Ferster's was the first nearly equal collaboration that fully engaged Skinner for several years. He and Ferster ran almost a dozen experiments simultaneously, 24 hours a day, with many exciting moments.

In a letter to Keller just a month after Ferster arrived, Skinner wrote, "Charlie Ferster has worked out wonderfully. In his quiet way he has vastly improved the basic design of most of our equipment. I have found it profitable to give him a full share in the design of experiments, too. We're starting to work up material for a long monograph on intermittent reinforcement."[11] This material turned out to be a book, *Schedules of Reinforcement* (Skinner & Ferster, 1957).

Despite their close and generally happy collaboration, Ferster was aware of Skinner's tendency to neglect students. In his lifelong reaction against being told what to do, Skinner constantly eschewed the role of what he called "Herr Professor," his stereotype of an autocratic German academician. He never explained where and how he was sensitized to this image since he never described such a person in his life. He seemed to have strived most of his life for independence, resenting any restraints. Apparently, Skinner never embraced a middle ground of undemanding guidance and empathy.

Ferster called Skinner's attention to an example of how confused his hands-off policy confused and upset some of his students. One asked for a "box," which Skinner asked Ferster to provide. Ferster gave the student a Sears ice-chest from which he and Skinner had adapted their experimental cages. But nothing else was furnished or described, and the student had to improvise all the other equipment needed. Rather than acknowledging his oversight about how he could have helped had he thought to, Skinner described the happy result whereby the student devised uniquely valuable experiments affected by the equipment he had to improvise. Skinner agreed with Karl Lashley that "any student worth teaching did not need to be taught" (Skinner, 1984, p. 89).

Ferster (1970) found that "Skinner usually built the first model from what was on hand, seldom waiting because parts needed to be ordered." With a more methodical view of equipment, Ferster maintained a much wider range of parts than Skinner was used to stocking. In his time with Skinner, Ferster (1970) found that "the teaching process was so natural but subtle, that I had no awareness that I was learning anything new or that the research we were carrying out was a departure from the existing body of knowledge" (n.p.). Only later did he realize that they were trail blazing.

"I think," Ferster continued, "that part of the reason for the delicacy and smoothness of the learning process was Skinner's natural style of creating the conditions which allowed learning to take place rather than teaching or telling me things" (Ferster, 1970). Further, Ferster thought that "Free of Skinner's praise, I was also free of his censure, real or imagined. Yet I still had the advantage of an inspiring model I could observe, whose behavior prompted me to greater accomplishments. I remember how easy it was for me to talk with Skinner about experiments and psychology in general."

Ferster (1970) also wondered how he adapted to

> *the feeling that almost anything [I] could do Skinner could do better. I think the reason I could contribute my portion without uneasiness was that I was never evaluated, rewarded or punished; nor was my behavior ever measured against his. I found Skinner's repertoire an ever-present source of prompts and supports which I could use whenever I was able to. It was a very fortunate young man from Columbia who had an opportunity to carry out his work with so much intellectual and practical support and with such exciting chances to "brainstorm."*

Skinner and Ferster conducted their experimentation with high energy and drive, and avoided criticism and argument. They did not have to participate together, even though most of their experiments were joint. "I don't know whether Skinner was conscious of the lack of personal praise in interpersonal relations in the laboratory. I certainly was not. My behavior was generated by the natural reinforcement of the laboratory activity. But some of the graduate students found the absence of personal support difficult" (Ferster, 1970).

By 1953, Ferster and Skinner had completed most of the research for a publication on *Schedules of Reward*, as they originally named the book, which they renamed *Schedules of Reinforcement* (1957). As they began to write, they turned the laboratory over to a couple of Skinner's favored graduate students, William Morse and Richard Herrnstein, although Skinner had thought that none could ever match Ferster.

Since Ferster was due to leave Harvard in June 1955, they set up for optimal writing production. Their room was dedicated to writing only. They discouraged interruptions. The pair worked only mornings (but then invariably). They never worried about what others would think or how their effort would turn out. What they were doing they considered a continuous experiment "that would bring results which we valued," Ferster (1970) wrote. Ferster concluded, "A potential reinforcing environment exists for every individual . . . if he will only emit the required performances on the proper occasions. One has merely to paint the picture . . . produce the machine, tell the funny story . . . and the world will respond . . . with prestige, money . . . [and recognition for scientific achievement]." He could have added: At least if you are working with Skinner—or learn to think as Skinner does.

While his research usually progressed well, mostly on his own or with his clear primacy, Skinner did not proceed as smoothly in his interactions with colleagues—and particularly with administrators. He successfully avoided almost all administrative or departmental committees or responsibilities. For five years, he did serve on one department committee, on educational policy, and held prestigious appointments such as on a National Research Council committee that visited, studied, and made reports on Russian science. A research internist-physician who made the latter trip with him reported that Skinner took the mission very seriously but did not interact much with members of the other disciplines represented in the group.

Rarely did Skinner express political opinions on controversial topics. Although he held firm views on social and political issues, he seldom stated them in public forums, as he did his professional and scientific beliefs. He criticized the notion that his nonprofessional convictions should gain any special credibility or attention because of profession. He also wanted to reserve his influence for issues where he could properly be respected as a scientist.

The principle did ordinarily protect him from confronting administrators when he disagreed with them, as he confronted Harvard President Pusey in 1956—to his everlasting regret. Skinner never doubted that he was right, but was sure he suffered continuing penalties. Soon after becoming president of Harvard, Pusey made public remarks about Harvard's Divinity School and Memorial Church being Christian. "He made the statement," said Skinner, "that all the professors at the Divinity School should be Christians. One of their most distinguished scholars was Jewish. . . . A committee of ten members visited him [Pusey] and said this is not one of the things we do at Harvard . . . [and] that this memorial church . . . was . . . given in memory of all the people who died in the second World War."[12]

Skinner remembered how McGeorge Bundy, Pusey's administrative assistant, after reading Skinner's letter, jogged across campus to make amends to Skinner. Once, answering a question for Pusey, McGeorge Bundy said, "'I'm sure that the president would say . . .' and he gave an answer like a parent speaking for a child."[13]

Later, Skinner wrote to Pusey to object to an "official attitude toward religion at Harvard" (Skinner, 1984, p. 127). He quoted from an article by E. B. White in the *New Yorker* magazine: "I hope that Belief never is made to appear mandatory." Skinner added, "I have thought it worthwhile, in the interests of good faith and intellectual honesty, to bring the matter to your attention" (p. 127). Although Skinner was far from alone in his view, he personalized it and thus gained a personal reaction.

Pusey replied that no one need worry that belief would ever be made mandatory at Harvard. But he continued to refer to "faith" as an essential ingredient for democracy and good citizenship. Skinner's suspicions strengthened. In 1956, he wrote in a notebook, "I feel that I am persona non grata here. Pusey has never shown it, but I believe he would be happy to see me leave if he were not blamed for my departure" (Skinner, 1984, p. 227).

Skinner continued to react negatively to Pusey as Pusey continued to talk about faith and the inner self that longed to learn and could be filled with "excited awareness." Such comments, Skinner wrote, never told "anyone how to teach more effectively" (Skinner, 1984, n.p.). For the rest of his life, Skinner believed that his shot at Pusey for his emphasis on Christian beliefs was held against him, and that because of it he was not given salary increases and other financial support awarded administratively.

Skinner also wrote, "I am unhappy about psychology at Harvard" (1984, p. 228). Yet he was simultaneously trying to "cultivate his own garden" (1979, p. 342), as his Minnesota friend Feigl had advised him about their disagreements (quoting Voltaire). He tried hard to keep his criticisms muffled and usually he succeeded. For a Harvard faculty professor to express himself critically was not, however, unusual. In his biography of Kissinger, for example, Walter Isaacson (1993) commented that his colleagues resented Kissinger's personality, which was "arrogant and abrasive even by Harvard standards." Skinner would not stand out as uniquely outspoken except in his own mind.

Despite what he viewed as penalties he incurred, Skinner was also granted important privileges to pursue his own interests, with waivers by the university of obstructive rules. Later, for example, he was allowed (against university rules) to retain faculty status without teaching, when he reached age 60 and took a federal career grant for personal research and writing.

Perhaps, with his unhappiness, Skinner was seeking justification for leaving Harvard to accept an offer from a new University of California campus being established at La Jolla, as he had rationalized leaving Minnesota to take a job at Indiana. It was a wonderful offer, to set up a department of psychology, with authorization to bring in two other full professors and three additional faculty. He could concern himself almost exclusively with the experimental analysis of behavior, with freedom to do his own work, and the option of deciding whether he would be chairman.

Against making the change, he listed "I like Harvard," "I have always loathed California," and "I have always feared lotus blossoms" (Skinner, 1984, p. 227). With Eve and Deborah, he made a second trip to look over La Jolla. He claimed to feel at home in the green hills of the East and foreign among the brown hills of California—hyperbole that seemed to have little to do with the topography of Cambridge compared with La Jolla. Only incidentally did he mention that Eve cried at the thought of leaving Cambridge. When it mattered to her, she usually did prevail, although Skinner seemed to minimize her impact, which she had exercised before about an offer from the University of Chicago. He was more affected by her feelings than he apparently wanted to admit.

In the mid-1950s, after reviving his interest in writing a novel by using a forthcoming sabbatical and hopefully a grant for that purpose, Skinner decided instead finally to complete his long-delayed book, *Verbal Behavior*. It was the closest he would return to his literary interest, describing how language was learned, rather than producing a novel itself. When Eve left on a tour of Egypt, Skinner set himself up for writing at an inn run by the school that Julie was attending in Putney, Vermont, while Deborah was boarding with a faculty family nearby.

Skinner made this a rigorous test of his self-discipline. He scheduled his writing as if he were entering a severely monastic life, living in one room, cold, with no alcohol, going to bed early, listening to classical music, reading to relax—with the overriding goal of maintaining as great efficiency as possible to complete the book. Assaying the pros and cons of his austere life-style, he felt reasonably contented with it. He had the freedom to wake and sleep as he wished, to come and go as he pleased, to visit with his daughters when he wanted to live inexpensively—and above all, to work entirely on his own terms, undistracted.

Verbal Behavior, the resulting book, was published by Prentice-Hall in 1957. Skinner had been working on it for 23 years, ever since he had been a fellow at Harvard. The earliest version of his classification of verbal responses was made in 1934. He continued to work on the manuscript while teaching courses on literary and verbal behavior through his years at Minnesota, and nine years later back at Harvard. He also used the work as the basis for lectures at the University of Chicago and Columbia. For much of that time, he had tried to do basic research that would give the book a scientific basis. He encouraged students to work on work associations and other operations that would fit in with his theory of verbal behavior. However, the students felt like failures as they became hopelessly enmeshed in word count complexities from which they found no way out.

Finally, he abandoned the notion of undergirding his book with research. He distributed several hundred mimeographed copies in its next to last rendition for his William James lectures at Harvard that led to his faculty appointment there. Late in his life, he told me, "My book *Verbal Behavior* is not a scientific book. There are no facts reported in it. . . . I took all [facts] out as well as reviews of the literature. It is an interpretation of human behavior where I was unable to get the kind of control and observation needed for a scientific analysis but interpreted as if that is what has happened. An evolutionary theory [it] is an interpretation of what probably happened in the light of genetics."[14]

In *Verbal Behavior*, Skinner described how operant conditioning could account for language behavior through selectively reinforcing emitted vocalizations. Essentially, he applied his theory of radical behaviorism to verbal responses, which he believed conformed to the same rules as other animal behavior. He defined a vocabulary to refer to the most important variables in determining how language develops. The most significant terms were *autoclitic*, meaning a verbal comment on a prior verbal comment by a speaker; *tact*, a verbal response that "makes contact with" the physical world; and *mand*, a verbal response that is reinforced by a consequence.

The many years he had worked on the book had taken their toll. It had gone on too long. "The whole thing is aversive . . ." he wrote after he finished it. "I am anxious to see the book appear but I seldom think of it or mention it. . . . I can understand how a mother might hate a baby who caused great pain" (Skinner, 1984, p. 130). But that feeling eventually passed after the book's publication, and Skinner came to consider it one of his three most important volumes. Sometimes, he referred to it as his *most* significant work.

Verbal Behavior received one of the most denunciatory and detailed criticisms of a professional book ever written, one which to many colleagues became more famous than the book itself. Noam Chomsky, a noted linguist at MIT and a leader in his field, wielded the axe. A skillful though often intensely subjective writer and debater, Chomsky (1959) wrote a 32-page review attacking Skinner's behavioristic views and advocating his own, which were far more popular among linguists. He argued that it was much more complicated for a child to learn language than was encompassed by Skinnerian principles of reinforcement and extinction. Learning language, Chomsky thought, had to be essentially innate and universal based on native potentialities. Children had only to learn the rules, which did not depend on reinforcement. Chomsky wrote,

> The goal of the [Skinner] book is to provide a way to predict and control *verbal behavior by observing and manipulating the physical environment of* *the speaker. . . . External factors consisting of present stimulation and the* *history of reinforcement . . . are of overwhelming importance, and . . .* *provide the basis for understanding the complexities of verbal behavior. . . .* *[But] . . . just as the attempt to eliminate the contribution of the speaker* *leads to a "mentalistic" descriptive system that . . . only . . . [blurs] impor-* *tant traditional distinctions, a refusal to study the contribution of the child* *to language learning permits only a superficial account of language acquisi-* *tion. (1959)*

The dichotomy between Chomsky's view of the blossoming of innate language powers and Skinner's view of the reinforcement of sounds and words continues. Estes believed it has been beneficial to linguistics generally (Hearst, 1979). When asked, after Skinner's death, whether he would add anything to his opinion of the book, Chomsky replied, "I don't think this paradigm is taken seriously or is influential in the major work in psychology."[15]

Among the strong defenders of Skinner's views, none was more scholarly and eloquent than his former student, later chairman of the psychology department at Minnesota, Kenneth MacCorquodale. MacCorquodale (1969) wrote,

> *"The argument in* Verbal Behavior *proceeds, inexorably and relentlessly, to the final overthrow of the speaker as an autonomous agent. . . . Chomsky did not grasp the differences between Skinnerian and Watsonian-Hullian behaviorism, and his criticisms . . . were mostly irrelevant. . . . This is a* great *book. The reader who is well acquainted with the technical experimental analysis of behavior will find real pleasure in watching its elegant argument unfold.*

Skinner claimed never to have heard of Chomsky before receiving his review, which Skinner did not read until long after it appeared. He did not defend himself until he thought he had to because of the stridency of the opposition. In the third volume of his autobiography, Skinner (1984) wrote that his former student John Carroll "is said to have [said], 'Behaviorism is dead and it was a linguist [Chomsky] who killed it'" (p. 155). "I am rather aghast," Carroll wrote me, "that Skinner never checked his sources. . . . I do not recall ever having said or written [it] . . . because I would not think it true. . . . I vaguely remember somebody else."[16]

The controversy continues. While Chomsky, with his continuing concentration on psycholinguistics, remains a strong voice in the field, a diminished contingent of psychologists still pursues research based on Skinner's theory. Estes's moderate view gives a place to both protagonists.

With the passing years, Skinner's interest in verbal behavior receded, and he increasingly moved toward larger social concerns as education, social living, and government. His interest especially in education intensified as he observed his own children in the classroom and the pressing need for improved methods. He had promised himself not to interfere with his daughters' schooling. But he soon objected to the system when Julie was told that she should study for two hours nightly in the ninth grade, which he thought was excessive. Many friends thought that the girls were spoiled and one still recalls with distaste that, when young, they openly called their grandmother "that SOB." Skinner regretted that he had spoiled them and that, perhaps as result, Julie spoiled her own children.

I have been very careful not to do things that my daughters can do for themselves. . . . Julie does too much for her children . . . driving them to college. . . . She's much too indulgent. . . . I think I let them grow up by themselves. . . . I would agree that we were very defective with Debs there. . . . She wasn't doing well. . . . We were absolutely sure it was the school's fault. . . . As a matter of fact, . . . the whole problem of Deb in school was responsible for all of my activity with the teaching machine and programmed instruction.

They went to a private school here. . . . I regret that I did it. It would have been much better if they had gone to the public school . . . and put the money to improve the public schools. It was Father's Day when I went to visit Deb's math class. The teacher's doing all the wrong things. I came back here and immediately began working on teaching machines.[17]

Previously, Skinner had written that the avoidance of punishment underlay most American education, that for most students low grades were more to be avoided than high grades were to be achieved. Other negatives were also built into the system: the teacher's displeasure, student ridicule of others' achievement, warnings to parents, and so forth.

He was further upset upon visiting Deborah's fourth-grade mathematics class to see the teacher walk up and down the aisles pointing out errors, keeping good students waiting impatiently to move ahead, and not handing back corrected papers until the next day when they were already working on new material. Each procedure violated a Skinner learning principle—using positive reinforcement, providing immediate feedback, and keeping students moving ahead as fast as possible but only after mastering prior lessons.

Shortly afterwards, in 1953, Skinner built a crude teaching machine that would automatically apply his learning principles to classroom education. Students placed an answer in the device, a light appeared if it was correct, and the next problem was not presented until the correct answer was inserted. At a Christmas party, staff members were fed peanuts for giving correct answers to questions.

Skinner developed instrumentation that provided rewards for learning the material. By the mid-1950s, he was talking widely on the subject of teaching machines, debating with protagonists for the "art" (as opposed to his technology) of teaching and being supported by Harvard Education Dean Keppel. He broke down the content of a subject into hundreds of small steps that moved the student toward mastery of a subject through reinforcement of correct answers.

Unknown to Skinner, in the mid-1920s, Sidney Pressey had invented a machine for presenting information to be learned, with candy as the reward. In 1954, Pressey, then on the faculty of Ohio State University, sent Skinner reprints of his articles from 1926 to 1932 on his teaching machines. Discouraged by gaining little attention for his teaching device despite publishing several positive articles, Pressey withdrew from the field. In 1932, Pressey noted that "the problems of invention are relatively simple . . . [but] one person alone can accomplish relatively little and he is regretfully dropping further work" (Skinner, 1984, n.p.).

Heretofore unaware of Pressey's work, Skinner discussed the machine with him and gained his support for a revival of the work that Skinner would advance with an improved apparatus. Even Garry Boring, the fastidious historian of psychology, erred in 1957 by attributing to Skinner the invention of the teaching machine. Skinner did carry Pressey's work forward by greatly improved technology and by making the choice of answers more deliberate than trial and error. Embarrassed by his ignorance of Pressey's work, Skinner traced the history of the machine even further back. Although Pressey may have been the first psychologist involved with it, another Skinner surnamed Halcyon received a patent in 1866 for a kind of teaching machine that presumably assisted learning more than taught.

In reviewing this history, Ludy Benjamin (1988) concluded that teaching machines in the 1920s did not catch on anywhere but at Pressey's university. Skinner was largely responsible for their resurrection in the 1950s and 1960s, but their use again declined until personal computers gained wide use in the 1980s.

Benjamin attributes the only sporadic popularity of teaching machines to their ineffectiveness. Although cultural inertia weighed down many of Skinner's inventive enterprises all of his life, he seldom succumbed to failure. Benjamin, however, wrote (1988) that "the teacher-student bond," the "living, breathing teacher" could never be replaced. His was a typical educational establishment view that Skinner would battle the rest of his life without much success. Only during periods of crisis such as World War II, when technical subjects needed to be taught fast, were teaching innovations like the machine used massively.

Another psychologist, George Buck, traced the teaching machine back to the first century A.D. in Rome, where gladiators were taught to use a weapon properly, the quaintain, by having it strike them if they used it incorrectly. He attributed the only intermittent popularity of such teaching methods to their indifferent results, except when there was very special need for efficient teaching (Buck, 1990, pp. 551–552).

Many critical educators believe that most learning programs are inadequate for teaching machines, even with relatively simple but basic subjects such as reading. Not enough is known, they believe, about how to teach, and therefore how to program the machines effectively. (In fact, Skinner preferred to call them *learning machines* rather than *teaching machines*.) Anyone who tries to follow even the most sophisticated and carefully developed teaching programs for computers quickly discovers that neither the language, the linkages, nor the required steps in instruction have kept pace in effectiveness with the simple use of reinforcements such as words, oral or printed, like "Very good!" or "You're close." Dean Keppel put Skinner in touch with a wealthy Harvard alumnus who connected him with IBM, which undertook to build at least 10 experimental models to try out at a school. They did little for a year, however, and only in 1957 did Skinner see the draft of a model. He prodded IBM with the information that *Life* magazine was planning an article on the machine. Meanwhile, others were building private models for experimentation.

Skinner tried hard to produce and apply learning-teaching programs. He talked with McGraw-Hill, the Ford Foundation, the National Science Foundation, the Carnegie Corporation, Harcourt Brace, the Comptometer Company, the Rheem Company, and others. Finally, IBM produced a usable model and asked that it be tested. When IBM then decided to terminate its agreement with Skinner and reassign the patent to him, Skinner desperately tried to get the young children of the president of IBM to try the machine.

All efforts failed—despite wonderful experimental results. Students received immediate reinforcement for correct answers, freedom to work at their own pace, early identification and correction of errors, and generally good study attitudes. He contrasted this with conventional methods: cramming, use of stimulant and relaxant drugs, fear of failure and consequent misbehavior, resistance, apathy, and other forms of anxiety about schooling that were the result of a punitive educational environment.

IBM continued to explore the possibilities of computer-centered learning. Seven years after IBM rejected Skinner's machine, he consulted a lawyer about a claim against the company. He was still angry that he could not do the work himself nor could he rouse the necessary support. "You are not paranoid enough for that kind of thing" (Skinner, 1984, p. 289), his lawyer told him. Thus ended his most strenuous efforts to promote teaching machines.

Skinner received a great deal of publicity, often misinterpreting what he was trying to do in education. Seldom did he discourage publicity, however. In fact, he was a master at obtaining and directing it. His goal was to make learning more pleasant, positive, and effective. But critics insisted that he was teaching through meaningless drill, mechanically and uninspired. The unspoken assumption of his adversaries was that most teachers taught through inspiration, and most students learned because of it. It is a myth that has not yet died, even though conventional education is generally considered seriously deficient. Inspired teachers are rare, though at least two of them—Ms. Graves and Dean Saunders—certainly were heroes to Skinner.

Despite lagging interest in teaching machines, exploiters appeared who used Skinner's methods—and his name—to sell inferior materials. He tried unsuccessfully to control what they did. A few good programs were created, but there were also terrible machines, poorly written materials, and ridiculous claims. The overriding criticism by intellectuals, however, was that Skinner's approach lacked depth and long-term effect and that the engineering depreciated human values. Yet the method itself, he declared repeatedly, could teach effectively whatever goals were desired, even values. It was the same old argument used against him for his lifetime—that he dehumanized humans in trying to shape their behavior even though his goal was to bring them satisfaction.

One year after Skinner returned to Harvard, in 1949, his first student at Minnesota, John Carroll, also arrived there for an appointment to the Graduate School of Education. Skinner promptly introduced him in the psychology department. Despite the fact that their offices were across the street from each other, they seldom met or socialized after that. Skinner did invite Carroll to see his teaching machine, which Carroll found "unimaginably primitive."

Carroll later developed his own more sophisticated apparatus for teaching foreign languages, but he could not interest Skinner in it. "Skinner apparently disowned me," Carroll wrote, "probably because there were deep disagreements . . . [and] Skinner disapproved of my going into psychometrics and the study of individual differences. I lost respect for his radical behaviorism, and I felt . . . that his ideas on education were unrealistic."[18]

Among the numerous jokes and cartoons about the teaching machine was this limerick:

> *The latest report from the Dean*
> *Concerning the teaching machine*
> *Is that Oedipus Rex*
> *Could have learned about sex*
> *By machine and not bothered the Queen. (Skinner, 1984, p. 200)*

Widespread use has since been made of programmed learning and teaching machines. Skinner and James Holland collaborated on a model programmed learning book *The Analysis of Behavior* (1961), which did not require a machine but used the same principles on the printed page. Pressey's words were prescient from his own terribly frustrating failure. The method has still not gained wide use as a substitute for, or even supplement to, conventional (and inefficient if not ineffectual) teaching methods. It was a relative failure that Skinner felt most keenly for the rest of his life, as public education became a consuming cause of his.

By the time he reached 60 years old in 1964, Skinner was tired of his usual academic activities. He wanted to quit teaching, give up his laboratory, and turn exclusively to his own office and writing. Reminiscing, he claimed that the biggest change in his life occurred in the "Dark Year" between college graduation and entering graduate school. It was then that he decided to become a scientist. Now at age 60, he would return to a form of writing, albeit not literary, based on his science of behavior, with which he was confident he could succeed in influencing the public.

Skinner obtained an exemption from teaching, which was a requirement at Harvard to retain faculty status, and was approved for the federal career grant that would provide for five years the equivalent of his annual $24,000 Harvard salary, renewable for another five years. That would take him to Harvard's mandatory retirement age of 70. He intended to write as clearly and persuasively as he could about why and how his "radical behaviorism," far from being incompatible with human freedom and dignity, was the surest insurance of it.

ENDNOTES

1. B. F. Skinner, personal interview.
2. From a letter to a friend, quoted in Skinner, 1983, p. 40.
3. B. F. Skinner, personal interview.
4. Unpublished personal communication with author.
5. Ibid.
6. University of Minnesota archives.
7. Unpublished correspondence with author.
8. Ibid.
9. Unpublished correspondence with author.
10. Unpublished correspondence with author.
11. Harvard archives.
12. B. F. Skinner, personal interview.
13. Ibid.
14. B. F. Skinner; personal interview.
15. Unpublished correspondence with author.
16. Ibid.
17. B. F. Skinner, personal interview.
18. Unpublished correspondence with author.

▶ 9

Middle Age at Harvard to Retirement

After 6 years at Harvard, and upon becoming 50 years old, Skinner assessed his status. First, he thought his relationship with Eve was improving, despite the fact that "mistakes have been made by both of us, but these have led to better understanding" with "growing mutual tolerance" based upon "less distrust" of the "other's interests" (Skinner, 1984, p. 71). Bland and careful comments at best and better serving his public image than candor would provide, they say nothing specific about his marriage and the sources of "mistakes" and "distrust." Skinner provides somewhat fuller accounts of his other close connections, as with Fred Keller, and his daughters. He was most guarded in personal comments about Eve.

When Fred courted Eve and early in their marriage, he admired her rich cultural background, especially in literature. Already he had been attracted to Ms. Graves and Dean Saunders for their cultural grounding, which helped compensate for his own keenly felt deficits. After marriage, however, his interest in behaviorism gradually became ascendant, and his social activities and friends centered around psychology. Although he and Eve did form a play reading group whose members ranged beyond psychology, his interest in literature declined.

Eve wanted to have a place in their life apart from Fred's professional activities (to which she remained cool all of her life). She avoided any semblance of a shadow wife, recognized because of her husband's prestige. Rather than answering questions about him and their relationship, she referred inquirers to her diaries. After they moved to Harvard, she took another step toward independence by training and functioning as an art docent.

Although Fred had always been more involved with their daughters than was Eve, he noted that "Eve's life [was] becoming more interesting with children growing up" (Skinner, 1984, p. 71) and that she had joined a group of women meeting for self-improvement. Like many professional men of his generation, Skinner grew impatient with his wife's homemaking role and wanted her to cultivate interests outside of their home and family. He wanted both a homemaker and an independent companion who would complement his life. He also realized that an autonomous wife would leave more freedom for him. He encouraged independence for Eve, just as he did for his students and himself.

After a few early years in their marriage, when Eve spent her time reading and in other mainly solitary activities, she began to develop her life outside her home. At Minnesota, she took writing classes, including one from Meridel LeSeur, a locally famous writer, and read to an almost blind older woman. Fred fretted about both too much and too little social life. His ambivalence about social activities showed itself throughout his life. He was offended when excluded, but also easily bored socially. His natural inclination was toward solitary activities, but his mother had influenced him with her sensitivity to social interactions. Eve turned increasingly to outside activities of her own choosing and often participated by herself. She also traveled overseas some-times without Fred, and began working as an art docent and lecturer in the Boston public schools.

Fred accepted Eve's broadening interests more than she did his. However, she had to accommodate to his consuming professional activities, even while remaining aloof from them. Early in their marriage, he had remarked that she should do more that was intellectually challenging. In reacting to the domi-nance of his professional one-mindedness, she must have decided to separate her identity from his and his growing fame.

The Skinner daughters grew up spirited and often rebellious, although Skinner thought that Deborah was too dependent on him. He had intervened for them at school and, on the basis of his research on learning, after visiting their classrooms. Mortimer Appley, a psychologist and former president of Clark University, observed Skinner's interaction with Appley's own children. Exceptionally apt at establishing rapport with them, Skinner took them on his lap, taught them to hum and whistle at the same time, and made paper pigeons for them. Much later, Skinner asked Appley, then Graduate Dean at the University of Massachusetts, if he could help Skinner's daughter Julie find a job near Cambridge.

Skinner's salary was insufficient to educate his daughters at the costly private schools he preferred for them at first, and he realized he would remain dependent on his mother for such expenses following his father's death. His only alternative was to make his writing "pay off" or to lower his family's living standard, which he never seriously attempted. He was also looking ahead to his retirement, not to loaf but rather for the time it would provide for him to work ever more independently.

Skinner had little interest in the Harvard Psychology Department and its increasing shift to introspective and "cognitive" theory that he found repugnant. His interest in his own teaching was still declining. If he taught at all, he preferred graduate courses, and considered offering postdoctoral apprenticeships for bright students eager to study with him. At best, he was energized to teach while he was developing his ideas and could use recordings and notes of his lectures as the basis for articles and books. He declared, "I was never successful in teaching seminars. I was not skillful in getting students to talk. . . . I talked too much myself" (Skinner, 1984, p. 300). In one seminar on verbal behavior, "only one or two students showed any interest. I refused to threaten, and we all wasted our time" (p. 300).

When he was about to take his Federal Career Award at age 60, Skinner wrote, "I have given my last lecture, held my last class. I said I would do it and I did. I have no regrets. I had a relatively short life as a teacher—27 years—but I had good students and it was worthwhile, I am sure . . . I will be more effective if I never teach again" (Skinner, 1984, p. 248).

While some, usually exceptional, students lauded his teaching and his influence on them, it was always a small minority that was devoted to learning. Those who most appreciated him often became outstanding psychologists. Skinner's enthusiasm, charisma, clarity, and creativity as a thinker and eloquent lecturer marked many of his students for life. His self-deprecatory remarks about his teaching skills stemmed from his boundless desire for perfection—and finally, to himself, he seemed to fall short. As is often the case with the great ones, he ended up more acutely aware of what he had been unable to do, visions unfulfilled, than what he had accomplished. Nowhere was this truer than with his teaching.

Skinner had published three respected books and was writing two more. He had good prospects for research funding. Increasingly oriented toward improving educational methods, he tried to move into the School of Education. Because of his involvement with his daughters' education and the teaching machine, and his desire to improve society, public education became a dominant theme for the rest of his life. He had, he believed, already discovered how to improve vastly the educational system.

Skinner was no longer attracted to the rigorous laboratory research that had earlier driven him. He was increasingly scrutinizing human behavior in larger realms of ethics, law, communal living, war, and government. He continued to attract and take pride in bright graduate students, especially William Morse and Richard Herrnstein, who worked in the laboratory on pigeons and reinforcement. Results were presented at various professional meetings, including the American Psychological Association in 1953, the National Academy of Sciences, the International Congress of Psychology in 1954, and many others.

He never did lose his interest in the arts. To the end, Skinner was listening to classical music, reading in French literature, play reading regularly with Eve and Harvard friends, and still hoping to write literary fiction—sometime in the future. He also formed a group for the first time since Minnesota to play chamber music. His star student, Herrnstein, played with the group. Although Skinner never did have many *close* friends, he socialized with a wide variety of colleagues at Harvard.

Friendships were easy to form within the community and at the university. Among his and Eve's friends were Edwin and Terry Land (of Polaroid fame), Al and Kathy Capp, Kate and Zero Mostel, John Kenneth and Kitty Galbraith, Elena and Harry Levin, and a few others. He valued prominent people among his acquaintances, and mentioned them throughout his autobiography. Partly, he remained the small-town boy who impressed people with his creative intelligence and was pleased to gain recognition for it despite his professed disinterest in his social standing.

Never completely abandoning his failed efforts (except for *Walden Two*) to publish literary fiction, Skinner was still trying as late as 1955 to obtain a grant from the Guggenheim Foundation to write a novel during his sabbatical leave. He would write the work to be "a fusion of scientific and literary approaches to the problem of human behavior" (Skinner, 1984, p. 78). He continued to write down ideas for stories, and even in his last year of life, to mention sometime getting back to writing fiction, still citing Robert Frost's early words of encouragement.

Only when he considered Eve was Fred troubled. As they aged together, he would have to adapt to her wishes, her different interests, even her pace in walking. With her, it "would undoubtedly be a better life . . . and the sacrifice . . . would still bring me out even" (Skinner, 1984, p. 80). He had not anticipated that toward the end of his life, he would deteriorate faster and further than she did, and Eve would monitor his care even though she, too, had serious physical problems. But when he spoke of changing his walking pace, it was at first because she could not keep up with him. It ended up the opposite.

He seemed to be assessing what he would gain from staying married to Eve. He judged his relations with others according to how they helped him. Sex with others obviously tempted him. In 1961, the FBI file reported a Manhattan phone book listing for him, which could not be confirmed. Never did he separate from her and he took pride in the marriage's longevity.

As for talking with his daughters about all of his experiences, "I think I am for honesty all the way. Tell the whole story? No, any 'whole story' told all at once is an inaccurate account. Some things should be untold. But admit the kinds of acts, point out all honest consequences" (Skinner, 1984, p. 81). This is a notable exception to his commitment to candor in writing about his life. Whether out of embarrassment about his sexual life or his inexplicable protectiveness of his daughters, he chose to keep his family's intimacies private and out of his autobiography. His daughters and wife were also extremely protective of their privacy.

Skinner's most enduring friendship after college was with Fred Keller. Their professional interests often intersected, although they communicated only sporadically in their later years. Keller, four years older than Skinner, retired in 1964 from Columbia, not being as clever as his friend in sustaining a paid career, although even at age 90 he was in far better shape physically. Keller received a paltry pension, as did almost all academics at the time he retired. Without telling Keller, Skinner recommended him for special jobs to supplement his income.

Skinner revisited Susquehanna several times late in his life to collect material for his autobiography. He never mentioned any sentimentality that may have drawn him there or that the trips generated. He went with each of his daughters, once at age 60 and twice in his early 70s, including a trip with an English TV crew filming a documentary on his life. Never did he go with Eve. He visited relatives but did not comment in his autobiography on any feelings the visits prompted. From comments in his autobiography, he might as well have been visiting Civil War battlefields or Iowa farmlands.

Love, sex, hostility, and shame are among the most sensitive subjects in any person's life. Clues are all about to question the fidelity of Skinner's relationship with Eve after their courtship, even as his support, loyalty (aside from superficial sex), and social attentiveness remained strong. He had always concentrated on his own work and satisfactions. This may have been selfishness and narcissism, but of a special sort since his efforts were devoted to improving the world. He did not strive for wealth, possessions, lavish living, or power.

These are difficult topics to probe. Skinner had a strong sexual drive and found temptations all around him. He probably resisted becoming dependent on Eve, seldom acknowledging ways he might have needed her—or anyone else. He did not publicly express or show affection; nor did Eve. If not already that way when they met, Eve soon became like Fred in cultivating her own interests, rejecting dependency, and seeking personally satisfying activities and attitudes. She tried to leave him alone and to live her own life as he said he wanted her to.

When someone's wife and children are alive, it is extremely difficult to balance objectivity with empathy, to remain focused on the greatness of the person and not on trivia. There is nothing revolutionary about trying to balance privacy with comprehensiveness. "We are both getting mature at last . . . and . . . I really hope and expect that an intelligent design for living can be worked out," he wrote (Skinner, 1984, n.p.). Skinner must have believed that marriage would be to his advantage as well as Eve's. He would have to take into account his predilection to play sexually with other women while avoiding commitments to anyone but Eve, in order not to threaten his marriage or his family life. He took great pride in both. His sexual relationship with Eve must have seemed insufficient to him, although he kept that secret. He referred almost entirely to equability between Eve and himself, while one of his best friends referred to their "open marriage."[1]

What did Skinner mean about not telling "the whole story"? He was obviously candid selectively, particularly about his relationship with Eve and his daughters. With Eve, it was sex that was thoroughly obscured; with his daughters, it was probably strong affection, which accounted for his anguish about having to discipline them and not doing so in ways he believed in.

Skinner did attempt to be honest, increasingly so as he aged, when family stability was ensured. He tried to rely on original sources (only) in his autobiography. But he withheld what he considered sensitive information. For example, he wrote to Julie about investments that "acting upon your request about privacy, I am destroying such letter when received."[2] When asked about it, he and Julie ignored the question, as he did for all of his life with other inquiries he chose not to answer. Occasionally, he claimed memory trouble, but that seemed to be an excuse he used only about questions he did not want to answer. Even his students from early in his teaching career recalled his selective memory deficits.

A fourth substantial book, *Cumulative Record: A Selection of Papers,* originally printed in 1959, was revised in its third edition in 1972. For this later edition, containing his major papers, he added a revised preface and included 18 papers with 2 deleted from the original version. He remarked that he was "dismayed" by his "boasting" in the original edition. His parents had warned him against bragging and he became increasingly sensitive to it as he aged. He was still in excellent shape mentally and quite narcissistic when he put this revision together, yet he edited out his most personal remarks without saying so and without repaginating since, he told me, that might have been noticed and called attention to the changes. Herrnstein thought it was "charming" in its original more personal form and should not have embarrassed Skinner.

What had so upset Skinner about the original edition of the book? He felt guilty about "advertising the 'Skinner Box,' dropping names, and showing off my Latin and my wit by *punning* in Latin. . . . [He concluded] Gone are the personal touches . . . gone is my acute shame in thinking about them" (Skinner, 1984, p. 165). He even considered writing under another name. Writing in 1966 that "I do not admire myself as a person. My successes do not override my shortcomings" (p. 410), he also noted that while he wrote *The Behavior of Organisms* in the first person, "I now stay in the third person (and envy those who use the first person gracefully)" (p. 410).

"I now see that I greatly exaggerated the extent to which the first edition of *Cumulative Record* was boastful and that I suffered unnecessarily" (Skinner, 1984, p. 410). Regret, even guilt about arrogance and aloofness, gnawed at him throughout his life. Avoiding most intimacy probably contributed to such feelings. Close friends would probably have reassured him, as Herrnstein did, about the irrelevance of such remorse. These moods may have been his equivalent of his father's depressive spells.

By 1966, *The Behavior of Organisms* was up to a seventh printing. Despite the vast expansion of the book's influence and applications, Arthur Koestler (1968) would still write that the experimental analysis of behavior "is comparable in its sterile pedantry to . . . counting angels on pinheads—although this sounds a more attractive pastime than counting the number of bar-pressings" (n.p.).

That same year, Skinner signed a contract to write his scientific memoirs, and the next year, he was asked to record 10 hours of reminiscences and self-analysis. "Was I not duty-bound to give a behavioristic account of myself?" (Skinner, 1984, p. 292), he asked himself. Instead, he returned the advance for his memoirs and started to consider a more comprehensive work that later became his autobiography. *Psychology Today* wanted to publish parts of his first volume to be titled "The Early Sex Life of a Behaviorist," which was the only public acknowlegment that his sex life contained anything of interest to the public.

In the early 1960s, Skinner was invited to lecture on programmed instruction in Germany. He had rejected earlier invitations to Germany because of his antipathy to Nazism—a position perhaps modified by a professor who insisted that such a movement could have developed in the United States. Skinner accepted this latest invitation of a German psychologist. Once there, challenged by the culture, Skinner thought some of its autocratic ways were close to the ambiance in which he grew up, and the "awful by-product is the ease with which a centralized control can . . . function, as under Hitler. . . . Could the culture be changed to preserve the efficiency and prevent the misuse?" (Skinner, 1984, p. 292). He thought he had solved the problem in *Walden Two* by eliminating any gains from power.

Besides serving on the Committee on Educational Policy at Harvard, Skinner was a member of the Council of the American Academy of Arts and Sciences but "it was not the kind of thing I took any interest in or did well" (Skinner, 1984, p. 165). The "Shop Club" was his only other systematic connection with the Harvard community—a group of 20 to 30 faculty members who dined together monthly and was addressed by a member about the speaker's work. It was an illustrious group—Nobel Prize–winning physicist Percy Bridgman, Pulitzer Prize–winning scholar and writer Howard Jones, and noted astronomer Harlow Shapley were among the members whom Boring invited Skinner to join.

Former Harvard president James Conant returned to the United States from administering Germany for the victorious allies, to study American high schools for the Carnegie Foundation. He tackled many questions except for what Skinner considered the most crucial one: "How can teachers teach better?" (Skinner, 1984, p. 166). Skinner asked to talk with Conant about teaching machines and sent Conant a chapter from his manuscript in which he described "a consumer's revolt . . . to demand better schools and more skillful teachers" (Skinner, 1984, p. 167). Conant opened their meeting by handing Skinner's manuscript back to him, remarking, "This is pretty shrill."

Conant said he wanted to drop an "atomic bomb" into the educational arena, beginning by improving reading in predominantly black elementary schools. Thinking that Conant would back his efforts to use teaching machines for this purpose, Skinner instead found Conant to be too pessimistic about their likely results to back such a project. Conant noted that there would be overwhelming resistance to such innovations, and furthermore, that if they were unsuccessful, the authorizing official would be held responsible for permanently damaging the students in the experimental group.

Trying to improve the educational system, Skinner was once again frustrated. Yet he did not show the tenacity and independence about performing research that would prove his case, as he did with his theory of learning. Strenuous efforts would be required for him to prevail. The forces of conservatism in public education continued to show enormous resistance to innovations, except in crises. As recently as 1994, Skinner's early student Marian Breland Bailey reported on "The Educational Ostrich and Behavioral Analysis" at the American Psychological Association convention in Los Angeles. Her message was that despite dozens of studies over 40 years proving the value of teaching machines, educators still resisted the behavior change methods.

Still, Skinner kept promoting teaching machines. He continued to accept invitations to lecture about them and at any opportunity he talked with businessmen who kept alive his faint hope of finding a manufacturer. Maintaining that "a good program in a good machine could teach twice as much in the same time and with the same effort as classroom instruction" (Skinner, 1983, p. 185), he visited a program where algebra was being taught. The students became so absorbed in learning that they didn't notice the teacher jumping on the platform to distract them. They learned and retained a full year of ninth-grade algebra in half that time and as eighth-graders. Mathematical logic was similarly taught at Yale Law School. Yet conventional education persisted in making classes smaller—but teachers no more efficient. As quickly as teaching machines demonstrated improved learning efficiency, the argument for the status quo would be shifted to unproved intangibles such as teacher inspiration, retention of the material, and generalizability.

The machine Skinner had designed was being sold and used though not in a mass market. General Motors wanted him to find a foundation to pay for it. Rheem Company wanted simpler machines, asked him to design them, then postponed production. One program tried, without consulting him, to stimulate students by playing martial music and nagging them. Purdue University began to broadcast courses but presented material at the same rate for all students and without reinforcement.

Skinner seldom totally abandoned his hopes to succeed at the enterprises he most valued. If an effort faltered or hit a stone wall, he would usually try a reasonable alternative, or he might temporarily accept the reality of implacable opposition or inertia. He had plenty else to work on. Not all of his persisting goals were highfalutin, however. He truly kept hoping, right up to his death, that he could write a novel, be consulted on political and administrative decisions, and get his baby-tender mass produced. The one project important to him on which he gave up completely was his pigeon bombsight. Yet even from that he squeezed significance. In receiving the Distinguished Scientific Contribution Award of the American Psychological Association (in 1958), he talked on "Pigeons in a Pelican," "The history of a crackpot idea, born on the wrong side of the tracks intellectually speaking, but eventually vindicated" (Skinner, 1984, p. 169). Like *Walden Two*, it was

> *a declaration of confidence in the technology of behavior . . . in which I have never lost faith. I still believe that the same kind of wide-ranging speculation about human affairs, supported by studies of compensating rigor, will make a substantial contribution toward that world of the future in which . . . there will be no need for guided missiles. (Skinner, 1984, p. 169)*

While nonprofessional activities almost always took a secondary position to his professional activities, Skinner finally and reluctantly sold the house on Monhegan Island, where his family had vacationed for years. It was the only place he took his family that Skinner described with much affection (tinged with sadness). It held great promise for sensuous pleasures, but they largely went unfulfilled. Repeatedly, he tried to view his vacation home as a haven of relaxation, but he eventually faced the fact that it failed him. He almost always ended up working hard there—the only times he expressed regret for his highly disciplined work habits.

Skinner wrote also of "the sadness of failure" (of an unspecified nature) in vacationing with his children, perhaps relating to their rebelliousness. And Monhegan "had never provided a really good summer for Eve" (Skinner, 1984, p. 171). So he ended up shutting off Monhegan as a failed part of his attempt to live happily with his family. Instead of relaxing there, they all preferred the attractions of larger cities and cultural activities. His original hopes for Monhegan seemed to be based on a romanticized view of living close to nature which, after his childhood, worked for him mainly in his daydreams. He idealized but never did accommodate to living Thoreau's values.

Skinner repeatedly expressed compassion for his daughters—for Deborah when she told a fib for which "she paid a wholly disproportionate price" (p. 170) in guilt, or did poorly at school because (he thought) her teachers had not yet learned how to teach properly (p. 171). When enrolling Deborah, he wrote to the private school: "Our present feeling is that Debbie's problem has always been one of slow maturation. . . . We had almost the same kind of problem with our older daughter" (p. 171). Since he had enjoyed his four years of high school Latin ("but I had a very different home discipline, and I could imagine Deb's despair" [p. 171]), Skinner got the school's permission for him to teach her the relations between Latin roots and affixes, and standard English words. He also worried about her forgetfulness and analyzed it behaviorally. Julie also was a source of concern to him, as she reacted defensively to making mistakes.

Neither girl displayed serious psychological problems; it was mainly Skinner's worrisomeness that was notable. He seemed to have no norms against which to assess his daughters. What stood out was that he so empathized with their problems and blamed himself for influencing them in troublesome ways. Despite his expressed indifference to the public outcry about the baby-tender and his adamant defense of it, he suffered pangs of remorse about being known for having placed Deborah in it. Publicly, he sensibly dismissed criticisms, but the misinformed accusations of mistreating her nonetheless bothered him throughout his life. He took heavy responsibility for the girls' rearing and could hardly bear even a hint of insensitivity about it.

Skinner's relations with his daughters impinged closely on feelings of somehow being treated unfairly by his own parents, which he never overtly acknowledged but reflected in other relationships. His attitude toward and treatment of his daughters were major inconsistencies in his life. Most of his attention related to his concern that they might not be well educated. Sometimes, however, he considered his daughters "spoiled," as both they themselves and others saw them. He seldom tried to discipline them and expressed regret that he had not insisted on more musical training for them. Skinner eschewed punishment early in Julie's rearing, and had completely rejected it by the time of Deborah's birth. Yet he was disturbed when they did not show the same self-discipline and desire to improve themselves that he did so extremely.

Skinner could also get carried away by his feelings about them. There was the time, for example, when, hearing that Deborah had marijuana, he called her at school late at night and pleaded, "If you love me, flush it down the toilet" (Skinner, 1984, p. 290). He was terrified that she might be arrested and that his name would be associated with hers in newspapers, damning them both.

When Julie married and had a daughter, Skinner instructed her to place a music box in the child's presence so she would happen upon it as if by chance, experiment with it, and learn to play it. By 1973, he tried to draw his girls closer to him geographically, writing Keller that "I'm trying to move Julie and Ernie (her husband) somewhere close so that we can see our grandchildren" (Skinner, 1984, n.p.). Six years later, he was recommending Julie for nearby jobs.

In old age, Skinner speculated that sons would have been more of a problem for him, that he might not have done as well with them, that emotional empathy with them would have been difficult. He had a soft spot for women, especially his daughters, and friends such as Miss Graves, Sister Annette Walters, and colleagues Eve Segal and Margaret Vaughan.

With his students overwhelmingly male, Skinner almost never blamed their environment nor himself for their problems. Predominantly he tried to enhance their independence so that they would control their environment as much as they could. To show compassion for them was incompatible with his theory of learning.

Two events prompted Skinner to consider further his learning theory: Watson's death and "cognitive" psychology. With Watson's death in 1958, Skinner was asked by *Science* magazine to write an obituary. Because of his commitment to the reflex and conditioning, Watson did not project his views into the wider environment and take genetics and introspection into account with behaviorism. Thus, "his brilliant glimpse of the need for, and the nature of, a science of behavior was all but forgotten," Skinner (Skinner, 1959b, p. 129) wrote. The magazine misreported that Watson was founder of the reinforcement theory that was Skinner's. Watson had *not* considered consequences as essential to behavior change; that was Skinner's contribution.

The growing popularity of cognitive psychology became an increasing annoyance to Skinner, who considered it merely a sophisticated return to a focus on introspection and mentalism, which he thought he had destroyed long ago. Yet here were his brilliant ex-students, Guttman and Herrnstein, writing about how humans acquired concepts beyond respondents and operants—concepts that Skinner thought did nothing to explain behavior.

He published a paper, "Why I am Not a Cognitive Psychologist" (1977), in which he wrote:

> *Having moved the environment inside the head in the form of conscious experience, and behavior in the form of intention, will, and choice, cognitive psychologists put them all together to compose an internal simulacrum of the organism . . . whose behavior is . . . called "subjective behaviorism."*
>
> *To escape the charge of dualism, cognitive scientists leaned heavily on "brain research". . . . I had learned to analyze behavior in its own right. . . . I was [not] opposed to physiological research. . . . An experimental analysis of behavior would give them a correct assignment, whereas cognitive science sent them looking for things they would never find. . . . Mentalists were superstitious in the sense that, having observed various states of their bodies just as they were about to behave, they concluded that the states caused the behavior. (n.p.)*

Since they were both concerned about stagnation in the Harvard Psychology Department, George Miller and Skinner discussed and agreed on shortcomings and Skinner submitted a paper suggesting changes. They must have covered over their differences only superficially, however, since Miller then collaborated on a proposal to found a center for cognitive studies at Harvard to be supported by the Carnegie Corporation. Skinner was alarmed by "how deep-seated mentalism is among our graduate students—supported, I am afraid, by the positions of Stevens, Bruner, and Miller" (Skinner, 1984, p. 194).

So his old hobgoblin—mentalism—had popped up again, reinvigorated, in the form of "cognitive psychology." Skinner blamed it on the computer, which had

> *emerged as a possible model of human behavior. . . . Psychologists no longer needed to worry about the difference between a perception and the world perceived; the mind simply processed information, the brain was a great computer, and the neurophysiologists would answer questions about the stuff of which it (and hence the mind) was made. It became fashionable to insert the word "cognitive" wherever possible. (Skinner, 1984, p. 194)*

The cognitive movement became Skinner's *bête noire* for the rest of his life. He had thought that mentalism had been superseded by his scientific "radical behaviorism," which he identified as the psychological equivalent of Darwin's theory of biological evolution. Much to his suprise, however, mentalism had revived and was flourishing despite the fact that "it could not be given the physical dimensions of what it was said to be about." But mentalism gave some promise through neurophysiology, which Skinner reluctantly acknowledged, then ignored, because it claimed too much by way of explaining behavior. Besides its other advantages, behavior therapy, Skinner thought, had helped psychologists in their conflict with psychiatry and psychoanalysis by clearly establishing psychologists' claim of creating the science of behavior shaping.

Claiming stress from "overwork" and invasion of his "intellectual privacy" from his promotion of teaching machines, Skinner at times became more ambivalent about battling for what he strongly believed in. He acted as if nothing much bothered him, even when it obviously did. He said he was not after acclaim, which he denied reinforced him. He wanted only for his arguments to prevail, especially when buttressed by practical provable success as from teaching machines, behavior shaping methods, utopian design, and so on.

Like a camel enduring without water, Skinner could sustain his efforts for long dry periods without reward. He even profited, he thought, from strenuous though unsuccessful "spade work" that he would not have done "if I had been as [conventionally] successful as my more distinguished contemporaries" (Skinner, 1984, n.p.). Narcissistic and egotistical as he was, Skinner envied some colleagues to whom success appeared to come easier than to him—a common enough misperception about one's peers.

The more widespread his fame, the more requests were made of him. At times, the requests became oppressive as he felt demands imposing upon his independence and his time. Many alternatives were attractive. He wanted to do it all—verbal behavior research, Walden Twos, programmed teaching, improving the social structure, and more. He stripped his life of lower-priority activities: classroom teaching, advising students, and laboratory research. He considered, then rejected, writing a new textbook with Herrnstein. It might pay well but collaboration would be "risky" and it would almost completely divert him. Lecturing and consulting seemed self-indulgent compared with creating new ideas to improve human society.

Skinner alternated between moods of pessimism and optimism, writing:

What does one do to make the best of the tag end of a life? Mostly what has been reinforced in the past, but much of it is on a lengthening ratio schedule. One tries harder and harder . . . to get the old familiar reinforcements. Aversive consequences pile up: the gourmet must cope with impaired digestion, the athlete with arthritis and sprains, the lover of . . . the arts . . . with failing vision and hearing. It is too late to undertake long courses of action. Fatigue comes more quickly, and lingers when one rests. (Skinner, 1984, p. 243)

He also wrote:

My plan for the next five to ten years is, I think, realistic and should be productive. I am still alive intellectually and I am still improving my intellectual efficiency. I have not been wholly successful in cutting out unproductive work. My correspondence could, in part, be turned over to a secretary. . . . I am getting things done. . . . Possible improvements: 1) Further reduction of office and departmental work. No lecturing. Minimal correspondence. 2) Organizing, filing, clarifying materials. . . . 3) Minimal social stimulation. 4) Unguilty relaxation. Light reading. TV. Music seems too disturbing. . . . 5) Better contact with psychology . . . (through initially forced reading and consequent clarification of my position). (p. 244)

The literary novel Skinner still wanted to write, though he didn't think of subjects or plots, should be a "behavioristic novel without referring to feelings, but rather to the actions from which the feelings were inferred. . . . Why not 'self-control' . . . the hero gradually discovering how to control himself by controlling the world in which he lives. . . . I was skeptical of inner struggle"

(1984, p. 246). He never could generate the passion or skill to drive him through the creation of a literary novel. Meanwhile, he associated with literary figures, including the distinguished comparative literature chairman at Harvard, Harry Levin, and Arthur Koestler, who visited Skinner.

Skinner flirted with drugs to gain pleasure per Aldous Huxley, Timothy Leary, and much earlier, as he discovered, the Goncourt brothers, French authors of the mid-nineteenth century. He was too energetic, too goal driven, too disciplined, to lapse into passive drug use, however. He never wrote why he didn't take to them more—nor what he did get from them—but predictably he rejected them after finding that he couldn't drive safely following his experiment with marijuana. In a later letter (December 16, 1989), he wrote, "It's positive at first, then it's negatively reinforcing to avoid withdrawal effects."[3] If he did try drugs extensively, he was unlikely to acknowledge it publicly.

However, he had been so influenced by drug-using literati as well as drug company propaganda—he was a consultant to drug manufacturer Merck—that he wrote that we were "entering the age of the chemical control of human behavior" (Skinner, 1984, p. 247). "In the not-too-distant future, the motivational and emotional conditions of normal life will probably be maintained in any desired state through the use of drugs" (Skinner, 1955). He regretted that brief lapse from his commitment to *self*-control.

Designed by the architect Yamasaki, the new behavioral sciences building at Harvard was being completed to house social relations as well as psychology. Herrnstein, the chairman of psychology, offered Skinner the best suite but Skinner chose a more modest one since he intended to take little part in departmental affairs. Even though he increasingly used his basement office at home, he continued to visit the Harvard space, which was expansive, with an entrance way, a secretarial room, and his inner area with large storage shelving.

Skinner turned down consultations in utopian communities because he and Eve chose not to live in them. "Unfortunately," he wrote,—and I say it with real regret—my life is full of so many interesting things that I could not possibly bring myself to break with it and wager the rest of my life on such a venture" (Skinner, 1984, p. 251). After a visit for the U.S. government to Russia in May of 1961, however, and being exposed to its innovative enterprises, he wrote to friends, "I am seriously thinking of starting a Walden Two. I still believe in non-political action and there is so much we need to know which can only be discovered from experimentation."[4] Finally, he decided that projects he had planned for his next five years would be more significant and enduring for "the eventual success of a radical reform of our way of life . . . than trying personally to implement *Walden Two*" (Skinner, 1984, p. 254). He kept being tempted to participate, however.

As usual, Skinner was criticized for not keeping up with psychology, even with his own field of operant conditioning. He agreed, but continued to draw large crowds for his lectures, no matter what the criticisms of him might have been. There was seldom enough room for his audience at American Psychological Association conventions.

Skinner's brand of behaviorism was attracting increasing attention among practitioners as well as scientists. Eighteen psychologists interested in the experimental analysis of behavior first met at Indiana when Skinner was there, then became part of the APA Division of Experimental Psychology. In 1964, Experimental Psychology became a separate division of the APA, with over 1,000 members. In 1968, it began to publish its own *Journal of Applied Behavior Analysis.* Skinner refused to become its first president, trying to avoid leading a cult. Yet, he remarked that "there is extraordinary neglect of our position. Students still go on in the old tradition. . . . [Isn't] there really an extraordinary advantage in my position? . . . The new division is off to a great start. I'm sure I have the measure of the psycholinguists. Etc., etc. It could be a very exciting decade" (Skinner, 1984, p. 264).

Publications and practical applications proliferated. When a Canadian psychologist, Werner Honig, published a book on Skinner's theory *Operant Behavior* (1966), with a wide range of authors, 28 years after Skinner's first work and reflecting the immense progress since then, Skinner reacted in a way puzzling even to himself: "It should have been a great moment in my life, but I was perfectly cold. Someday I may get a thrill, but not now" (Skinner, 1984, p. 266). Skinner did not analyze or speculate about the feeling; he simply cut it off as inexplicable. Once again, he seemed trapped between a sense of success and a sinking feeling about self-aggrandizement.

Soon after, Skinner flagellated himself even more severely following an invited lecture to the Royal Society in London. Lecturing on "The Technology of Teaching: Its Nature and Some Problems Encountered in Its Use," he described methods derived from his theory to solve a variety of educational problems. He went to bed believing he had handled himself well, but the next morning he was appalled when he thought of how offensive he must have been. He had drunk only one glass of sherry and little other wine, but he had ignored his host's request to discuss teaching machines informally, and had been critical of scientific prizes in the presence of prize winners. He was becoming increasingly sensitive to the egoism he had been mostly oblivious to in the past.

"The articles in *Time* and *Life,* the profile in *Harper's,* and my 'successes' in Texas, Arizona, and Washington," Skinner wrote, "have plunged me into a sustained depression. Feelings I can vaguely describe as guilt and anxiety overwhelm me. . . . Much of this is the result of losing control. Flushed with success I go too far. It was once a more devastating flaw; it could still destroy me" (1984, p. 265). At the same time, he relished his past toughness and wrote that "the danger was the temptation to relax and enjoy. It would be a mistake simply to give people what they expected to hear. I resolved to present more and more technical material" (p. 271). He became aware of the vast potential of operant conditioning applied to wage schedules in industry. "Fixed- or variable-ratio wage systems were prohibited by unions or governments; they were so powerful they were dangerous. Less threatening uses were usually acceptable. For example, a free lottery ticket received each day upon arrival at work, with a weekly or monthly drawing, reduced absenteeism" (p. 273).

Concerned that incentives might be misused in industry solely for the benefit of employers, Skinner refused to write an article for a business magazine about their use. Of course others did so anyway, applying Skinnerian theory but on so limited and self-serving a basis that no one paid much attention to their immense potential power and possibilities for abuse. The enormity of cultural lag in resisting innovations ensured that Skinner's views would not quickly sweep the world, even though they slowly infiltrated most aspects of society. Under heightened scrutiny generated by severe economic pressure, industry occasionally opened to radical change, but reinforcement theory will probably always be suspect by organized labor. It may flourish only in a cooperative system where powerful and selfish control is not a threat.

Skinner was beginning to experience some medical scares. In 1970, he could no longer read with his left eye and discovered that he had glaucoma in the right. Because of the retinal lesion, he covered part of his left lens. Would he have to adapt to blindness and depend on services to the blind? "No, the trick is to change my style of life," he wrote. "I am driven back upon *myself*" (1984, p. 329). The glaucoma was medically controlled, and with medical help he could see with one eye though he misjudged distances and locations, and carried a cane for reassurance.

During promotional events for *Beyond Freedom and Dignity* in 1971, Skinner developed anginal pains, which led him to ease up on his activities and reduce his weight by 10 percent—as his physician recommended and Julie pursued. His physician diagnosed it as "rusty pipes," and reported that one-third of those with his condition would be dead in five years. Skinner "almost broke down" (1984, p. 330) when he told his daughters about it—Eve was away on a trip.

In 1964, Skinner for the first time designated a literary executor for his books. He asked Herrnstein to act as his trustee in case he didn't survive to finish his book, *The Technology of Teaching* (1968). "That was before he turned in that strange way against me, wrote the paper about post-Skinnerian behaviorism and so on,"[5] Skinner stated. "Then I eventually made Julie my executor."[6] At the same time, he drew up an irrevocable family trust, which "was my will, really," which included money his mother had left him in 1960. He designated a secretary as his literary executor before appointing daugher Julie.

Skinner promptly began to review his records with Julie, who was by then a behavioral psychologist. He also discovered a growing tumor near his ear, which proved to be cancerous and required radiation to cure. When Eve returned from her trip to Africa, she supervised his exercise and diet regimen. Upon completing the manuscripts he had underway, his anginal symptoms disappeared and did not return. Despite his failing senses and coordination, he persisted in his productive intellectual habits, and also in walking regularly, rejecting help except from whatever aids he could buy or improvise (and thus control).

He remained unregenerate in referring specifically to the control of human behavior. Others tried to ameliorate the negative impact of the word *control* by substituting a more benign word such as *influence* or *educate*. Although he also used *behavior modification* and *behavior changing*, Skinner meant *control* and did not hesitate to use the term. This upset humanitarians and democrats who identified the word with malevolence, curtailed freedom, and abusive power. Skinner stubbornly defended the exercise of control in a salutary, benign, and voluntary way, except with criminal or psychotic behavior when it posed an imminent danger to the self or others.

Another death brought a poignant moment to Skinner's life. Intermittently, he had interacted with physicist Percy Bridgman about private and public perceptions in science. They had exchanged manuscripts, Skinner sending Bridgman his *Science and Human Behavior,* Bridgman sending Skinner his *The Way Things Are,* appending the comment, "Here it is. Now do your damnedest" (Skinner, 1984, p. 280). Bridgman already was failing and was distressed about talking erratically. Skinner noted, "He has lived too long" (p. 280). Soon after, Bridgman committed suicide by gun.

Once again, Skinner took a death personally, feeling deeply contrite: "I failed Bridgman in his old age. It was the dilemma of the individual. He found himself shrinking" (1984, p. 281). It is difficult to understand why Skinner would feel guilty, and what he could have done about it except to communicate more, which he seldom did with anyone. It may have related to his suppressed feelings, perhaps about his father. When he himself was dying, Skinner wrote that he was unperturbed by it, and tried to prepare for death by seeing his brief life in perspective, talking with those closest to him, and by obtaining the means to commit suicide to avoid extreme pain.

Skinner's differences with professional psychology were sharpening, but they took the form of increasing alienation from colleagues and organizations rather than direct anger at attacks from a wide variety of critics. Jacques Barzun, Joseph Krutch, Arthur Koestler, Paul Goodman, and many others from the humanities especially took sharp shots at his presumed inhumanity, desire to control, and insensitivity to human will and feelings, particularly following publication of *Beyond Freedom and Dignity.* His irritation with his own profession most specifically occurred in his department at Harvard, where he tried to keep aloof from the misdirections he perceived. "The energy I save from not fighting my colleagues is better spent elsewhere, but my pretending to be part of the *status quo ante* is rather absurd" (1984, p. 286). He was also unhappy with the American Psychological Association, where he declined to run for president on grounds that he was afraid he'd be elected and wouldn't like the work. His friends in experimental psychology could no longer get elected, however, so he didn't think he could either. Clinical practitioners had become dominant.

Skinner grew depressed by national psychological meetings because so little attention was paid to matters he considered important, and also because "so little attention was paid to *me*" (1984, p. 288). But he admitted that when he was forced to sit through meetings he would not have otherwise attended, "I discover interests, formulations, theories I would otherwise neglect. . . . I have promised myself, as part of my Career Award Project, to maintain a more intimate contact with current psychology for practical reasons" (p. 288).

Each of his last attempts to get a company to work on teaching machines and programmed instruction he thought of as a final effort. Nonetheless, he could not resist a possible opening. The publisher Appleton-Century-Crofts wanted a program on "verbal arts" to include handwriting, spelling, and reading. Many problems occurred because teachers were not trained to teach with machines and because drills had fallen into disrepute (because, he thought, they were conducted punitively instead of with reinforcement and with ink that might be toxic). In the end, only the reading program survived, taught at several hundred learning centers in schools through the United States. They were his only major practical success in the field. Harvard's Committee on Programmed Instruction was eliminated when Skinner took up his Career Award.

In supporting Skinner's application for the federal Career Award, Richard Elliott, who had by 1963 retired from the University of Minnesota, wrote, "I would rank him number one among contemporary psychologists in the influence he has had upon the development of this subject. And more specifically on basic behavioral theory."[7] It is curious that Skinner called on Elliott, long gone from his life, to support his grant request. He knew that Elliott invariably supported his proposals and respected his intellect, but why had no one yet replaced him for this purpose? Even though Skinner's regrets for his sometime arrogance were high at this time in his life, he must have known he could easily have offended even Elliott by leaving Minnesota as he did.

At age 65, after his five-year Career Award was renewed for another five years, Skinner read that people in their fifties were worn out, and he noted that his classmates had begun to retire. "Yet I have never worked more efficiently" nor been "thinking more clearly. . . . I probably have five good years left" (Skinner, 1984, p. 306). Depression must have been clouding his judgment, for he had another 21 productive years left. His manuscript on freedom and dignity was going well, and he looked forward to writing his autobiography. Not until his seventies, however, in his second and final retirement, did he finally complete it.

Skinner was then bouncing back to consider a literary career. It kept popping up. He still yearned to write a novel, continued to lack a plot or passion, and would forever equivocate: "I am quite serious about leaving psychology . . . but am I ready (and able?) to take such a definite step" (1984, p. 306). In this respect, he remained arrested where he was when he graduated from college. A British psychologist, T. H. Pear, surveyed colleagues and friends for recent novels in English by fully trained psychologists, and *Walden Two* was most often mentioned. But to Skinner, it was not a *literary* novel but more like a psychological treatise. He believed that it caught the theme of post-World War II United States, and that "after the destruction of the current order must come rebuilding . . . [as] possibly in *Walden Two*" (n.p.).

While "the freedom and dignity book," as he called it, was progressing (his major commitment for the Career Award), he believed that his mind and thinking were as clear as ever, though he could not work efficiently as long as he used to. Calculating carefully, as usual, he determined that he was spending more time per word on the new manuscript than the two minutes per word he had taken on *The Behavior of Organisms* and *Verbal Behavior*—but only by an extra half a minute per word.

He suffered from the writing, not being able to think about it at times, and had a stomachache most of the time. "I often wonder," Skinner wrote, "whether I can finish it" (Skinner, 1984, p. 309). He had never complained as much about any other writing, though *Verbal Behavior* stretched out over many more years. Although he and Eve went on a cruise with friends, he was still writing the book, and upon returning, "For a day I was numb, unable to think of much of anything. I am getting anxious," he wrote. "I want the book to appear. . . . What will people say? There is no chance at all that it will be understood and liked by everyone" (pp. 309–310). How unlike that "solipsist," as Elliott had designated him to Boring about his first book. The rocklike self-confidence and narcissism of this youth and middle age were diminishing as he noted his powers declining.

Negotiations for publishing the book proceeded better than with most of his others. With a choice of offers, Skinner selected Knopf because he remembered that it printed the most prestigious books in his youth. His editor there, Robert Gottlieb, suggested that the tentative title be changed to indicate its break with conventional notions. *Beyond* popped into Skinner's head to add to *Freedom and Dignity*, and that addition clinched its final name. He had a knack for choosing apt titles—euphonious, appropriate, and with a bite. *Beyond Freedom and Dignity* conveyed clearly what he had in mind by suggesting that feeling free was not enough to make "freedom" reality, since it was not objectively validated—that even while being crucially influenced by their environment, humans could both think they were free of it and be able to transcend it by learning to deliberately use it to their advantage.

With publication of the paperback edition of *Walden Two* in 1963, Skinner took renewed interest in the way it related to his new book on freedom. With special pride, he noted that unlike other utopias, it had no leader. He tried to safeguard the notion of freedom from manipulators, dictators, even advisers. "The designer has arranged his own demise as leader. . . . Who is to control? No one" (Skinner, 1984, p. 313). That did not ensure him against attacks from the seriously philosophical to hostile descriptions of him as fascist, God, controller. Few understood how antimanipulative he insisted on being, how repugnant it was to him to control any human being—or to be so controlled himself.

Simultaneously, Skinner was repelled by the turmoil generated by activist youth at Harvard. The emotion of the rebelliousness and what he viewed as its negativism, even destructiveness, seemed personally offensive to him, so disciplined and coolly rational was he in handling his own reactions even when angry. He sympathized with the students' plight, however, which he thought resulted from having nothing positive to inspire them in their discontentment with the status quo and their idealistic desire for change.

He wanted the students to latch on to *Walden Two,* to want to create a better society, not merely to reform Harvard, which he had long ago given up on:

> *They have nothing to do. . . . Is it any wonder they turn to drugs or violence. . . . Why is there no world to* engage *these people. What must be done to build such a world? . . . They were not misbehaving because they had disturbed personalities, were alienated or rootless. . . . They were suffering from a lack of positive reinforcement. One had only to look at what happened when they went home or stayed at home . . . to school . . . to work. . . . The consequences, mostly punitive, bred the escape and defection we were seeing. (1984, pp. 315–316)*

Skinner missed the positive goals the students had. They wanted to eliminate the ROTC, which they viewed as contributing to a warlike stance, and they wanted a Black Studies Department. Above all, they wanted change, and they wanted it now. They were offended by the deadly conventionality of those seeking, above all, to preserve order, to follow the rules, who urged patience, evolution, and tact to change university structure and policies.

Skinner seemed to have no firsthand connections to students except for his daughters, and his empathy was more theoretical than concrete. He knew only what he read and heard from colleagues, and the administration was at war with its rebellious students. At a graduation ceremony he had to attend, he was given written instructions to sit in an aisle that would block students if they tried to reach the stage uninvited.[8] He was almost totally out of touch with and untouched by the turmoil, even when the police were called in to campus by the administration and beat up some students. He believed that a respected dean and former student of his, Franklin Ford, had a heart attack during (and because of) the student turmoil, and that outraged him, as did all forms of violence. But what about the confrontation between police and students? He had never so directly faced conflict and probably could not imagine doing so. He seemed conventionally more concerned with manners than were the students. He lacked the empathy one might have expected from one with his personal attitudes.

Beyond Freedom and Dignity (1971) almost immediately attracted wide attention, often intensely unfavorable, sometimes highly favorable. Representing an apogee of his ideas and influence, it explained as well as he could why the behaviorism and control he espoused from his first book, to his last, extended the concept of human freedom. He pushed beyond the notion of self-determination, to include controlling and directing environmental influences from which one could never be free.

Acknowledging the powerful effects of environment on humans, one could intentionally incorporate them into one's efforts to control one's life. But so pervasive was the idea that self-determination must mean freedom from or transcending environment that many devotees of humanism insisted that Skinner's views were bleakly malevolent and that he was a menace to democracy and personal freedom.

At a high point of attention to his ideas, *Time* magazine on September 20, 1971, printed his picture on its cover under the caption "B. F. Skinner says: We Can't Afford Freedom." His head was framed by insets of a pigeon with a ball, a rat with lever pressing lights, a control box, and an idyllic landscape, presumably a Walden Two. Predominantly, its many reviewers viewed the book with alarm and denounced it as inhumane. Reviewer Christopher Lehman-Haupt wrote, however, in the *New York Times*, "If you plan to read only one book this year, this is probably the one you should choose" (Skinner, 1984, p. 318). Many more were caustic, worried, or sarcastic, angry about Skinner's desire to control human behavior and his simple-mindedness, his old adversary Chomsky heading the parade. One cartoon pictured Skinner's face on a rat's body, and another, on a pigeon's. The accompanying article quoted him as saying his life was pleasant, "yet I am unhappy." The omitted part of this quotation added that he was unhappy because so few others shared his enviable environment.

Following the publication of *Beyond Freedom and Dignity*, Skinner drew large and lively audiences. He had touched a nerve of the intelligentsia. Outselling all of his other books immediately, it was on the *New York Times* best-seller list for 20 weeks. He was greeted more enthusiastically by public and student audiences than by peers, but his critics were overwhelmingly outnumbered by appreciative members at the annual meetings of the American Psychological Association.

Skinner gleefully noted the fall of major political adversaries of the book. Congressman Cornelius Gallagher, soon imprisoned for income tax evasion, had questioned Skinner's federal Career Award because he was "advancing ideas which threaten the future of our system of government by denigrating the American traditions of individualism, human dignity" (Skinner, 1984, p. 323). Gallagher was joined by Vice President Spiro Agnew, soon to resign his post in dishonor, who declared that "Skinner attacks the very precepts on which our society is based" (Skinner, 1984, p. 323). But many more illustrious humanistic critics also attacked him.

Only late in life did Skinner report blithefully on such adversaries. He also became self-conscious about his success, "a winning ticket" as he reported it:

> *I read a few pages of* Beyond Freedom and Dignity *and for the very first time felt resentment at my critics. It is a good book—a great book, I believe. Every sentence is as clear and honest as I could make it. There are no appeals to emotion. No rhetoric. No padding. . . . I found myself weeping slightly, not in anger at the vicious criticism, but in gratitude for having been able to write the book. That is something granted to very few men. (Skinner, 1984, p. 324)*

Accepting the inevitability that the course of his remaining life would be set by his scientific bent and his desire to improve the world, he wrote,

> *I am overwhelmed by one ruthless fact:* I can't stop now. *My dream of a more relaxed intellectual life, of exploring my own history in an autobiography, of writing a novel, is quite shattered. Too much remains to be done. The extraordinary misunderstanding shown by the critics of* Beyond Freedom and Dignity *demands rectification . . . by presenting the operant position at a more popular level. (1984, p. 324)*

When a silver trophy was awarded to him by the Kennedy Foundation for Mental Retardation, the citation especially pleased him: "Dr. Skinner has developed, *on the purely practical level,* teaching and therapeutic methods that have proved extraordinarily effective in work with mentally retarded persons" (1984, p. 325). He appreciated the word *practical,* and thought even *compassion* (which was also used) could be reinforced by its "fortunate by-products" if he could help where it was most necessary—and lacking—with "small children, the chronically ill, the aged, the psychotic and retarded, and prisoners" (p. 325).

Proceeding despite his occasionally bleak moods, he returned to his next three books. Writing the autobiography was so seductively easy and satisfying that he allowed himself to work on it only an hour a day. The popular explanation of his theory, tentatively titled *Primer of Behaviorism,* was ultimately published as *About Behaviorism* (1974), and a proposed book on intellectual self-management ended up as an article ("How to Discover What You Have to Say—A Talk to Students") (1981).

By his mid-sixties, Skinner became aware of a significant hearing loss and tried out a hearing aid he found among his mother's possessions. He would not repeat his father's resistance to help. He attempted to adapt a cheap pocket aid to his ear, and tried other devices that were too much nuisance because of tiny controls and short-lived batteries. He wrote a manufacturer, suggesting ways to improve these devices and he visited the factory but he had little impact. By age 66, he began to use a conventional fitted aid anyway, and later, two of them. Still, he withdrew from social events because of hearing difficulties.

The problem of punishment continued to plague Skinner. Just as the public associated "discipline" with punishment, so it also identified punishment with conditioning and behavior modification. To many, conditioning was synonymous with aversive methods to eliminate undesired conduct, rather than, as he tried invariably to demonstrate, to reward desired activity. The most dramatic example of aversive conditioning was portrayed in the movie *Clockwork Orange,* where a psychopath was conditioned to become nauseated when viewing violent sexual scenes. Anthony Burgess, author of the novel on which the film was based, stated, "It is preferable to have a world of violence undertaken in full awareness—violence chosen as an act of will—than a world conditioned to be good or harmless" (Skinner, 1984, pp. 334–335).

Defending his position "that we needed good environments, not good people" (1984, p. 335), Skinner found an echo in Bill Clinton's 1992 campaign rhetoric when Clinton remarked that he'd prefer good character in the presidency more than in the president. Clinton was as misunderstood on this issue as Skinner was.

Skinner was constantly misinterpreted. To his dismay, the *Manchester Guardian* newspaper reported that "behavior modification programs are going on in the United States in schools, hospitals, and prisons and electric shock as well as candy" (1984, p. 335). True, they did go on, but not with Skinner's approval. He utterly rejected them. Colleagues and ex-students had established the selective effectiveness of punishment. He strongly believed that he could prevail more effectively with positive reinforcement alone and could eschew punishment. Punitive measures, so widespread in U.S. education, and indeed throughout its institutions, even if effective in the short term, produced hostile and destructive reactions later, Skinner believed.

Applications of operant conditioning were constantly expanding under Skinner's concept of self-direction, producing salutary results beyond those from undirected freedom that humanitarians fought to preserve. Sometimes amorphous freedom seemed like anarchy to Skinner. *Biofeedback* became a popular term for operant conditioning applied to autonomic responses. It was used for the self-control of pulse rate, blood pressure, and other physiological functions. It remains a hopeful field of research and treatment.

In 1972, the Center for the Study of Democratic Institutions headed by Robert Hutchins, retired president of the University of Chicago, sponsored a week-long conference on *Beyond Freedom and Dignity.* Skinner was both attacked and defended vigorously by distinguished scholars of various professions. Defenders included John Platt, Dennis Pirages, Arthur Jensen, and Joseph Schwab, in person. Adversaries were Michael Novak, in person, and, in writing, Arnold Toynbee, Chaim Perelman, Karl Pribram, and Max Black. Platt wrote:

> Beyond Freedom and Dignity *is a revolutionary manifesto. It proposes the design of a new society using new methods for improving the behavior and interactions of human beings. It has been roundly condemned . . . by humanist critics who at other times call for improved human interactions. In fact, Skinner may have had the worst press of any scientist since Darwin.* (Skinner, 1984, p. 337)

In an example of "the extraordinary violence shown by some of my critics" (wrote Skinner), Black remarked that the book was a "melange of amateurish metaphysics, self-advertising technology, and illiberal social policy" (1984, p. 338). Skinner felt hopeless to contend with the criticism, and concluded his official reply with a remark about the poisonous eucalyptus trees among which the host center was housed: He said he had received a strange message, "'Will you join me in a cup of eucalyptus?' signed, 'Socrates.' "

A later conference on the subject at Yale "was stacked even more heavily against me" Skinner wrote. "I am defending my position. I must hold to my plans for the future if I am to save myself," not to offset a sense of failure, but "to offset extinction" (1984, n.p.). There were always alternatives to revitalize him. Inquiries were coming in about making *Walden Two* into a movie, which he referred to the trust he had created for his daughters for his royalties. The movie never was made, but the revived interest in the book generated a District of Columbia committee that founded a Virginia community named Twin Oaks and produced a book (Kinkade, 1973).

Despite consigning himself to the periphery of the Harvard Psychology Department to avoid the distraction and frustration of administration, Skinner was upset by the department's skittish association with Social Relations under a single administrator. Administrative juggling had split Social Relations, Sociology, and part of Anthropology from Psychology in 1947. In 1965, they reunited as the Center for the Behavior Sciences under one director but as separate entities except for administrative details. Eventually, Social Relations was eliminated as a department, although when Skinner retired at age 70, it was as Professor of Psychology and Social Relations Emeritus.

Years earlier, when the new building, William James Hall, Psychology's current home, was ready for occupancy, Skinner refused to move from ancient Memorial Hall, where he had started at Harvard. Eventually, he complied with a direct order from the president's office to do so. He wanted to stay at the old place, physically aloof and independent in the decrepit but spacious basement.

His administrator for almost 15 years referred to Skinner as "an operator," "never embroiled in fights," with "a flair for self-promotion." "Everyone liked him," and he was "sweet-tempered" but "considered himself only." And "most students would consider him 'great.' "9

Attending the first meeting of the joint department, which Skinner had presumably abjured when embarking on his career grant, he found it "a distressing experience" because the disparate divisions found little in common. He spoke pejoratively of the structure—and ignored it—though various administrators thought they protected him at times from his own aloofness. While he had occupied one of the most prestigious chairs in psychology at Harvard as Edgar Pierce Professor, he was never awarded the most honored rank at Harvard of "University Professor."

Half-way through the Career Award, he received a letter from Harvard President Pusey asking him to stay on until age 70. "I don't know why," Skinner remarked, "unless he felt guilty. . . . Maybe [it's] his way of accepting the . . . [Career] Award. Harvard didn't like those . . . it took people off the teaching rolls." [But] "I could never get a grant after I was 70 though they would give them to 75."10

Skinner was concerned about what his income would be after he had to retire completely at 70 years of age. "We live at a level," he said, "we couldn't live at if I . . . [depended on] my teacher's annuity. . . . I get a little over a thousand a month from Harvard and Social Security. I still get royalty checks. . . . I gave that to the girls from *Beyond Freedom and Dignity*."11 He was fortunate to have his best-selling books. It was his only way to make much money and that may have prompted some of his late books addressed to the public, especially *Enjoy Old Age* (Skinner and Vaughan, 1983). But *Walden Two* and *Beyond Freedom and Dignity* remained the big sellers—and money-makers.

Toward the end of his Career Awards, when he would finally have to retire totally, he wrote to Dean Dunbar in 1971, stating his "touch of sadness" about his little changed salary for the next year, on which his award was based. He believed it was because he was (still) *persona non grata* to President Pusey.

Named "Humanist of the Year" by the American Humanist Association in 1972 over many objections, Skinner maintained that "Behaviorism was simply effective Humanism" designed to "actualize the human potential." He declared that "if Humanism meant nothing more than the maximizing of personal freedom and dignity, then I was not a Humanist. If it meant trying to save the human species, then I was" (Skinner, 1984, p. 343).

The primer for the public that he promised himself to write during his career appointment to advance a wider and more accurate understanding of his viewpoint was published as he was turning 70 years old (*About Behaviorism*, 1974). As usual, it stirred the kind of vehement controversy he encountered all of his life. His hope of disarming his adversaries and dissipating popular mythology about his theory by answering 20 wrong-minded charges against him only rekindled the old criticisms.

Computer scientist Weizenbaum wrote in his *New York Times* book review (July 14, 1974) that "large and significant sections of the scientific community have for many years insisted on calling attention to the difference between the spectacular achievements of Dr. Skinner, the master animal trainer, and the 'science' of Professor Skinner, the constructor of utterly vacuous theories." The obvious connection the reviewer ignored was: How else could Skinner have become "the master animal trainer" except through his theory?

In honor of his final retirement in 1974 at age 70 to emeritus status, a large, elegant party was held in the courtyard of Harvard's Fogg Museum. It was a formal affair, with an orchestra and effusive tributes from colleagues. The prize gift to him was a first edition of Thoreau's original *Walden*. Little changed in his life, however. He continued seamlessly with his work. He paid for a former secretary part time and other office expenses at home, but retained his Harvard office since nobody asked him to move out. He enclosed a card with his correspondence announcing that he could no longer answer letters freely nor accept other commitments. Nonetheless, he soon found it necessary again to employ a full-time secretary, and continued an extensive correspondence.

He was settling into old age in a pattern of activity, which he talked about changing but took little action upon. Much more stressful adjustments had occurred earlier, in his sixties, as he accommodated to serious curtailments of his sight, hearing, and movement. His zest for pleasures, creative expressions of his theory, and practical ways of improving the lot of humankind persisted to his death. He never quit trying.

ENDNOTES

1. Harry Levin, unpublished correspondence with author.
2. Harvard archives.
3. Unpublished correspondence with author.
4. Harvard archives.
5. B. F. Skinner, personal interview.
6. Ibid.
7. University of Minnesota archives.
8. Harvard archives.
9. Telephone conversation with author.
10. B. F. Skinner, personal interview.
11. Ibid.

▶ 10

The World as His Oyster

1974–1990

After he retired from Harvard for the second time, at age 70, Skinner continued to work in his usual ways. However, he soon realized that he was "plagiarizing" himself, so he tried to continue to develop in three somewhat modified directions: (1) He extended his scope to more social venues, commenting, for example, on how enemies of world order could be reinforced toward positive activities instead of being punished; (2) He tried harder to explain his theory and principles to the public, and to answer his critics; and (3) He sought out new arenas to apply his theory where he was less likely to repeat himself, such as in ethics and in adapting to old age.

Skinner started to write a book on ethics that would explain the rules of social behavior in terms of reinforcement, which he thought might be as innovative and influential as his first book. His collaborator was Margaret Vaughan, with whom he wrote *Enjoy Old Age* (Skinner and Vaughan, 1983). But he soon discovered that he lacked the energy and intellectual power to follow through, and abandoned it after writing a prospectus, which he later destroyed after circulating it to friends, including myself.

Much of Skinner's working time was spent trying to answer criticisms, the most voluminous of which were contained in *The Selection of Behavior* (Catania & Harnad, 1988). It contained 6 of his "canonical papers"; 143 "commentaries" by a wide variety of critics, followed by Skinner's replies to each; and 2 extended evaluations by the co-editors, which were also answered by Skinner. A more exhaustive critique of his life's work is hard to imagine.

Skinner's exasperation with this comprehensive review is summed up in his last words in the book (Catania & Harnad, 1988):

> *It has been my experience that when I write something in one setting at one time and come back to it in a different setting at a different time I see other implications and relations. I had thought that something of the same sort would happen when other people read these papers. . . . Too often, this has not happened. . . .*
>
> *Why have I not been more readily understood. . . . I worked very hard on these papers, and I believe they are consistent. . . . The central position, however, is not traditional, and that may be the problem. To move from an inner determination of behavior to an environmental determination is a difficult step. . . .*
>
> *Why is discussion in the behavioral sciences so often personal? I do not believe that Einstein, finding it necessary to challenge some basic assumptions of Newton, alluded to Newton's senility. . . . Why has it been so tempting to say, as one commentator does, that I am "strangely provincial," that my reluctance to acknowledge something or other is "quixotic". . . .*
>
> *I have tried to keep the personal tone out of my replies . . . at a few points I have failed. . . . In any case, I have been unable to avoid spending time and space on the simple correction of misstatements of fact and of my position. . . . Whatever current usefulness this volume may have, it should at least be of interest to the future historian as a sample of the style of discussion among behavioral scientists near the end of the 20th century. (pp. 487–488)*

The last paragraph of this quote represents Skinner's strenuous effort to write positively despite resentment. Exasperation is perhaps the most benign characterization of his reaction to criticism. He bristled about it and did not easily give up correcting it. He held grudges into the last years of his life, though he was mellowing considerably and seeking more conciliatory relationships with some of his critics with whom he had personal connections. Like his father, he remained "bumpy," which can be updated to "defensive," however well justified. He reflected the criticisms by trying even harder to write clearly, directly, and simply, but that didn't help much either, since his professional writing almost always had been careful and of high quality.

Usually a courteous man, Skinner was also deeply involved in trying to serve humankind—and to gain acceptance for his views. His awareness of his "bumpiness" made his rewards all the more important to him. Despite his deprecation of awards and denial of the importance to him of other common reinforcers, he often acknowledged his sensitivity to them: compliments that Robert Frost gave his early writing; designation as "Humanist of the Year"; award from the Kennedy Foundation for Mental Retardation; invitations to address the American Psychological Association conventions; and others.

Throughout his life, he would seldom attempt to conciliate directly with his critics. Although Skinner readily argued with them, he thought he was quite forbearing. He sometimes got carried away with clever or acerbic wit, which he later regretted because he might have antagonized colleagues. But he also took pride in his forthrightness in confronting critics.

Like everyone, Skinner changed with age. He became both more touchy about criticism and more mellow as it receded in time. He became ever less accepting of requests made of him and more protective of his working time. He took longer to accomplish what he undertook and more careful of what he wrote. He forgot matters that he would remember at other times. He made many errors in his initial or informal writing, of fact and even grammar, while he continued to take pride in his writing skill.

What happens to the brain structurally and functionally as it ages is being extensively studied. It matters increasingly as the human population's longevity is extended, protracting the likelihood that old people will hold positions of responsibility. Increasingly, areas of the brain are being correlated with external behavior and of deterioration with age. As Skinner concluded long ago, however, mapping the brain's relationships to external behavior so far remains much less useful for changing specific behavior than controlling the environment. It is known, for example, that language skill remains relatively unaffected by aging, compared with problem solving in new circumstances; that the creation of novel concepts is associated with early adulthood; and that struggle, crime, misery, drug use, and other major behavioral problems are related to youth. Changing behavior in these areas with environmental rewards, however, is still far more powerful, most of the time, than trying to change it by manipulating the brain physiologically, mechanically or chemically.

Skinner's greatest theoretical contribution to psychology occurred with publication of his first book when he was 34 years old. His later books fleshed out and applied his theory and principles; he occasionally modified them but basically changed them little. He repeated in his own life the progression of human mental aging, moving toward both greater generalization and particularization, trying to accommodate to conflicting conclusions, and emphasizing his own views and ignoring dissonant ones. Skinner attempted to reconcile with some divergent views of people he liked, but he commented more acerbically than ever about criticism from people he didn't know or like.

Skinner often contradicted himself, usually in relatively unimportant ways. For example, he ranked the importance of his various books differently from time to time, among *The Behavior of Organisms*, *Verbal Behavior*, *Beyond Freedom and Dignity*, and the prospective one on ethics, calling each the most important at different times. He expressed more antagonisms, which he had ignored or suppressed in the past. He reestablished his old friendship with Marian Breland Bailey, despite his annoyance with her ethological view in the

"Misbehavior of Organisms" (1961), and he emphasized his collegial relationship with William Estes, despite his lack of sympathy with Estes's mathematical theories.

How did his aging change the nature of his work from age 70 in 1974, when he officially became emeritus at Harvard, until his death in 1990? Most dramatically, Skinner came to doubt his ability to conduct the last major work he contemplated and had outlined—a book to "modernize" ethics. He had rarely dropped a project before—and never at so early a stage and so irrevocably. He began to consider who would complete his work. There was no question of leadership for his theory, however. He always abjured the notion of a "school" devoted to advancing his theory, and downplayed his role with the Association for Behavior Analysis and its journal. Although Skinner always denied his personal importance for his theory to flourish, he nevertheless was always its leading light.

Charles Catania, who co-edited the massive review of Skinner's theory and research with a wide range of critiques and answers by Skinner (Catania, 1988), could have been a leader. Another possibility was Richard Herrnstein, who succeeded to Skinner's animal laboratory, became chairman of the department, and was, when Skinner seriously considered his mortality, named Skinner's first literary executor. But when Herrnstein wrote critically of Skinner's theory, claiming to update it to encompass contemporary research, he mortally offended Skinner. Herrnstein himself wrote me that he still did "reject the notion that something untoward or regrettable happened between us when I 'crossed him,' to use your phrase. As I see it, science marches on, and the people involved in it owe loyalty only to the truth as best they can discern it, not to each other. I was surprised and disappointed at Fred when he took my article so personally."[1] Herrnstein's co-authorship of *The Bell Curve* with Charles Murray (1994) was even more controversial than his offense to Skinner.

In 1977, when Skinner was 73 years old, a student offered to compile a bibliography of his publications. After a summer's work, Robert Epstein from the University of Maryland was invited to stay on as a graduate student at Harvard. Not only did he produce the bibliography but he also worked prodigiously on compiling indices for the first two volumes of Skinner's autobiography, which the author had inexplicably omitted, as he did from several other books. He would never answer my question of why he did so. An index was included in the third volume but it was inadequate in Epstein's view, so he compiled a more comprehensive one.

Although the source of the increasing strain between Epstein and Skinner is unclear, the index situation provides a clue. Skinner usually had strong reasons for acting as he did—or they became strong when under criticism, even when he would not articulate them. Epstein overrode whatever objections Skinner had to indices, not only making them available for the first two volumes but also for the third after Skinner had agreed to let the publisher include one. Additionally, Skinner did not want a museum or statue dedicated to him, which Epstein initiated nonetheless. Whatever the cause, Epstein annoyed, even offended, Skinner in proceeding over Skinner's objections.

Epstein also organized Skinner's cursory comments in his notebooks, editing them into a publishable volume with Skinner's approval (*Notebooks*, Skinner, 1980) and collaborated on research with Skinner, later filmed, on teaching pigeons to "talk." Along with Skinner, he also contributed editorial notes to a 1982 textbook, *Skinner for the Classroom*.

Over Skinner's demur, Epstein also founded a Skinner museum on the edge of the Harvard, campus and had a bust of Skinner commissioned over Skinner's objections to being so glorified. Skinner would not serve on the Board of the museum. In the museum, Epstein displayed an early baby tender, a teaching machine, and other artifacts of Skinner's creative mind. Eve also disliked Epstein, but Skinner could not bring himself directly to reject so eager and useful a helper. Finally, Skinner enlisted an administrator to ease Epstein out of any relationship to him.

Epstein persisted in maintaining the museum himself, despite Skinner's rebuffs. He did complete his doctorate degree at Harvard, with Herrnstein. The museum is a unique tribute to Skinner's inventiveness, containing early versions of his various devices and other memorabilia that would interest students of his as well as historians of psychology. An adviser of Epstein's noted that "[Epstein] and Fred had a falling out at some point."[2] Whatever the differences between them, Epstein provided many valuable services to Skinner, which were somehow distasteful to Skinner despite their obvious usefulness. Skinner was probably correct about his luck in not having sons.

Skinner and his family and his few close friends, such as Fred Keller, wanted to protect his reputation and integrity as a faithful husband, so they kept quiet about his sexual peccadilloes. Unlike Skinner, his Harvard psychology colleague, Henry Murray wanted his own long affair revealed after his death, and even prepared a biographer to do it (Robinson, 1992). He considered it a key to his life's story and wanted careful attention paid to it in his biography. "Sex and Secrecy at Harvard College," published in *Harvard Magazine* (Pattullo, 1992), described the administrative handling of sexual problems at Harvard.

Putting Skinner's sexual peccadilloes in prespective, while necessary to portraying his character, should cast no pall on his brilliant contributions to society and his loyalty to his family. His sexual proclivities will surely leak out further, however, considering all of the women involved and the many others who heard rumors, including, at one time, much of the student body at Radcliffe College.

Nothing in a human's sexual behavior necessarily affects his or her major contributions to the world—any more than do eating or grooming habits. Sexual activity may, however, distract from creativity or activity, may inhibit public or professional acceptance of the subject's importance, may suggest socially impaired views or insensitive treatment of other human beings, may produce severe penalties and constraints (such as the bar on behaviorist J. B. Watson from academia), and may dismay surviving family members. It seemed to have little effect on Skinner's circumstances except for his eventual enhanced self-control and in whatever modified reactions his family had.

Sexual behavior in recent years has been greatly publicized. Consider innumerable recent notables such as Franklin Roosevelt, John Kennedy, Pablo Picasso, Havelock Ellis, Robert Graves, Truman Capote, Anais Nin, Dwight Eisenhower, Gore Vidal, and Albert Ellis. Sigmund Freud may have had a lifelong affair with his sister-in-law. It is likely that many creative people are more energetic sexually—as well as in other ways—than the norm. They may also attract sexual affairs because of their fame.

Skinner's sexual behavior was largely unknown in academia, even to many of his professional colleagues or by the public who knew of him. His references to sex in his autobiography were minimal and oblique, and he eschewed any comments at all about his sex life after his marriage. He was proud of his family and his 54-year-old marriage. At rock bottom, his family and Fred Keller were his major emotional connections in life and he would not want to offend them. They would not have respected him for such behavior, even if it did not impinge on them except for Eve.

Skinner's lifelong extramarital experiences deserve comment because of their very persistence, their deviation from his own habitual standards of honesty and candor, their unusual breadth for one otherwise so fastidious, their possible impediment to favor at his universities, and the flaw they revealed in his sensitivity to human relationships. In his maturity and especially in his old age, his sexual behavior was increasingly criticized as the feminist movement began to take hold. Skinner simply wanted to be left alone to live his life as he would. Acceptable attitudes generally toward women and sex changed radically during his lifetime, as evidenced by the case of Charles Bird, Skinner's colleague at Minnesota over a half century ago, who was not promoted by his chairman because he was divorced.

In the two years Skinner took off between college and graduate school, when he lived in Greenwich Village and traveled in Europe, he had brief affairs that gave him experience, apparently in quantity but not quality. He ended up believing he had learned what he needed to gain sexual satisfaction, but never considered himself to be a good lover. A brisk note in John Kenneth Galbraith's autobiographical *A Life in Our Times* (1981) recollects Skinner as a graduate student at Harvard. Galbraith was living in Harvard's Winthrop House as one of the resident tutors who met each morning "often to hear from

B. F. Skinner, who would become the most famous and innovative of social psychologists, of his imaginative exploits of the night before. Presently Fred fell in love, and we were enthralled no more."

Skinner's exploits did not cease, however. No one else seems to have mentioned them publicly besides Galbraith, and that was late in Skinner's life. Faculty sexual involvement with students, employees, and clients violates not only standards of professional ethics but often state law as well. With students, colleagues, admirers, and others, there often is no governing law, not even tough university regulation. In his survey of research data available on psychologists and psychiatrists, Gary Schoener (Schoener et al., 1989) found that close to one-sixth of male and half that number of female psychologists had sexual contact with current or former clients. Over half of malpractice insurance payouts were spent on alleged sexual exploitation. This situation involves practitioners; Skinner never was one, but many of his academic colleagues practice clinically part time, and the standard with students should be similar because of the power involved in giving grades.

When the president of Harvard, caught up several years ago in the apogee of the feminist movement, sent out guidelines for proper professorial conduct with students, John Kenneth Galbraith retorted with his usual wit: "Just over forty-five years ago, already a well-fledged member of the Harvard faculty . . . I fell in love with a young female student . . . we were married. So, and happily, we have remained. . . . As a senior member of this community . . . I must do everything possible to retrieve my error. . . . What would you advise?" The dean referred to the old churchly practice of selling indulgences and suggest endowing a chair. Even such wit seems obsolete.

One older professional woman who knew of Skinner's pursuit of women at professional conventions commented only that "boys will be boys," it was so common. She believed that with Skinner there was no gross exploitation, that what occurred was mutually agreeable. She had heard from her "sister school" classmates that Skinner did play around, was easily put off, and no special attention need be paid to him for it.

In 1983, Harvard's Dean Rosovsky wrote what essentially became the current regulation: "Amorous relationships that might be appropriate in other circumstances are always wrong when they occur between any teacher or other officer of the university and any student for whom he or she has a professional responsibility." The words *always wrong* have since been replaced with *always have inherent dangers* (Pattullo, 1992, p. 68). At Harvard, the persistance of Skinner's overtures to secretarial staff, faculty wives, and students continued after he had retired. Once, potential scandal was silenced when a secretary was dissuaded by the administration from bringing charges against Skinner. This happened when he was in his eighties. His department chairman discussed it with him, which was apparently the only such administration action during Skinner's career.

Is it significant that Skinner had these affairs? Given his apparently rather prim attitudes toward moral behavior (for example, gossiping was barred in his utopia), one must say yes, although sex itself was practiced rather freely from a young age in *Walden Two*. He was firmly committed to honesty and staunchly against any exploitation of students—or anyone else—and showed no admiration of or any special attention to others' sexual exploits. He lived quite privately, he was not very sociable in frivolous ways, he did not appear to make any kind of advances to women publicly except perhaps in intimate groups, and generally he did not talk or write about sex except in rather serious intellectual ways. Even though most colleagues seldom received public attention for sexual behavior, Skinner maintained a special devotion to his wife and daughters, which would seem to preclude extramarital relations. There is no evidence at hand to indicate that any of his sexual relationships was other than temporary, superficial, honest, and nondemanding with the women involved, as they have attested to me.

It was Skinner's vitality, energy, curiosity, and inventiveness that transcended all else about his presence—and, privately, sexual eagerness. As Gore Vidal stated:

> By and large I'm not interested in other people's sex lives, but in history. There are times when you think, Something's got to explain why someone is doing what he's doing. . . . All the hysteria that our poor historians have is because they think that they have to transform all of our great Presidents into Ivory Soap monuments. The real subject is sexual energy. . . .
>
> Everybody thinks everybody else has about the same degree of sexuality as he himself has. It isn't true. Reading Reckless Youth *about Jack Kennedy; I mean, there was going to be a different girl every day. . . . And all this oohing and aahing. . . . At first I thought it was sheer hypocrisy; then I realized, these people writing reviews had very low sex drives. You can't just settle down with Myrtle and three children . . . and really do much of anything"* (1993, p, 19)

Sex must have been the way Skinner felt he cut loose from the masses, when he acted recklessly against convention and for his own pleasure. Anyone who knew about his sex life has publicly ignored it, even those who are antagonistic to him. Skinner took chances; he even came very close to suffering administrative sanctions at Harvard. By then, he was willing to comply or become more discreet to accommodate to an administrative warning. When he was young, he might have flaunted the challenge to reform his behavior, as he did with warnings about his Ph.D. thesis, although his family concerns would probably have overridden his bravado.

Other than in his work, passion was never a conspicuous feature of Skinner's. He did his research as a rigorous scientist dedicated to enlarging the scope of behaviorism; nothing distracted him from that deeply or for long. He himself mentioned "passion" in connection with his work only in his writing of *Walden Two*. His career—in terms of freedom, money, and status (status was most important because it gained him the first two)—figured heavily in the major decisions of his life. Regarding his sexual escapades, he would have wanted his daughters to hold the highest opinion of him. Like Eve, they didn't respond to my questions on the subject. Nor did Eve ever show detectable concern that Skinner might leave her. His sexual activities apparently were mere blips in a cohesive family life.

ENDNOTES

1. Unpublished letter to author.
2. Personal conversation with author.

▶ 11

The Last Months
1990

Skinner's intimations of his mortality came relatively early—in his sixties—when his sight and hearing began to deteriorate significantly. His bouts with cancer (cured) and heart symptoms had long since disappeared, but his failing senses and unsteadiness grew slowly worse. Skinner used a powerful circular magnifying glass-lamp for reading, two strong hearing aids, and a cane for walking. By the time of my last visit, his wife had prevailed on him never to walk alone and to amble even around his own neighborhood only with company, which he tried to do daily to keep limber. On our final visit, he asked if I would accompany him on his daily walk since a neighbor who usually did, could not. I did and we both got lost temporarily in that maze of meandering streets, within three or four blocks of his home. But his thinking showed no deficiencies.

Skinner wrote articles on an ever-expanding list of human enterprises: training animals, educating children, community living, political functions, training the disabled, teaching, and gaining personal satisfactions in old age. Outcomes were his everlasting goal; they had priority over understanding.

After he fainted while Eve was being treated for an embolism, blood studies were performed on him. In November 1989, he wrote to me, "I have some other serious news to report about myself. . . . I now have leukemia and am existing from week to week on somebody else's blood. I will steadily lose resistance to disease but am not quite sure yet how soon that will occur. If you like, we can discuss the feelings that are by-products of news of that sort."[1] After transfusions, Skinner would be restored to a sense of good health, which gradually declined until he had to have another. It was a lengthy process during which he listened to taped music. In between treatments, he worked

175

at home close to his usual schedule. All guests were handed a sheet of instructions that included hand washing so that they wouldn't infect him during this vulnerable time.

Skinner himself was quite tranquil. When we talked about death, he stated that he was reconciled to it, that he and Eve had chosen a lovely location in Cambridge for burial, and that he considered himself just a speck in the evolutionary process. It was humans who thought they were important, who couldn't accept the notion of their own obliteration, he declared. Leukemia was his final disability. He wanted no heroic measures taken to save his life but he did agree to total blood transfusions regularly to revive him. He was more sensitive than usual to his feelings, which he had generally ignored, but contemplating his own death was a new experience for him.

His most pervasive emotional response had been related to women, particularly his daughters. The death of friends had also produced a powerful emotional reaction in the past. At deaths of close ones, Skinner paid moving tributes, including to Sister Annette Walters, a student of his at Minnesota and later a colleague, to whom he wrote "It is at times like these that one wished one could pray" (Skinner, 1984, p. 372).

Toward the end of his life, there seemed to be a total acceptance and comfort between him and Eve. He maintained a regular work schedule, in his basement office at home mainly, although he occasionally used his Harvard office till his death. He slept in his Japanese stackable box, which he had barely gotten into his basement, going to bed for three hours, waking and working for a couple of hours, then going back to sleep for another three hours or so. He paid for his own daily secretarial help. His correspondence with me was regular and prompt. He also continued to publish articles that drew on what he already knew. Additionally, he gave talks almost annually at the American Psychological Association convention, which drew large, enthusiastic crowds eager to see the mythic figure who was a landmark in the history of psychology. It didn't matter whether they agreed with him.

In 1987, when I decided to write his biography and began to correspond with him about it, I wanted immediately to visit with Skinner. He was hospitalized when I reached him in Boston in 1988. He reported that he had lost his balance when reaching above the refrigerator and fallen back on his head. (There were other explanations also, such as that he fell down the basement stairs.) Skinner suffered a concussion, required surgery to repair the brain damage, and in the process became infected, was reoperated on, and took a long time to recover.

During our visit in the Massachusetts General Hospital while he was convalescing the first time, he spoke clearly and his memory seemed good. I had lunch with daughter Julie at that time and also talked with Eve. We corresponded frequently thereafter, and visited together in his Harvard office at first, then in his home as he spent increasing work time there. We got along very well, and he wrote, "I would be glad to look at it [your manuscript] if you like, although not to veto anything except clear inaccuracies."[2]

He also wrote, "Don't be afraid to ask me questions; it is all in a good cause, I hope."[3] He also volunteered a letter for publishers, which stated:

> *I first met Daniel Wiener in the early 1940s when I was on the faculty of the Department of Psychology at the University of Minnesota. I have recently been in contact with him for about three years during which he has been writing a biography. We have had many interviews, and he has interviewed my former colleagues and students. I have no doubt of his intelligence, good will, and dedication to the task. I think he understands my position in the general field of psychology and behavioral science.*"[3]

It was touching to me that he would volunteer such an endorsement, since he had almost always been cautious in the past about recommendations.

Skinner was always cordial to me. He continually added to my knowledge with his responsive letters, as did Deborah. We shared many experiences as I carried messages to him from conversations with old mutual acquaintances such as Paul Meehl, Herbert Feigl, and William Heron, and correspondence with Marian Bailey, Stuart Cook, and John Carroll. We also shared mutual interests and activities, such as living in small towns, our yearning to write literature, critical views of our profession, and even the lullabies our mothers sang to us.

About influences in his life, he wrote:

> *Cuthbert Daniel, who influenced me greatly as a scientist when he was working with D. W. Bridgman, took Freud seriously for a time and that is perhaps why I did too. When I taught a course in the psychology of literature at Minnesota, I padded it with Freudian analyses of* Sons and Lovers, The Brothers Karamazov . . . *and so on. As you say . . . we are all to some extent Freudians—as I am still to some extent Presbyterian. I don't think either one is admirable but merely inevitable after a given history. . . .*
>
> *I feel no affinity whatsoever with James and consider him a baleful influence. Wundt and Titchner were better because they could be disproved. James said nothing that could really be tested but it got into Western thought in spite of that shortcoming. . . .*
>
> *Peter Gay wrote two excellent volumes on the Enlightenment, but I think his retreat to a Freudian analysis a tragedy. I can see how Freud attracts him, because Freud was indeed primarily a literary artist. In contributing to an understanding of human behavior, good literature has some of the effect of direct personal contacts with people, but I do not think it contributes to a science of behavior.*[5]

For a man who wrote with and worked at independence as much as Skinner did, it was remarkable that he never learned how to type efficiently. He wrote all of his manuscripts by hand, except for *Walden Two* (1948). Especially as he aged, he depended increasingly on secretarial help. In 1955, while writing his verbal behavior book under monastic circumstances, he wrote to Elliott that he was learning touch typing, with a bastardized system where he looked at the keyboard and made many errors. My later letters from him all were typed by secretaries.

Skinner published five pieces in the decade before his death, including the final volume of his autobiography. *Enjoy Old Age* (Skinner and Vaughan, 1983) was his last book. It grew from a paper he delivered at the annual meeting of the APA in 1982 on "Intellectual Self-Management in Old Age." The book elaborated anecdotally on ways he had discovered of remaining productive and satisfied despite the ravages of aging. What he considered to be a much more important paper he delivered at the same meeting, "Why We Are Not Acting to Save the World," received much less attention and fewer letters.

He used all the aids he could find or create to supplement his failing senses, and he developed rules and habits that helped maintain his productivity. One was to try to enter new fields, since that way he was least likely to repeat himself. Skinner also developed methods of clarifying his thinking, making up large charts, for example, to keep clear on categories of his efforts. He (with Vaughan) wrote in *Enjoy Old Age*, "Young people now . . . are . . . planning better for *physical* old age, but a different kind of planning is necessary for the *enjoyment* of it" (Skinner & Vaughan, 1983, p. 153).

Skinner attached an "Appendix" to the end of that last book: "A Note on the Language in Which This Book Is Written" (pp. 155–157). In three short pages, he added definitions from his theory to the "everyday English" in which the book was written—terms such as *behavior, reinforcers, needing, thinking about,* and so on. Then he referred readers to his books *Science and Human Behavior* and *About Behaviorism.*

The last paragraph in *Enjoy Old Age* captured Skinner's spirit as he was dying: "And if you yourself have constructed the world that permits you to live a tranquil, dignified, and enjoyable life, you will be doubly admired—not only for a great performance, but for writing a last act that plays so well" (1983, p. 153).

Skinner always seemed aware of himself on the stage of his life, taking a prominent role. He invented a technology to extract the most he could from his talents, then applied it to improve the world at large, promoting it partly to gain attention to himself but mainly for what he had managed to create—to gain maximum enjoyment for others and himself. Always a scientist, he based his theory on shaping behavior that he observed first in rats and pigeons, then in humans.

Skinner played the last act as well as the preceding ones with his usual aplomb—an elegant style that pleased him. He created a technology for himself first, and for all other humans, designed to bring them the greatest satisfactions they could obtain from their lives by choosing and using the environments that would shape them as they wished. That would include sensuous pleasures—music, art, food, sex, all of it.

By the time of my last visit, Julie was providing each visitor with a list of instructions designed to protect her father from infections to which his leukemia left him extremely vulnerable. He professed little concern about impending death. As usual, Skinner made the best of his living conditions and continued to plan ahead on his writing and his talk to the APA.

On August 10, 1990, Skinner received a gold medal from the APA at its annual convention as the most prominent psychologist of the century. He spoke as part of his "last act," eight days before his death as it turned out. At his family's request, the Association tried to isolate him from crowds and the danger of infection by ushering him, his wife, and Julie about "like movie stars," he remarked. As usual, the crowd overflowed the scheduled room and another that had been opened next to it. As he entered, the audience rose and applauded. It finally had to be interrupted. He had no written text or even notes, and yet his fragility vanished as he approached the podium and he spoke fluently and with vigor.

Skinner talked for about 15 minutes and was videotaped for posterity. He challenged conventional thinking throughout his speech, drawing an analogy between his theory of behavior as evolutionary and Darwin's theory of "natural selection by consequences." "So far as I'm concerned, cognitive science is the creationism of psychology," he declared (Skinner, 1990). He could not have damned more succinctly the most popular current view of human behavior. The applause, as he finished, did not match that at the beginning.

Skinner's last moments were described in a lovely tribute written by daughter Julie (Vargas, 1990). She wrote of their loving relationship. She admired his sturdy work ethic and yet tried to protect him from it in his last days. Again, he refused final lifesaving efforts, but at the end, when his mouth was dry, Julie noted that "upon receiving a bit of water he said his last word: 'Marvelous'" (n.p.).

ENDNOTES

1. Unpublished correspondence with author.
2. Ibid.
3. Ibid.
4. Ibid.
5. Ibid.

References

Benjamin, L. (1988, September). The history of teaching machines. *American Psychologist, 703–712.*

Boring, E. G. (1950). *A history of experimental psychology.* Englewood Cliffs, NJ: Prentice Hall.

Boring, E. G., & Lindzey, G. (Eds.). (1967). *A history of psychology in autobiography* (Vol. 5). New York: Appleton-Century-Crofts.

Braybrooke, N. (Ed.). (1989). *Seeds in the Wind.* San Francisco: Mercury House.

Breland, M., & Breland, K. (1961). The misbehavior of organisms. *American Psychologist, 16,* 661–64.

Breland Bailey, M. (1994). *The educational ostrich and behavioral analysis.* Report given at the American Psychological Association convention, Los Angeles, August 13.

Buck, G. (1990). A history of teaching machines. *American Psychologist, 45*(4), 551–552.

Catania, C. A. (1988). The behavior of organisms as work in progress. *Journal of the Experimental Analysis of Behavior, 50,* 277–281.

Catania, C. A., & Harnad, S. (1988). *The selection of behavior: The operant behaviorism of B. F. Skinner: Comments and consequences.* Cambridge: Cambridge University Press.

Chomsky, N. (1959). Review: *Verbal behavior. Language, 35,* n.p.

——— (1967). A review of B. F. Skinner's *Verbal behavior.* In L. A. Jakobovitz & M. S. Miro (Eds.), *Readings in the psychology of language* (n.p.). New York: Prentice Hall. (Originally printed in *Language,* 1959).

Comunidad Las Horcones. (1989) Walden Two and social change: The application of behavior analysis to cultural design. (Trans. S. Roberts). *Behavior Analysis and Social Action, 7*(1–2), 35–41.

Coleman, S. R. (1985a). B. F. Skinner, 1926–1928: From literature to psychology. *Behavior Analyst, 8,* 77–92.

——— (1985b). When historians disagree: B. F. Skinner and E. G. Boring, 1930. *Psychological Record, 35,* 301–314.

——— (1987). Quantitative order in B. F. Skinner's early research program, 1928–1931. *The Behavior Analyst, 10,* 47–65.

Detroit News, January 18, 1979. n.p.

Dews, P. D. (Ed.). (1970). *Festschrift for B. F. Skinner.* New York: Appleton-Century-Crofts.

Dinsmoor, J. A. (1987). A visit to Bloomington: The first conference on the experimental analysis of behavior. *Journal of the Experimental Analysis of Behavior, 48,* 441–445.

Eissler, K. (1983). *The assault on truth: Freud's suppression of the seduction theory.* Farrar, Straus & Giroux.

Elliott, M. (1952). M. Elliott. In E. G. Boring & G. Lindzey (Eds.), *A history of psychology in autobiography* (Vol. 4). New York: Appleton-Century-Crofts.

Elms, A. C. (1981). Skinner's dark year and *Walden Two. American Psychologist, 36,* 470–479.

Epstein, R. (Ed.). (1980). *Notebooks: B. F. Skinner.* Englewood Cliffs, NJ: Prentice Hall. (Also listed under Skinner, 1980).

———— (Ed.). (1982). *Skinner for the classroom.* Champaign, IL: Research Press.

Ferster, C. (1970). Schedules of reinforcement with Skinner. In P. B. Dews (Ed.), *Festschrift for B. F. Skinner* (n.p.). New York: Appleton-Century-Crofts.

Galbraith, J. K. (1981). *A life in our times.* Boston: Houghton-Mifflin.

Harvard University Archives, Pusey Library.

Hearst, E. (Ed.). (1979). *The 1st century of experimental psychology.* Dist. by Halsted Press Division, Wiley. Hillsdale, NJ: L. Erlbaum Associates.

Herrnstein, R. (1977, December). The evolution of behaviorism. *American Psychologist,* n.p.

Herrnstein, R., & Murray, C. (1994). *The bell curve.* New York: Free Press.

Hilgard, E. R. (1939). Review of *The behavior of organisms. Psychological Bulletin, 36,* 121–125.

Isaacson, W. (1993). *Kissinger: A biography.* New York: Simon & Schuster.

Keller, F. S. (1970). Psychology at Harvard (1926–1931): A reminiscence. In P. B. Dews (Ed.), *Festschrift for B. F. Skinner* (pp. 29–36). New York: Appleton-Century-Crofts.

———— (1986, Fall). A fire in Schermerhorn Extension. *Behavior Analyst, 9,* 139–146.

———— (1990). Burrhus Frederic Skinner (1904–1990) (A thank you). *Journal of the Experimental Analysis of Behavior, 54,* 155–158.

Kinkade, K. (1973). *A Walden Two experiment: The first five years of Twin Oaks community.* New York: William Morrow.

Klaw, S. (1963, April). Harvard's Skinner: The last of the Utopians. *Harper's,* 45–51.

Koestler, A. (1968) *Ghost in the machine.* New York: Macmillan.

MacCorquodale, K. (1969). B. F. Skinner's *Verbal behavior:* A retrospective appreciation. *Journal of the Experimental Analysis of Behavior, 12,* 831–841.

———— (1970). On Chomsky's review of Skinner's *Verbal behavior. Journal of the Experimental Analysis of Behavior, 13,* 83–99.

———— (1975, September 26). Some history of Minnesota psychology. From a transcript of talk given at the University of Minnesota for the orientation of new students (Fall Quarter, 45 Nicolson Hall).

Masson, J. (1984). *The Assault on truth: Freud's suppression of the seduction theory.* New York: Farrar, Straus & Giroux.

Meehl, P. (1989). Paul Meehl. In G. Lindzey (Ed.), *A history of psychology in autobiography* (Vol. 8) (n.p.). Stanford, CA: Stanford University Press.

Minnesota, University of, archives.

New York Times, November 7, 1989, n.p.

New York Times Book Review, July 14, 1974, n.p.

Pattullo, E. (1992, January–February). Sex and secrecy at Harvard College. *Harvard,* 67–70.

Rabin, A. I., et al. (Eds.). (1990). *Studying persons and lives.* New York: Springer.

Random House Dictionary. (1987 edition). New York: Random House.

Robinson, F. G. (1992). *Love's story told.* Cambridge, MA: Harvard University Press.

Russell, B. (1927). *Philosophy.* New York: Norton.

Schoener, G., et al. (1989). *Psychotherapists' sexual involvement with clients.* Minneapolis, MN: Walk-In Counseling Center.

Shakow, D. (1947). *Report of APA committee on training in clinical psychology.* American Psychological Association.

Skinner, B. F. (1931). The concept of the reflex in the description of behavior. *Journal of General Psychology, 5,* 427–458.

———— (1932a). Drive and reflex strength. *Journal of General Psychology, 6,* 22–48.

———— (1932b). On the rate of formation of a conditioned reflex. *Journal of General Psychology, 8,* 274–286.

———— (1933a). On the rate of extinction of a conditioned reflex. *Journal of General Psychology, 9,* 114–129.

———— (1933b). The measurement of spontaneous activity. *Journal of General Psychology, 9,* 3–23.

———— (1934). Has Gertrude Stein a secret? *Atlantic Monthly, 153,* 50–57.

———— (1936). The verbal summator and a method for the study of latent speech. *Journal of Psychology, 2,* 71–107.

———— (1938). *The behavior of organisms: An experimental analysis.* New York: Appleton-Century.

———— (1939). The alliteration in Shakespeare's sonnets: A study of literary behavior. *Psychological Record, 3,* 186–192.

———— (1945, June). The operational analysis of psychological terms. *Psychological Review,* n.p.

———— (1945, October). Baby in a box. (The machine age comes to the nursery! Introducing the mechanical baby-tender). *Ladies Home Journal,* 30–31, 135–136, 138.

———— (1948, 1976) *Walden two.* New York: Macmillan.

———— (1950). Are learning theories necessary? *Psychological Review, 57,* 193–216.

———— (1952). A case history in the scientific method. *American Psychologist, 11,* 221–223.

———— (1953). *Science and human behavior.* New York: Macmillan.

———— (1954a). The science of learning and the art of teaching. *Harvard Educational Review, 24,* 86–97.

———— (1954b). A critique of psychoanalytic concepts and theories. *Scientific Monthly, 79,* 300–305.

———— (1955). *The control of human behavior.* New York Academy of Sciences.

———— (1956). A case study in scientific method. *American Psychologist, 11,* 221–133.

———— (1957). *Verbal behavior.* New York: Appleton-Century-Crofts.

———— (1959a). *Cumulative record.* New York: Appleton-Century-Crofts. (Revised in 1972).

———— (1959b). John Broadus Watson, behaviorist. *Science, 129,* 197–198.

———— (1960). Pigeons in a pelican. *American Psychologist, 16,* 28–37.

—— (1961). The design of cultures. *Daedalus, 90,* 534–546.

—— (1963a). Behaviorism at fifty. *Science, 140,* 951–958.

—— (1963b). Operant behavior. *American Psychologist, 18,* 503–515.

—— (1967). B. F. Skinner. In E. G. Boring & G. Lindzey (Eds.), *A history of psychology in autobiography* (Vol. 5) (pp. 387–413). New York: Appleton-Century-Crofts.

—— (1968). *The technology of teaching.* New York: Appleton-Century-Crofts.

—— (1969). *The contingencies of reinforcement: A theoretical analysis.* New York: Appleton-Century-Crofts.

—— (1970). Creating the creative artist. In A. J. Toynbee et al. (Eds.), *On the future of art* (pp. 61–76). New York: Viking.

—— (1971). *Beyond freedom and dignity.* New York: Knopf.

—— (1972). *Cumulative record* (3rd ed.). New York: Appleton-Century-Crofts.

—— (1973). Answers for my critics. In H. Wheeler (Ed.), *Beyond the punitive society* (pp. 256–266). San Francisco: Freeman.

—— (1974). *About behaviorism.* New York: Knopf.

—— (1976a). *Particulars of my life.* New York: Knopf.

—— (1976b). Walden Two revisited. In *Walden Two.* New York: Macmillan.

—— (1977). Why I am not a cognitive psychologist. *Behaviorism, 5,* 1–10.

—— (1978). *Reflections on behaviorism and society.* Englewood Cliffs, NJ: Prentice Hall.

—— (1979). *The shaping of a behaviorist.* New York: Knopf.

—— (1980). *Notebooks: B. F. Skinner.* Englewood Cliffs, NJ: Prentice Hall. (Also listed under Epstein, 1980).

—— (1981a). How to discover what you have to say—A talk to students. *The Behavior Analyst, 4,* 1–7.

—— (1981b). Skinner's dark year and *Walden Two. American Psychologist, 36*(5), 470–479.

—— (1982). *Skinner for the classroom.* Champaign, IL: Research Press. (Also listed under Epstein, 1982).

—— (1983, September). Origins of a behaviorist. *Psychology Today,* 22–33.

—— (1984 (© 1983)). *A matter of consequences.* New York: Knopf.

—— (1987 (© 1986)). *Upon further reflection.* Englewood Cliffs, NJ: Prentice Hall.

—— (1989). *Recent issues in the analysis of behavior.* Columbus, OH: Merrill.

—— (1990, August). Speech given at the annual APA convention.

—— (1992). Superstition in the pigeon. *American Psychologist,* 272–274. (Reprint of original 1948 article).

Skinner, B. F., & Barnes, T. C. (1930). The progressive increase in the geotropic response of the ant *Aphaenogaster. Journal of General Psychology, 4,* 102–112.

Skinner, B. F., & Ferster, C. (1957). *Schedules of reinforcement.* New York: Appleton-Century-Crofts.

Skinner, B. F., & Heron, W. T. (1937). Effects of caffeine and benzedrine upon conditioning and extinction. *Psychological Record, 1,* 340–346.

Skinner, B. F., & Holland, J. (1961). *The analysis of behavior.* New York: McGraw-Hill.

Skinner, B. F., & Rogers, C. (1956). Some issues concerning the control of human behavior. A symposium. *Science, 124,* 1057–1066.

Skinner, B. F., & Vaughan, M. E. (1983). *Enjoy old age.* New York: Knopf.

———— (1971, September 20). Skinner's Utopia: Panacea or path to hell? *Time,* pp. 47–53.

Thompson, T. (1988) Retrospective review: Benedictus behavioral analysis: B. F. Skinner's magnus opus at fifty. *Contemporary Psychology, 33,* 397–402.

Vargas, J. S. (1972, January/February) B. F. Skinner: Father, grandfather, behavior modifier. *Human Behavior,* 16–23.

———— (1993). B. F. Skinner: glimpse of the scientist as a father. *Behaviorology,* 55–60.

———— (1990, Winter). B. F. Skinner: The last few days. *Journal of Applied Behavioral Analysis,* 409–410.

Vidal, G. *The Nation* (magazine), July 5, 1993, p. 19.

Watson, J. B. (1913). Psychology as the behaviorist views it. *Psychological Review, 20,* 158–177.

Ziemba, M. (1977). Contrasting theories of Utopia: An analysis of *Looking Backward* and *Walden Two.* Thesis (Ph.D.), American University.

Also used as a reference were Skinner's Minnesota and Washington, DC, FBI files.

Skinner Bibliography

1930

The progressive increase in the geotropic response of the ant *Aphaenogaster. Journal of General Psychology, 4,* 102–112. (With T. C. Barnes).

On the inheritance of maze behavior. *Journal of General Psychology, 4,* 342–346.

On the conditions of elicitation of certain eating reflexes. *Proceedings of the National Academy of Sciences, 16,* 433–438.

1931

The concept of the reflex in the description of behavior. *Journal of General Psychology, 5,* 427–458.

1932

Drive and reflex strength. *Journal of General Psychology, 6,* 22–37.

Drive and reflex strength: II. *Journal of General Psychology, 6,* 38–48.

On the rate of formation of a conditioned reflex. *Journal of General Psychology, 7,* 274–286.

A paradoxical color effect. *Journal of General Psychology, 7,* 481–482.

1933

On the rate of extinction of a conditioned reflex. *Journal of General Psychology, 8,* 114–129.

The rate of establishment of a discrimination. *Journal of General Psychology, 9,* 302–350.

The measurement of "spontaneous activity." *Journal of General Psychology, 9,* 3–23.

"Resistance to extinction" in the process of conditioning. *Journal of General Psychology, 9,* 420–429.

The abolishment of a discrimination. *Proceedings of the National Academy of Sciences, 19*, 825–828.

Some conditions affecting intensity and duration thresholds in motor nerve, with reference to chronaxie of subordination. *American Journal of Physiology, 106*, 721–737. (With E. F. Lambert and A. Forbes).

1934

Has Gertrude Stein a secret? *Atlantic Monthly, 153*, 50–57.

The extinction of chained reflexes. *Proceedings of the National Academy of Sciences, 20*, 234–237.

A discrimination without previous conditioning. *Proceedings of the National Academy of Sciences, 20*, 532–536.

1935

The generic nature of the concepts of stimulus and response. *Journal of General Psychology, 12*, 40–65.

Two types of conditioned reflex and a pseudo type. *Journal of General Psychology, 12*, 66–77.

A discrimination based upon a change in the properties of a stimulus. *Journal of General Psychology, 12*, 313–336.

1936

A failure to obtain "disinhibition." *Journal of General Psychology, 14*, 127–135.

The reinforcing effect of a differentiating stimulus. *Journal of General Psychology, 14*, 127–278.

The effect on the amount of conditioning of an interval of time before reinforcement. *Journal of General Psychology, 14*, 279–295.

Conditioning and extinction and their relation to drive. *Journal of General Psychology, 14*, 296–317.

Thirst as an arbitrary drive. *Journal of General Psychology, 15*, 205–210.

The verbal summator and a method for the study of latent speech. *Journal of Psychology, 2*, 71–107.

1937

Two types of conditioned reflex: A reply to Konorski and Miller. *Journal of General Psychology, 16*, 272–279.

Changes in hunger during starvation. *Psychological Record, 1*, 51–60.

The distribution of associated words. *Psychological Record, 1*, 71–76. (With W. T. Heron).

Effects of caffeine and benzedrine upon conditioning and extinction. *Psychological Record, 1*, 340–346. (With W. T. Heron).

1938

The behavior of organisms: An experimental analysis. New York: Appleton-Century. (See also 1966).

1939

An apparatus for the study of animal behavior. *Psychological Record, 3,* 166–176.

Some factors influencing the distribution of associated words. *Psychological Record, 3,* 178–184. (With S. W. Cook).

The alliteration in Shakespeare's sonnets: A study of literary behavior. *Psychological Record, 3,* 186–192.

1940

The rate of extinction in maze-bright and maze-dull rats. *Psychological Record, 4,* 11–18. (With W. T. Heron).

A method of maintaining an arbitrary degree of hunger. *Journal of Comparative Psychology, 30,* 139–145.

1941

The psychology of design. In *Art education today* (pp. 1–6). New York: Bureau Publications, Teachers College, Columbia University.

A quantitative estimate of certain types of sound-patterning in poetry. *American Journal of Psychology, 54,* 64–79.

Some quantitative properties of anxiety. *Journal of Experimental Psychology, 29,* 390–400. (With W. K. Estes).

1942

The processes involved in the repeated guessing of alternatives. *Journal of Experimental Psychology, 30,* 495–503.

1943

Reply to Dr. Yacorzynski. *Journal of Experimental Psychology, 32,* 93–94.

1945

The operational analysis of psychological terms. *Psychological Review, 52,* 270–277, 291–294.

(October). The machine age comes to the nursery! Introducing the mechanical baby-tender. *Ladies Home Journal, 62,* 30–31, 135–136, 138.

1947

An automatic shocking-grid apparatus for continuous use. *Journal of Comparative and Physiological Psychology, 40,* 305–307.

Experimental psychology. In W. Dennis et al., *Current trends in psychology* (pp. 16–49). Pittsburgh: University of Pittsburgh Press.

1948

"Superstition" in the pigeon. *Journal of Experimental Psychology, 38,* 168–172.

Walden two. New York: Macmillan.

1950

Are theories of learning necessary? *Psychological Review, 57,* 193–216.

1951

How to teach animals. *Scientific American, 185,* 26–29.

The experimental analysis of behavior. *Proceedings and Papers of the 13th International Congress of Psychology,* 62–91.

1953

Some contributions of an experimental analysis of behavior to psychology as a whole. *American Psychologist, 8,* 69–78.

Science and human behavior. New York: Macmillan.

1954

The science of learning and the art of teaching. *Harvard Educational Review, 24,* 86–97. A critique of psychoanalytic concepts and theories. *Scientific Monthly, 79,* 300–305.

1955

The control of human behavior. *Transactions of the New York Academy of Sciences, 17,* 547–551.

1955–56

Freedom and the control of men. *American Scholar, 25,* 47–65.

1956

A case history in scientific method. *American Psychologist, 11,* 221–233.

What is psychotic behavior? In *Theory and treatment of the psychoses: Some newer aspects* (pp. 77–79). St. Louis: Committee on Publications, Washington University.

Some issues concerning the control of human behavior: a symposium. *Science, 124,* 1057–66. (With Carl Rogers).

1957

The psychological point of view. In H. D. Kruse (Ed.), *Integrating the approaches to mental disease* (pp. 130–133). New York: Hoeber-Harper.

The experimental analysis of behavior. *American Scientist, 45,* 343–371.

A second type of superstition in the pigeon. *American Journal of Psychology, 70,* 308–311.

Concurrent activity under fixed-interval reinforcement. *Journal of Comparative and Physiological Psychology, 50,* 279–281. (With W. H. Morse).

Verbal behavior. New York: Appleton-Century-Crofts.

Schedules of reinforcement. New York: Appleton-Century-Crofts. (With Charles Ferster).

1958

Diagramming schedules of reinforcement. *Journal of the Experimental Analysis of Behavior, 1,* 67–68.

Some factors involved in the stimulus control of operant behavior. *Journal of the Experimental Analysis of Behavior, 1,* 103–107. (With W. H. Morse).

Reinforcement today. *American Psychologist, 13,* 94–99.

Teaching machines. *Science, 128,* 969–977.

Sustained performance during very long experimental sessions. *Journal of the Experimental Analysis of Behavior, 1,* 235–244. (With W. H. Morse).

Fixed-interval reinforcement of running in a wheel. *Journal of the Experimental Analysis of Behavior, 1,* 371–379. (With W. H. Morse).

1959

John Broadus Watson, behaviorist. *Science, 129,* 197–198.

The programming of verbal knowledge. In E. Galanter (Ed.), *Automatic teaching: The state of the art* (pp. 63–68). New York: John Wiley and Sons.

Animal research in the pharmacotherapy of mental disease. In J. Cole & R. Gerard (Eds.), *Psychopharmacology: Problems in evaluation* (pp. 224–228). Washington, DC: National Academy of Sciences–National Research Council.

Cumulative record. New York: Appleton-Century-Crofts. (Revised 1961, 1972).

1960

Special problems in programming language instruction for teaching machines. In F. J. Oinas (Ed.), *Language teaching today* (pp. 167–174). Bloomington, IN: Indiana University Research Center in Anthropology, Folklore, and Linguistics.

Concept formation in philosophy and psychology. In S. Hook (Ed.), *Dimensions of mind: A symposium* (pp. 226–230). Washington Square, NY: New York University Press.

The use of teaching machines in college instruction (Parts II–IV). In A. A. Lumsdaine & R. Glaser (Eds.), *Teaching machines and programmed learning: A source book* (pp. 159–172.). Washington, DC: Department of Audio-Visual Instruction, National Education Association. (With J. G. Holland).

Pigeons in a pelican. *American Psychologist, 16,* 28–37.

1961

The design of cultures. *Daedalus, 90,* 534–546.

Why we need teaching machines. *Harvard Educational Review, 31,* 377–398.

Learning theory and future research. In J. Jysaught (Ed.), *Programmed learning: Evolving principles and industrial applications* (pp. 59–66). Ann Arbor: Foundation for Research on Human Behaviors.

Teaching machines. *Scientific American, 205,* 90–122.

The analysis of behavior. New York: McGraw-Hill. (With J. Holland).

1962

Technique for reinforcing either of two organisms with a single food magazine. *Journal of the Experimental Analysis of Behavior, 5,* 64.

Operandum. *Journal of the Experimental Analysis of Behavior, 5,* 224.

Squirrel in the yard: Certain sciurine experiences of B. F. Skinner. *Harvard Alumni Bulletin, 64,* 642–645.

Two "synthetic social relations." *Journal of the Experimental Analysis of Behavior, 64,* 531–533.

1963

Conditioned and unconditioned aggression in pigeons. *Journal of the Experimental Analysis of Behavior, 6,* 73–74. (With G. S. Reynolds and A. C. Catania).

Behaviorism at fifty. *Science, 140,* 951–958.

Operant behavior. *American Psychologist, 18,* 503–515.

Reply to Thouless. *Australian Journal of Psychology, 15,* 92–93.

Reflections on a decade of teaching machines. *Teachers College Record, 65,* 168–177.

L'avenir des machines à enseigner. *Psychologie Française, 8,* 170–180.

1964

New methods and new aims in teaching. *New Scientist, 122,* 483–484.

Man. *Proceedings of the American Philosophical Society, 108,* 483–485.

1965

The technology of teaching. *Proceedings of the Royal Society, 162,* 427–443.

Stimulus generalization in an operant: A historical note. In D. I. Mostofsky (Ed.), *Stimulus generalization* (pp. 193–209). Stanford, CA: Stanford University Press.

(October 16). Why teachers fail. *Saturday Review, 48,* 80–81, 98–102.

1966

The phylogeny and ontogeny of behavior. *Science, 153,* 1205–1213.

An operant analysis of problem solving. In B. Kleinmuntz (Ed.), *Problem solving: Research, method, and theory* (pp. 225–257). New York: John Wiley and Sons.

Conditioning responses by reward and punishment. *Royal Institution of Great Britain, Lecture Summary, 41,* 48–51.

Contingencies of reinforcement in the design of a culture. *Behavioral Science, 11,* 159–166.

What is the experimental analysis of behavior? *Journal of the Experimental Analysis of Behavior, 9,* 213–218.

Some responses to the stimulus "Pavlov." *Conditional Reflex, 1,* 74–78.

The behavior of organisms: An experimental analysis. New York: Appleton-Century-Crofts. (See also 1938).

1967

B. F. Skinner. In E. G. Boring & G. Lindzey (Eds.), *A history of psychology in autobiography* (Vol. 5) (pp. 387–413). New York: Appleton-Century-Crofts.

(January 5). Visions of utopia. *The Listener, 77,* 22–23.

(January 12). Utopia through the control of human behavior. *The Listener, 77,* 55–56.

The problem of consciousness—A debate. *Philosophy and Phenomenological Research, 27,* 55–56.

1968

The science of human behavior. Twenty-five years at RCA Laboratories, 1942–1967, 92–102.

Teaching science in high school—What is wrong? *Science, 159,* 704–710.

Edwin Garrigues Boring. *Yearbook of the American Philosophical Society,* 111–115.

The design of experimental communities. In *International encyclopedia of the social sciences* (Vol. 16) (pp. 271–275). New York: Macmillan.

The technology of teaching. New York: Appleton-Century-Crofts.

1969

Contingency management in the classroom. *Education, 90,* 93–100.

(April). The machine that is man. *Psychology Today, 2,* 22–25, 60–63.

Contingencies of reinforcement: A theoretical analysis. New York: Appleton-Century-Crofts.

1970

Creating the creative artist. In A. J. Toynbee et al. (Eds.), *On the future of art* (pp. 61–76). New York: Viking.

1971

(May/June). Humanistic behaviorism. *The Humanist, 31,* 35.
Autoshaping. *Science, 173,* 752.
A behavioral analysis of value judgments. In E. Tobach, L. R. Aronson, & E. Shaw (Eds.), *The biopsychology of development* (pp. 543–551). New York: Academic Press.
(September 30). B. F. Skinner says what's wrong with the social sciences. *The Listener, 86,* 429–431.
Beyond freedom and dignity. New York: Knopf.

1972

Some relations between behavior modification and basic research. In S. W. Bijou & E. Ribes-Inesta (Eds.), *Behavior modification: Issues and extensions* (pp. 1–6). New York: Academic Press.
A lecture on "having a poem." In B. F. Skinner, *Cumulative record* (3rd ed.) (pp. 345–355). New York: Appleton-Century-Crofts.
(July/August). Humanism and behaviorism. *The Humanist, 32,* 18–20.
Freedom and dignity revisited. (August 11). *New York Times,* p. 29.
Compassion and ethics in the care of the retardate. In B. F. Skinner, *Cumulative record* (3rd ed.) (pp. 283–291). New York: Appleton-Century-Crofts.

1973

The freedom to have a future. The 1972 Sol Feinstone Lecture, Syracuse University.
Reflections on meaning and structure. In R. Brower, H. Vendler, & J. Hollander (Eds.), *I. A. Richards: Essays in his honor* (pp. 199–209). New York: Oxford University Press.
Answers for my critics. In H. Wheeler (Ed.), *Beyond the punitive society* (pp. 256–266). San Francisco: Freeman.
Some implications of making education more efficient. In C. E. Thoresen (Ed.), *Behavior modification in education* (pp. 446–456). Chicago: National Society for the Study of Education.
Are we free to have a future? *Impact, 3,* 6–12.
(Winter). Walden (one) and Walden two. *The Thoreau Society Bulletin, 122,* 1–3.
The free and happy student. *New York University Education Quarterly, 4,* 2–6.

1974

Designing higher education. *Daedalus, 103,* 196–202.
About behaviorism. New York: Knopf.

1975

Comments on Watt's "B. F. Skinner and the technological control of social behavior." *The American Political Science Review, 69,* 228–229.
The shaping of phylogenic behavior. *Journal of the Experimental Analysis of Behavior, 24,* 117–120. (Also published in *Acta Neurobiologiae Experimentalis, 35,* 409–415).

The steep and thorny way to a science of behavior. *American Psychologist, 30,* 42–49.
The ethics of helping people. *Criminal Law Bulletin, 11,* 623–636.

1976

Farewell, my LOVELY! *Journal of the Experimental Analysis of Behavior, 25,* 218.
Particulars of my life. New York: Knopf.
Walden two revisited. In *Walden two* (paperback edition) (pp. v–xvi). New York: Macmillan.

1977

The force of coincidence. In B. C. Etzel, J. M. LeBlanc, & D. M. Baer (Eds.), *New developments in behavioral psychology: Theory, methods, and application* (pp. 3–6). Hillsdale, NJ: Lawrence Erlbaum Associates.
The experimental analysis of operant behavior. In R. W. Reiber & K. Salzinger (Eds.), *The roots of American psychology: Historical influences and implications for the future (Annals of the New York Academy of Sciences)* (Vol. 291) (pp. 374–385). New York: New York Academy of Sciences.
(July 26). Freedom at last, from the burden of taxation. *New York Times,* p. 29.
(Fall). Why I am not a cognitive psychologist. *Behaviorism, 5,* 1–10.
(September). Between freedom and despotism. *Psychology Today, 11,* 80–82, 84, 86, 90–91.
Herrnstein and the evolution of behaviorism. *American Psychologist, 32,* 1006–1012.

1978

Reflections on behaviorism and society. Englewood Cliffs, NJ: Prentice Hall.
(March). Why don't we use the behavioral sciences? *Human Nature, 1,* 86–92.

1979

The shaping of a behaviorist. New York: Knopf.
(March). My experience with the baby tender. *Psychology Today, 12*(10), 28–31.
(Winter). A happening at the annual dinner of the Association for Behavioral Analysis, Chicago, May 15, 1978. *The Behavior Analyst, 2*(1), 30–33.
Le renforgateur arrangé. *Revue de modification au comportement, 9,* 59–69. (Translated into French by Raymond Beausoleil).

1980

Symbolic communication between two pigeons. *Science, 207,* 543–545. (With R. Epstein and R. P. Lanza).
Resurgence of responding after the cessation of response-independent reinforcement. *Proceedings of the National Academy of Sciences, 77,* 6251–6253. (With R. Epstein).

Notebooks: B. F. Skinner. Englewood Cliffs, NJ: Prentice Hall. (Edited by R. Epstein).

The species-specific behavior of ethnologists. *The Behavior Analyst, 3,* 51.

1981

Pavlov's influence on psychology in America. *Journal of the History of the Behavioral Sciences, 17,* 242–245.

Self-awareness in the pigeon. *Science, 212,* 695–696.

Charles B. Ferster—A personal memoir. *Journal of the Experimental Analysis of Behavior, 35,* 259–261.

How to discover what you have to say—A talk to students. *The Behavior Analyst, 4,* 1–7.

Selection by consequences. *Science, 213,* 501–504.

The spontaneous use of memoranda by pigeons. *Behavior Analysis Letters, 1,* 241–246. (With R. Epstein).

1982

Contrived reinforcement. *The Behavior Analyst, 5,* 3–8.

"Lying" in the pigeon. *Journal of the Experimental Analysis of Behavior, 38,* 201–203. (With R. P. Lanza and J. Starr).

Skinner for the classroom. Champaign, IL: Research Press. (Edited by R. Epstein).

1983

(March). Intellectual self-management in old age. *The American Psychologist, 38*(3), 239–244.

(Spring). Can the experimental analysis of behavior rescue psychology? *The Behavior Analyst, 6*(1), 9–17.

(September). Origins of a behaviorist. *Psychology Today,* 22–33.

Enjoy old age. New York: Knopf. (With Margaret E. Vaughan.)

A better way to deal with selection. *The Behavioral and Brain Sciences, 3,* 377.

A matter of consequences. New York: Knopf.

1984

The evolution of behavior. *Journal of the Experimental Analysis of Behavior, 45,* 115–122.

(December). Canonical papers of B. F. Skinner. *The Behavioral and Brain Sciences, 7*(4), 473–724.

The shame of American education. *American Psychologist, 39*(9), 947–954.

1985

Toward the cause of peace: What can psychology contribute? *Applied Social Psychology Annual*, 21–25.

(Spring). News from nowhere, 1984. *The Behavior Analyst, 8*(1), 5–14.

Cognitive science and behaviorism. *British Journal of Psychology, 76*, 291–301.

(Spring). Reply to Place: "Three senses of the word 'tact'." *Behaviorism, 13*(1), 75–76.

1986

Some thoughts about the future. *Journal of Experimental Analysis of Behavior, 4*, 568–574.

(May). What is wrong with daily life in the western world? *American Psychologist, 41*(5), 568–574.

(Summer). Sleeping in peace. *Free Inquiry, 6*(3), 57.

(October). Programmed instruction revisited. *Phi Delta Kappan, 68*(2), 103–110.

Upon further reflection. Englewood Cliffs, NJ: Prentice Hall.

1987

(May 8). Outlining a science of feeling. *The Times Literary Supplement*, 490–496.

1988

Whatever happened to psychology as the science of behavior? *Counselor Psychology Quarterly, 1*(1), 111–122.

1989

Recent issues in the analysis of behavior. Columbus, OH: Merrill.

Whatever happened to psychology as the science of behavior? *American Psychologist, 42*(8), 780–786.

1990

(Fall). To know the future. *Behavior Analyst, 13*(2), 103–106.

(November). Can psychology be a science of mind? *American Psychologist, 45*(11), 1206–1210.

Some issues concerning the control of human behavior. *TACD Journal, 18*(1), 79–102. (With C. R. Rogers).

1992

Superstition in the pigeon. *American Psychologist*, 272–274. (Reprint of original 1948 article appearing in *Journal of Experimental Psychology, 38*, 168–172).

Index